TIMBER BOOMS AND INSTITUTIONAL BREAKDOWN IN SOUTHEAST ASIA

This book explores three puzzles: Why did the Indonesian, Malaysian, and Philippine governments disastrously mismanage their forests? Why have the governments of many developing states done the same? And why do states generally squander their natural resources?

In this study, Michael L. Ross draws on the new institutional economics, the theory of rent-seeking, and examples from Southeast Asia, to show how the volatility of international markets can damage the institutions of developing states – and lead to the plunder of natural resources.

Michael L. Ross is Assistant Professor of Political Science at the University of Michigan, Ann Arbor.

POLITICAL ECONOMY OF INSTITUTIONS AND DECISIONS

Series Editors

Randall Calvert, Washington University, St. Louis
Thráinn Eggertsson, Columbia University and University of Iceland

Founding Editors

James E. Alt, Harvard University
Douglass C. North, Washington University of St. Louis

Other books in the series

Alesina and Howard Rosenthal, *Partisan Politics, Divided Government
and the Economy*
Lee J. Alston, Thráinn Eggertsson and Douglass C. North, eds., *Empirical
Studies in Institutional Change*
Lee J. Alston and Joseph P. Ferrie, *Southern Paternalism and the Rise of the
American Welfare State: Economics, Politics, and Institutions, 1865–1965*
James E. Alt and Kenneth Shepsle, eds., *Perspectives on
Positive Political Economy*
Jeffrey S. Banks and Eric A. Hanushek, eds., *Modern Political Economy:
Old Topics, New Directions*
Yoram Barzel, *Economic Analysis of Property Rights, 2nd edition*
Robert Bates, *Beyond the Miracle of the Market: The Political Economy
of Agrarian Development in Kenya*
Peter Cowhey and Mathew McCubbins, eds., *Structure and Policy in Japan
and the United States*
Gary W. Cox, *The Efficient Secret: The Cabinet and the Development
of Political Parties in Victorian England*
Gary W. Cox, *Making Votes Count: Strategic Coordination in the
World's Electoral System*
Jean Ensminger, *Making a Market: The Institutional Transformation
of an African Society*
David Epstein and Sharyn O'Halloran, *Delegating Powers: A Transaction Cost
Politics Approach to Policy Making under Separate Powers*
Kathryn Firmin-Sellers, *The Transformation of Property Rights in the Gold
Coast: An Empirical Analysis Applying Rational Choice Theory*
Clark C. Gibson, *Politicians and Poachers: The Political Economy of
Wildlife Policy in Africa*

Continued on page following index

TIMBER BOOMS AND INSTITUTIONAL BREAKDOWN IN SOUTHEAST ASIA

MICHAEL L. ROSS

University of Michigan, Ann Arbor

CAMBRIDGE UNIVERSITY PRESS

PUBLISHED BY THE PRESS SYNDICATE OF THE UNIVERSITY OF CAMBRIDGE
The Pitt Building, Trumpington Street, Cambridge, United Kingdom

CAMBRIDGE UNIVERSITY PRESS
The Edinburgh Building, Cambridge CB2 2RU, UK
40 West 20th Street, New York, NY 10011-4211, USA
10 Stamford Road, Oakleigh, VIC 3166, Australia
Ruiz de Alarcón 13, 28014 Madrid, Spain

Dock House, The Waterfront, Cape Town 8001, South Africa

http://www.cambridge.org

First published 2001

Printed in the United States of America

Typeface Sabon 10/13 pt.   *System* QuarkXPress [BTS]

A catalogue record for this book is available from the British Library

Library of Congress Cataloging in Publication data
Ross, Michael Lewin, 1961–
Timber booms and rent seeking in southeast Asia / Michael L. Ross.
   p.   cm. – (Political economy of institutions and decisions.)
Includes bibliographical references (p.).
ISBN 0-521-79167-7
1. Forest management – Environmental aspects – Asia, Southeastern.   2. Forest
policy – Environmental aspects – Asia, Southeastern.   3. Logging – Economic aspects
– Asia, Southeastern.   4. Timber – Economic aspects – Asia, Southeastern.   5. Rent
(Economic theory)   I. Title.   II. Series.
SD387.E58R67   2001
333.75'137'0959–dc21

                                                                    00-037922

ISBN   0 521 79167 7   hardback

For Sophie

"The economies of frontier countries are storm centers to the modern international economy."

Harold Innis (1956: 382)

Contents

Illustrations

Tables

Preface

This book grew out of my dissertation, which in turn reflected my concern about tropical deforestation in Southeast Asia. In 1994 I visited the region's leading timber-exporting states – the Philippines, Indonesia, and Malaysia – to learn more about their forests and forestry policies. Unlike some observers, I believed that these governments were wise to authorize logging on at least a limited scale, and to convert a portion of their forests into agricultural land. The United States had done much the same thing in an earlier era, using its abundant forests to spur development; why should not developing states today make a similar choice?

I was initially impressed by the forest policies of these three states – or, rather, four states, since in Malaysia forest policies are made at the state level, and most of Malaysia's timber came from the autonomous states of Sabah and Sarawak on the island of Borneo. I was also struck by the dedication of many of their foresters. Yet I gradually realized that the policies of their forestry departments were systematically ignored by politicians, particularly when it came to distributing timber concessions. As a result, these governments had at times authorized logging at rates far above the sustained-yield level, even in forests that were ostensibly set aside for "sustainable" forestry. The story began to make sense only after I uncovered documents – including previously confidential reports from the archives of the U.N. Food and Agriculture Organization (FAO) in Rome – that showed evidence of fierce internal struggles in these states between forestry officials, who sought to protect the institutions and policies of sustained-yield logging, and the politicians who sought to dismantle them. Almost invariably, the politicians won.

My dissertation chronicled the policy failures of the four governments, and drew on the new institutional economics and the theory of patron-client relations to help explain them. My advisors and colleagues seemed satisfied with my work, and urged me to publish my dissertation and get on with future projects. Yet I was dissatisfied with my analysis and was reluctant to part with it. My argument was narrowly tailored to my four cases, and said little that was new or enlightening to scholars who worked on more general topics, such as the sources of institutional change, or the problems of natural resource exporters. I also lacked a good explanation for some of the most puzzling aspects of the four cases, including why their policy failures varied over time and from case to case.

I consequently began to study other types of commodity booms in other states, to see if the policy failures that beset Southeast Asia's timber exporters fit into a larger category of phenomena. Most prior studies of commodity booms were produced by economists, who were preoccupied with an intriguing puzzle: While standard economic theories suggested that commodity booms should have a positive (or at least, neutral) effect on a country's economic development, often their impact was harmful. Sometimes this harm was caused by a condition known as the Dutch Disease; yet many studies found that policy failures were at fault. A major study of Dutch Disease states by economists Neary and van Wijnbergen (1986: 10–11), for example, concluded,

In so far as one general conclusion can be drawn [from our collection of empirical studies] it is that a country's economic performance following a resource boom depends to a considerable extent on the policies followed by its government. . . . [E]ven small countries have considerable influence over their own economic performance.

The policy failures described by these studies were – at least to my political scientist's eye – strikingly similar across regions, commodities, and regime types. Moreover, they suggested a beguiling paradox: Why should the good fortune of a commodity windfall lead to bad policy-making? This book draws on the theory of rent seeking to offer a general explanation for this paradox, and uses the cases of Southeast Asia's timber exporters to illustrate my argument.

In preparing this book I incurred an absurdly large number of debts. Most of them date back to 1993–6, when I first studied the politics of forestry in Southeast Asia and wrote my dissertation. I was immeasurably aided by my three dissertation advisors: Atul Kohli, John Waterbury, and George Downs. Now that I have the privilege of advising graduate students myself, I do my best to replicate the wisdom, patience, candor, and good humor of my own advisors.

Preparation for my initial field work was supported by an International Predissertation Fellowship from the Social Science Research Council, which was made possible by a grant from the Ford Foundation. The field work itself was supported by a fellowship from the Institute for the Study of World Politics, and my final year of dissertation writing was underwritten by a Woodrow Wilson Fellowship. The Center of International Studies at Princeton University provided me with additional support during the 1995–6 academic year, thanks to a grant from the MacArthur Foundation. A 1993 trip to the FAO archives in Rome – which proved to be critical for my research – was made possible by an International Environmental Institutions Fellowship provided by Harvard's Center for International Affairs, which received funding from the Rockefeller Brothers Foundation. Finally, at Princeton I was fortunate to be supported and housed by the Center for Energy and Environmental Studies, which was beneficently directed by Robert Socolow.

As one with no prior experience in Southeast Asia, and no prior knowledge of forestry, I was exceptionally dependent on the assistance of others during my field work. In Rome, Franca Monti dependably guided me through the FAO's archives. At the Universiti Malaya, I was fortunate to be sponsored by Dr. Mohamad Abu Bakar and Dr. Norazit Selat. I am especially indebted to Dr. Jomo Kwame Sundaram for his help and companionship, and to Clive Marsh for his assistance while in Sabah. In Indonesia I was graciously housed and assisted by the Center for International Forestry Research in Bogor; I am grateful to Neil Byron and Jeff Sayers for making this possible. My research was repeatedly aided by Dr. Rizal Ramli, Colin MacAndrews, and Jim Douglas, and my stay was enriched by my friendship with William Sunderlin, by the extraordinary hospitality of the extended Soedjatmoko family, and by the warmth and companionship of Bama Athreya, Robert Lang, and their cat Gregor. In the Philippines I was lucky to receive the help and hospitality of Marites Vitug, whose extensive research on Philippine logging politics made my own efforts possible. Chip Barber of the World Resources Institute also went out of his way to help me in both Washington, D.C., and the Philippines, and I owe him a special debt of gratitude.

I received insightful comments on my dissertation from many friends, advisors and colleagues; they included Tom Banchoff, Katrina Burgess, Lisa Curran, Alastair Fraser, Robert Keohane, Suzi Kerr, David Kummer, Miriam Lowi, Kate McNamara, Richard Robison, James Scott, Jeff Vincent, and John Walker. Pieces of the book manuscript were read by

Preface

Pradeep Chhibber, Robert Franzese, Michael Leigh, William Liddle, Ann Lin, Robert Pahre, and Nancy Peluso, all of whom offered helpful advice. My Michigan colleagues John Campbell and Jennifer Widner were both kind enough to read the full manuscript and both gave me thoughtful suggestions. Susan Go cheerfully guided me through the University of Michigan's vast Southeast Asia collection, and tracked down obscure but critical materials from other collections around the world. Uwe Deichmann and Polly Means kindly offered their help with the map and graphs, respectively. Four anonymous reviewers (two for Cambridge, two for another press) gave me extensive feedback, which led to important clarifications in the manuscript. One reviewer in particular – who I wish I could thank by name – drew on his encyclopedic knowledge of the region to save me from more than a few missteps, particularly in the chapter on Indonesia.

Several people deserve special mention. William Ascher has been a marvelous source of advice during all stages of the research and writing process, and made many suggestions that shaped the final manuscript. Chris Barr was kind enough to share early drafts of his Master's thesis with me, and to review my own work on Indonesia; his scholarship has greatly influenced mine. David Fairman helped me understand many subtle aspects of both natural resource use and the new institutional economics; through our lengthy discussions of Philippine forestry politics, we also became close friends. Finally, Alex Holzman skillfully threaded my manuscript through Cambridge University Press's approval process; Alissa Morris patiently fielded my impatient queries; and Laura Lawrie deftly edited the manuscript and prepared it for publication.

Some of the people and institutions I have thanked may disagree with all or parts of this book. I alone am responsible for its contents, including all remaining errors in fact and lapses in judgment.

January 2000, Washington, D.C.

I

Introduction

Three Puzzles

Between 1950 and 1995, the Philippines, Indonesia, and Malaysia each enjoyed periods of booming timber exports. Each had forests that contained trees from the *Dipterocarpaceae* family – trees that grew tall and straight, resisted wood-boring pests, and could be milled into high-quality lumber and plywood. While Indonesia's forestry institutions were weak, the Philippines and Malaysia had relatively strong forestry institutions, at least initially. Both had forestry departments that were led by well-trained professionals, that enjoyed a high degree of political independence, and that restricted logging to sustained-yield levels.

Yet over time the forestry institutions of all three states broke down. After timber exports began to boom, the Philippine, Malaysian, and Indonesian forest departments lost their political independence; the quality of their forest policies dropped sharply; and each government began to authorize logging at ruinously high rates – as high as ten times the sustainable level. Why did the forestry institutions of these three states break down? And why did these governments become so eager to squander their forests?

The breakdown of forestry institutions in the Philippines, Malaysia, and Indonesia is the central puzzle of this book; in answering it, though, I seek to cast light on two larger puzzles. One is the puzzle of poor forest management in the developing world. Since the 1950s, virtually all developing states with commercially valuable forests – in Latin America, the Caribbean, West and Central Africa, and Southeast Asia – have logged them unsustainably. A landmark 1988 study by economists Repetto and Gillis found that across the tropics, the misuse and waste of forest resources was, in part, caused by government policies. Yet the reasons for these self-defeating policies are elusive. According to one survey, attempts to explain poor forest policies have been "extremely frustrating, with suspicious or extremely poor quality data and missing data omnipresent" (Bilsborrow and Geores 1994).

This book suggests that in the Philippines, Malaysia, and Indonesia, a boom in timber exports helped cause a decline in the quality of the state's forestry institutions and policies. This argument may at first seem paradoxical: Why should an export boom hurt a state's institutions and policies? Should not governments manage their resources with *greater* care when their commercial value rises? In fact, in developing states, resource booms are commonly followed by a decline in the quality of the state's resource institutions and policies – which points us to the book's other major puzzle.

Scores of developing states rely heavily on natural resource exports, which can range from agricultural goods to zinc. Since international markets for these goods tend to be volatile, these states periodically undergo export booms and busts, which can flood or deprive their economies of export revenues.

Since the 1950s, economists have been divided about the merits of commodity booms. Classic theories of economic development – including the "big push" theory and the "staple theory" of economic growth – argued that commodity booms would help developing states grow quickly.[1] Others warned that sharp fluctuations in resource exports would turn developing regions into "storm centers to the modern international economy" (Innis 1956: 382).

Most developing states have assembled a wide range of institutions – including marketing boards, price stabilization funds, and "stabilizing" export taxes – to ensure that resource booms turn out to be an asset, not a curse. Yet despite these institutions, governments tend to respond poorly, even perversely, to resource booms. According to Lewis (1989: 1560), "Few governments have been able to manage (commodity booms) in a manner which, ex post, seems consistent with the objectives those governments set for themselves." Collier and Gunning (1999: 51) find that positive trade shocks often lead, paradoxically, to fiscal crises in the postshock period, due to "substantial policy errors." As a result, developing states tend to be harmed by booming natural resource exports. Policy errors help turn the blessing of resource wealth into a curse.

It would not be hard for political scientists to explain why govern-

---

1 On the big push theory, see Rosenstein-Rodan (1943) and Murphy, Shleifer, and Vishny (1989); on the staple theory, see Watkins (1963).

ments respond badly to *negative* economic shocks. But why should they respond so poorly to *positive* shocks? Should not extra revenue make it *easier* for officeholders to govern prudently, enabling them to build support for long-term policy goals, buy off their critics, and strengthen state institutions?

This book suggests the answer is "no," but for reasons that may not be obvious.

Observers commonly offer two explanations for the ill effects of commodity booms on government policies. The first is that sudden wealth leads to short-sighted, euphoric behavior among policymakers, who thereby cease to act rationally. Nurske (1958) and Watkins (1963), for example, suggest that commodity booms produce a "get-rich-quick mentality" among businessmen and a "boom-and-bust" psychology among policymakers; Karl (1997) argues that Venezuela's oil boom caused a type of "petromania" among policymakers. Similar arguments have been used to explain the perverse forest policies of the Philippines, Malaysia, and Indonesia. According to one foreign consultant, the Malaysian government's short-sighted forest policies were caused by the jubilant belief that "since there seems no obvious resource shortage today there is no apparent need for concern for the future" (Baird 1987: 12).

The second argument is that on receiving commodity windfalls, governments are overwhelmed by pressures from influential individuals, classes, interest groups, or other "rent seekers." In states with weak political and legal institutions, these pressures are said to lead to the breakdown of fiscal discipline and the dissipation of the windfall on patronage, corruption, and pork barrel projects. Tornell and Lane (1999) use a formal model to develop this argument, showing how a positive shock can be dissipated when "powerful groups" attack a state with a "weak legal-political infrastructure." Observers have used a similar argument to account for the harmful forest policies of Southeast Asia's governments – suggesting that powerful logging firms, and the clients of leading politicians, manipulated government policies to capture control of the windfall (Rush 1991; Broad 1995; Dauvergne 1997).

This book suggests that while both of these effects may occur, they are insufficient to explain the postboom policy failures of many developing states, including states whose institutions were previously strong. It offers a third explanation: Windfalls encourage politicians themselves to engage in a type of rent-seeking behavior, which I call *rent seizing*. I define rent seizing as *efforts by state actors to gain the right to allocate rents*.

Scholars generally recognize two types of rent seeking: rent creation, in which firms seek rents created by the state, by bribing politicians
and bureaucrats; and rent extraction, in which politicians and
bureaucrats seek rents held by firms, by threatening firms with costly regulations.[2] This book identifies a third type of rent seeking – rent seizing
– which occurs when state actors seek rents that are held by state
institutions.

There are two key differences between standard types of rent seeking
(including both rent creation and rent extraction) and rent seizing. First,
rent seekers seek out rents; rent seizers seek the right to allocate rents to
others. Rent seizing might be seen as "supply-side" rent seeking: when
private actors compete to acquire rents, state officials compete to supply
them.

Second, when private actors engage in rent seeking, they usually con-
front a battery of institutional devices that were designed to thwart them
– such as anticorruption laws, regulations that promote transparency,
bureaucratic insulation from political pressures, and meritocratic norms.
But unlike private actors, state actors may hold rule-making authority
over the institutions that would otherwise restrain them. For rent seekers,
state institutions are exogenous; but for rent-seizing politicians, state
institutions are endogenous and can hence be dismantled when they
obstruct the rent-seeking process. Rent-seizing politicians need not storm
the fortress: They are already inside the walls.

For scholars of institutions, international political economy, natural
resource policymaking, and Southeast Asia, this book makes a series of
interlinked claims. At the broadest level it addresses a neglected question
about institutional change. In recent years, the study of institutions has
received new attention across the social sciences. One body of scholarship has tried to explain how institutions develop.[3] A second is concerned
with how they become stable.[4] Scholars of the developing world,
however, are painfully familiar with a third problem: Ostensibly stable
institutions may unexpectedly collapse. Of course, state institutions may
break down for many reasons. This book seeks to explain a single type

2 See Tullock (1967); Krueger (1974); Bhagwati and Srinivasan (1980); Tollison
(1982); and McChesney (1987).
3 See, for example, North and Thomas (1973); Libecap (1989); Riker and Sened
(1991); Steinmo, Thelen, and Longstreth (1992); Knight (1992); Greif, Milgrom,
and Weingast (1994).
4 See, for example, Axelrod (1984); March and Olsen (1984); North (1990);
Tsebelis (1990).

of institutional collapse, which comes about when institutions become endogenous to a rent-seeking process.

The book also addresses the longstanding question of how international economic forces influence domestic political institutions. The question is of special concern for developing states, which often depend heavily on exports for growth, and tend to be more vulnerable to international market forces. Developing states that export primary commodities are perhaps the most vulnerable of all, since global commodity markets are exceptionally volatile. For decades, scholars have tried to tease out the causal links between international markets and domestic policy failures in commodity-exporting states – faulting declining terms of trade, multinational corporations, class alliances between First World and Third World elites, and the high asset-specificity of extractive industries.[5] This book suggests that international markets can harm developing states through a different mechanism, by creating positive economic shocks that lead to rent seizing and institutional breakdown.

The book also speaks to the problem of natural resource policymaking in developing states. Three-quarters of all developing states rely on natural resource exports for at least half of their export income. Yet natural resource policy failures are ubiquitous; most developing states govern their resources so poorly that the blessing of resource wealth routinely becomes a curse (Sachs and Warner 1995; Ross 1999). There are many types of natural resource policy failures (Ascher 1999). This book scrutinizes one: the policy failures caused by international market shocks. States that hope to use their natural resource wealth to promote development must find ways to mitigate this problem. Some options are discussed in the conclusion.

Finally and most centrally, this book concerns the devastation of Southeast Asia's forests and forest-dwelling peoples. Other scholars have described the loss of the once-valuable forests of the Philippines, Malaysia, and Indonesia, and the harm done to the people who lived in them. Yet they have not fully explained why these governments did so much to promote the misuse of their own resources.

Some observers have blamed these policy failures on ignorance or myopia, suggesting that government officials lacked the information, training, or intelligence to manage their forests on a sustained-yield basis. One of the central goals of this book is to refute this claim. The case

---

5 See, for example, Baran (1952); Gunder Frank (1966); Wallerstein (1974); Cardoso and Faletto (1979); Shafer (1994).

studies show that both the Philippines and Malaysia had strong forestry institutions until their timber booms began – institutions designed to thwart corruption and political interference, and to manage the forests on a sustained-yield basis. The cases also use government documents, many previously classified, to show that since the 1950s the Philippine, Malaysian, and Indonesian governments have been well informed about the dangers of forest misuse. Indeed, for half a century, leading foresters from each state, and from international organizations, have pleaded with these governments to manage their forests in accordance with sustained-yield principles. Once their timber booms began, these pleas were ignored.

Other observers have argued that nonstate actors, including multinational firms and domestic rent seekers, pressured these governments to adopt the logging policies that eventually brought their forests to ruin. This book confirms some of these accounts.

It also shows, however, that a great deal of damage was caused by rent seizing, as government officials dismantled their states' forestry institutions to obtain control of the timber rents. When timber prices began to create supranormal profits (i.e., rents) for logging firms, state officials began to disassemble the legal and regulatory mechanisms that had previously served to protect the forests and its inhabitants: mechanisms that had kept logging to sustained-yield levels and protected fragile soils and watersheds (in the Philippines and Malaysia); that had guarded the traditional rights of forest dwellers (in Malaysia and Indonesia); and that had insulated the forestry bureaucracy from political pressures (in the Philippines and Malaysia). At the moment these institutions were most needed, they were taken apart. The result was the devastation of Southeast Asia's forests and forest-dwelling peoples.

OUTLINE OF THE BOOK

This book has eight chapters. Chapter 2 maps out the broad domain of the problem. It describes the number and characteristics of states that rely heavily on natural resource exports, the types of institutions they have, and how they respond to export booms.

Chapter 3 discusses two alternative explanations for the policy failures of resource exporters. It then develops a theory of rent seizing, specifying its key assumptions, how it differs from other types of rent seeking, and what its observable implications are. It also explains the use of the Philippine, Malaysian, and Indonesian timber sectors for the case studies.

Chapters 4 through 7 are case studies of the forestry institutions of the Philippines, the Malaysian states of Sabah and Sarawak, and Indonesia.[6] Each chapter describes fluctuations in timber revenues (the independent variable); the subsequent rent-seizing behavior of state actors (the causal mechanism); and the resulting breakdown in the institutions of sustained-yield forestry (the dependent variable). Each also considers other explanations for the weakening or breakdown of the state's forestry institutions, including myopia and pressure from nonstate actors.

Chapter 8 is the conclusion. It summarizes the findings of the four case studies, and revisits the hypotheses spelled out in Chapter 3. It also describes some of the book's implications for the protection of tropical forests, the political economy of development, and the study of political institutions and rent seeking.

6 In Malaysia, forestry policies and institutions reside at the state level, rather than the federal level. Sabah and Sarawak are Malaysia's two largest states and harbor most of its forest resources; they also hold an exceptional degree of autonomy from the federal government in Kuala Lumpur. Chapters 5 and 6, consequently, focus on the independent timber booms of Sabah and Sarawak.

2

The Problem of Resource Booms

Before explaining *why* resource booms lead to the breakdown of institutions, it is important to define my terms and map out the domain of the problem. This chapter describes some basic facts about states that rely heavily on the export of natural resources: it explains what commodity booms are, and how they can create rents; it describes the types of institutions that developing states use to manage their commodity sectors, and to cope with export booms; and it reviews earlier research on the performance of these institutions.

The chapter has three central points: many developing states face periodic booms in their natural resource exports; many of these states have institutions that include features designed to help manage these booms; and despite these institutions, states respond poorly to resource booms.

It may be helpful to mention some of the claims this chapter does *not* make. It does not claim that all developing states undergo natural resource booms. It does not claim that all booms are followed by institutional collapses. It does not suggest that resource booms are the only source, or even the principal source of failure in these institutions.[1] Finally, it does not try to prove that resource booms cause institutional breakdowns: that is the task of the case studies in Chapters 4 through 7. This chapter lays out the scope of the problem. The rest of the book examines its source.

---

1 In the developing world, commodity institutions suffer from a wide range of maladies, apart from the ones described here. See, for example, Lele and Christiansen (1989); Ascher and Healy (1990); Auty (1990, 1993); Ascher (1999); Ross (1999).

NATURAL RESOURCE EXPORTERS

How many states depend on natural resource exports?

Table 2.1 provides some basic data on the reliance of states, by region and income, on the export of natural resources. Three points are noteworthy. First, reliance on resource exports varies widely by region: the highest concentrations of resource-reliant states are in Africa, the Middle East, and Latin America; the lowest concentrations are in East Asia and

Table 2.1. *States and Resource Exports, 1970 and 1990*

Region	Number of States	Over 50% Total Exports[a]	Resource Exports 1970[b]	Resource Exports 1990
South America	13	11	93.2	69.8
Central America, Caribbean	20	17	83.6	54.0
Sub-Saharan Africa	45	41	94.3	86.6
North Africa	6	3	92.9	86.6
Middle East	14	10	99.8	83.1
South and East Asia[c]	24	9	53.7	21.4
Oceania	9	7	67.4	72.5
Least Developed States	45	38	86.6	83.6
All Developing States	131	98	80.4	44.6
East Europe and Former Soviet Union	8	2	31.0	41.5
Advanced Industrial States	24	4	25.3	18.6
ALL STATES	163	104	36.2	25.9

[a] Number of states that receive over 50 percent of their export income from unprocessed natural resources, based on a three-year average (1989–91). The 1989–91 average is the most recent available from the United Nations Conference on Trade and Development.

[b] Export of natural resources as a percentage of regional exports.

[c] Excluding Japan.

Note: Commodity or resource exports, defined by the United Nations Conference on Trade and Development (UNCTAD), includes unprocessed minerals (including petroleum), agricultural products, and timber. Figures listed here include only states with populations over 100,000.

Source: Compiled from UNCTAD (1995).

Europe. Second, there is a rough correlation between level of development and natural resource reliance. The advanced industrial states and the high-growth states of East Asia rely little on resource exports, while the least developed states are exceptionally dependent on them. Third, the developing world as a whole has grown less dependent on resource exports. From 1970 to 1990, the number of developing states that received at least half of their export income from primary commodities dropped from 116 (89 percent) to 98 (75 percent); the fraction of the developing world's export income derived from commodities dropped from 80 to 45 percent. Yet there was little change in the dependence of the least developed states, on resource exports.

RESOURCE BOOMS

A resource boom is any sharp financial gain generated by the export of an unprocessed commodity, including hard rock minerals, petroleum, agricultural products, fish and animal products, and timber. It may be created by either an increase in a resource's export price, or by an increase in the quantity exported. In either case, resource booms can flood an economy with new revenues – a commodity or resource windfall.

Most commodity windfalls produce economic rents.[2] Rents are supranormal profits – profits in excess of the normal cost of extracting (or producing) a good, which includes a "normal" profit. The suppliers of natural resources can earn rents in three ways: They may earn scarcity rents if they control resources that are in demand, and have inelastic supply curves; they can earn differential rents if they control deposits of unusually high quality, or unusually low extraction costs; and they can earn monopoly rents if they are a monopoly or oligopology supplier. Few if any natural resource exporters have monopolies and can earn monopoly rents. Some earn differential rents. When resource prices boom, exporters earn scarcity rents.

Most resource booms are caused by the exceptional volatility of international commodity markets. Both the supply of and demand for basic

---

2 Scholars have long been concerned about the political and economic consequences of rents. In *Principles of Political Economy* (1848) John Stuart Mill suggested that the theory of rent

is one of the cardinal doctrines of political economy; and until it was understood, no consistent explanation could be given of many of the more complicated industrial phenomena. The evidence of its truth will be manifested with a great increase of clearness. (XVI:3)

commodities tend to be inelastic – that is, they respond sluggishly to changing conditions. As a result, small shifts in either supply or demand can produce large changes in price. Figure 2.1 compares changes in the price of manufactured goods with changes in the price of primary commodities between 1900 and 1986; it illustrates the higher volatility of commodity prices.

In recent decades, some developing states have grown less susceptible to commodity price shocks thanks to the growth of their manufacturing exports. Between 1970 and 1990, almost one-quarter of all developing states (31 out of 131) grew less dependent on commodities, reducing

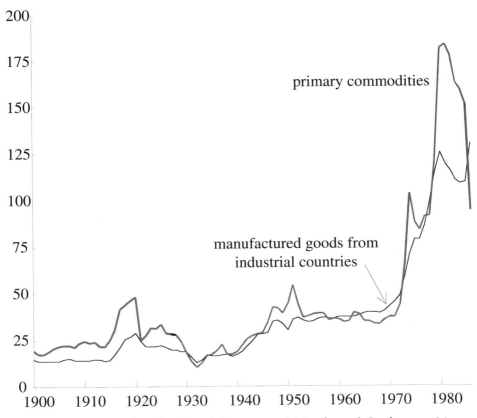

Figure 2.1. Price Indices for Natural Resources and Manufactured Goods, 1900–86. *Source*: Grilli and Yang (1988).

the fraction of their export income from commodities by at least 25 percent.[3]

Still, since 1970 most developing states have grown *more* susceptible to commodity market fluctuations, for two reasons. First, the volatility of all major commodity groups has increased (Reinhart and Wickham 1994). Second, since the 1950s many developing states have national-ized foreign corporations in their resource sectors, leaving their economies and governments more exposed to fluctuating resource prices. Until the 1960s the resource sectors of many developing states, includ-ing virtually all mineral exporters, were dominated by foreign corpora-tions. By the mid-1970s, many states had nationalized these firms. Before nationalization, foreign corporations often absorbed and repatriated a large fraction of any resource rents, including those created by resource shocks. This "drain" of wealth was much resented by developing-state governments. Yet, ironically, the private appropriation of resource windfalls insulated these governments from the volatility of international commodity markets. By expropriating foreign corporations – at a time when resource prices were growing even more variable – resource-exporting governments unwittingly exposed themselves to the hazards of trade shocks.

RESOURCE INSTITUTIONS

Scholar have long disagreed about the value of resource booms. Accord-ing to the staple theory of growth, resource booms should promote economic development, by drawing labor and capital to underdeveloped areas; as the boom proceeds, the profits from the core resource sector should be invested in value-added industries and local infrastructure, building a diversified pattern of growth (Innis 1956; Watkins 1963). Similarly, the "big push" literature suggests that poor states tend to get caught in low-income equilibrium traps. To escape, they need a large expansion in demand – a sustained "big push" – that can induce entrepreneurs to bear the fixed costs of industrialization. A commodity boom should provide this boost (Rosenstein-Rodan 1943; Murphy et al. 1989).

Other observers have worried about the impact of resource booms on developing states. Introducing a special issue of *Kyklos* in 1958 devoted

---

3 Calculated from data in UNCTAD (1995).

to the issue of commodity shocks, Ragnar Nurske (1958: 143) suggested that

> The instability of export markets for primary commodities makes any steady development policy difficult; discourages investment in primary production itself; generally limits the "economic horizon," and destroys the sense of continuity so necessary in private as well as public planning.

To guard against the dangers of export instability, developing states have looked toward both international and domestic institutions. Beginning in 1954, commodity exporters worked under the purview of the United Nations Conference on Trade and Development (UNCTAD) to negotiate International Commodity Agreements that could smooth out fluctuations in international markets. In the 1960s and 1970s, commodity price stabilization was part of the agenda of developing states for a New International Economic Order. The most ambitious commodity agreements – those that governed the trade of tin, cocoa, and natural rubber – created international buffer stocks designed to offset market volatility. Both the cocoa and tin buffer stocks broke down within three years of their founding. The exporters of some two dozen other commodities signed weaker accords, or failed to reach agreements at all (Gilbert 1996).

With no international institutions to reduce the volatility of commodity markets, states have been forced to rely on their own domestic institutions. These resource institutions take many forms and often have many functions. Many agricultural commodity exporters have marketing boards, marketing agencies, or price stabilization funds designed to collect the windfalls generated by commodity shocks, and use them to subsidize the prices paid to farmers when international prices later fall. Mineral-exporting states usually govern their resource sectors through state-owned enterprises, which supervise the extraction process and capture any resource rents; some also have stabilization funds. Timber-exporting states rely on their forestry departments to regulate the extraction and export of timber, and to collect resource rents when export prices are high.

Some of these institutions date back to the colonial era. Others were designed, or extensively reconfigured, in the 1950s, 1960s, and 1970s, with the assistance of the World Bank and the U.N. Food and Agriculture Organization (FAO). Both organizations urged developing states to protect their private sectors from resource shocks by using "stabilizing" export taxes and commodity stabilization funds. When international prices were high, export taxes would capture any windfall and place it in a stabilization fund; when international prices fell, the government could draw down this fund to subsidize the prices that the private sector received. If the commodity was owned by the state (such as minerals and timber), commodity institutions could smooth out government revenue flows and help the state maintain stable fiscal policies.

The effort in the 1960s and 1970s to build resource institutions was undergirded by a widespread belief that states were more likely than private actors – ranging from peasant farmers to transnational corporations – to use these windfalls in socially optimal ways. There have been five common arguments to support this claim. In the 1960s and 1970s, many scholars claimed that foreign corporations had a harmful influence on Third World development. Often these corporations repatriated the rents they captured; even if they invested them locally, some argued that these investments produced an inferior, "dependent" form of development (Baran 1952; Cardoso and Faletto 1979; Evans 1979).

A related argument was that economic growth in developing states required a move away from the export of primary commodities, and toward value-added processing and industrialization; and that to accomplish this, states would have to capture resource windfalls themselves, and use the revenues to subsidize export diversification (Hirschman 1958, 1977; Baldwin 1966).

A third argument was that governments were less likely than private actors to squander windfalls. Economists suggested that governments would be better at recognizing the temporary nature of short-term price shocks, and to respond with the appropriate caution; private actors might not recognize the transience of the windfall, and would be more likely to embark on a wasteful spending spree. According to Nurske, "The violent fluctuations of the export trade may well be a major cause of the speculative attitude and the 'get-rich-quick' mentality so widespread among businessmen in underdeveloped countries" (1958: 143).

More recently, economists have noted that even if both the state and private actors recognize that a price shock is temporary, the state is often better able to pool risks, and has access to insurance mechanisms (such as forward contracts and futures markets) that typically are unavailable to private actors in developing states (Schiff and Valdes 1992).

In the 1980s, concern about the "Dutch Disease" led to a fourth argument for state intervention. The Dutch Disease is an economic condition that sometimes follows a major export boom, and can make a commodity exporter's nonbooming sectors lose their international competitiveness (Corden and Neary 1982; Neary and van Wijnbergen 1986). Some economists suggest that states should offset the Dutch Disease by using revenues from a booming sector to temporarily subsidize nonbooming export sectors.[4]

Finally, in the 1980s and 1990s, a renewed interest in the economics of exhaustible resources led to a fifth argument: that when a windfall comes from an exhaustible resource whose depletion is imminent – such as minerals, timber, and fish – governments should capture any resource rents and invest them in ways that can offset the drop in national income that will follow resource depletion (Hartwick 1977; Vincent, Panayotou, and Hartwick 1997).

In short, there has been a broad consensus that developing states should have institutions that can buffer their economies against international market shocks, capture resource windfalls, and use them to mitigate the effects of export instability. Rather than leave windfalls in the uncertain hands of private actors, both economists and state officials have agreed – at least, until recently – that state institutions are needed.[5]

MEASURING INSTITUTIONAL PERFORMANCE

How well have these resource institutions performed? To answer this question, we need a common way to measure the performance of institutions that take different forms in different states and sectors, and are sometimes designed to achieve different clusters of policy objectives. Data on the performance of these institutions is often scarce, which constrains the choice of indicators further still.

---

4 Guarding against short-term deindustrialization may be important if a temporary drop in manufacturing output results in a long-term loss of comparative advantage – which may occur if there are industry-specific learning-by-doing effects that are external to the firm. See van Wijnbergen (1984) and Krugman (1987).
5 There has been a handful of dissenters from this consensus; they include Newbery and Stiglitz (1981), and Bevan, Collier, and Gunning (1993). Collier and Gunning (1999) discuss in greater detail the economic arguments for and against state windfall capture.

The common indicator I use is the ability of a resource institution to limit the pace at which a windfall is disbursed. Although states use their windfalls for a variety of purposes, in all cases they must refrain from using it overrapidly.

If the state's goal is stabilizing the prices that producers receive for their goods, then a resource institution must save a windfall for use when prices drop. If the goal is managing the economy with countercyclical fiscal policies, the state should save the windfall until a recession looms. In either case, disbursing the windfall too soon will have a procyclical effect, overheating the economy and leaving the state with fewer resources for countercyclical use.

Even when a state's goal is to subsidize a nonbooming export sector (to offset the Dutch Disease), a state must exercise fiscal restraint. Too much economic stimulation can raise the exchange rate by boosting the demand for imports, and by triggering inflation; a higher exchange rate will hurt any effort to aid nonbooming export sectors.

Economists often urge states to use their resource windfalls for investment, not to boost consumption.[6] Even when states heed this advice, they face the same constraints on the pace of windfall use. Economies have a limited ability to efficiently absorb new investments; in developing states, this absorptive capacity is often low. The greater the size, and the faster the pace of investments, the more likely they will produce a low or negative rate of return.[7] Investment booms – though classified as "savings" and not "spending" – can also have the same harmful effects as overrapid spending, leading to an overheated economy, a diminished capacity to counteract future recessions, and an overvalued exchange rate.

Finally, overrapid windfall use can also lead to budget deficits. It is easier to raise government spending than to reduce it; state budgets tend

6 This assumes that windfalls are temporary, which they typically are. Note that states can use windfalls to boost consumption in two ways: directly by increasing government spending, and indirectly by cutting taxes or increasing wages.

7 More precisely, governments should only promote investment until the rate of return is driven down to the discount rate (which in this case may be the mean rate of return from overseas investments), at which point they are better off investing the windfall abroad and repatriating it in the future. Cross-national studies suggest that the rate of return on investments has an important impact on the economic performance of developing states (Easterly 1991; Lal and Myint 1996).

to be "sticky downward." When the windfall is gone, governments often find it politically difficult to reduce their budgets commensurately, and engage in deficit spending.

To avoid these problems, economists recommend that states use their resource windfalls slowly and countercyclically. If the windfall is large relative to a state's domestic economy, the government should temporarily place the windfall in higher-yielding foreign assets until it can be "smoothly" repatriated and invested in domestic projects (Salant 1995; Varangis, Akiyama, and Mitchell 1995).

In short, the slow and deliberate liquidation of a temporary windfall is necessary (though certainly not sufficient) for states to achieve a wide range of policy goals. When states liquidate their windfalls too quickly, they cause themselves more harm than good.[8]

For these reasons, many commodity institutions are designed, in part, to protect windfalls from overrapid use. Moreover, in a world of rational actors, we might expect institutional constraints on windfall use to enjoy public support. Restraint is needed, but only when times are good and the economy is already enjoying the benefits of a booming resource sector. As long as citizens recognize that a windfall is temporary – and there is plenty of evidence that they do[9] – they should also recognize the value of saving windfalls for later use.

How well, then, do states and their institutions respond to resource windfalls? How often do they restrain the pace of windfall spending?

Many studies in the 1980s and 1990s addressed these questions. Two cautions are in order. First, most of these studies describe windfall policies but say little about institutions. We might infer that when states spend their windfalls quickly despite the presence of institutions charged with windfall sequestration, then the institutions have failed; still, our evidence is indirect. Second, some of these studies may suffer from a common type of selection bias. Policy failures attract the attention of scholars, while policy successes often go unnoticed. Most of these studies describe policy failures, but we cannot infer that failure is the norm – only that these failures have attracted attention.

---

8 Perhaps the only exception is when states use their windfalls to pay off debts.
9 See, for example, Knudsen and Parnes (1975); Bevan, Collier, and Gunning (1993); Morduch (1995); Townsend (1995).

Multisector Studies

The largest multisector study of windfall policies was carried out by Collier and Gunning (1999); the authors covered nineteen states that experienced positive trade shocks between 1964 and 1989.[10] They found that government responses to these shocks were "remarkably diverse" on most issues, including taxation, trade, and monetary policy. Most states heeded the advice of economists and saved a large fraction of their windfalls, at least initially. Yet in most cases these savings were quickly spent, or overspent, producing a fiscal crisis within several years. "Far from governments stabilizing the economy in the face of shocks," they concluded, "the shocks appear to have destabilized the budget" (Collier and Gunning 1999: 45).

Using regression analysis, Collier and Gunning found that windfalls raised investment by an average of 3.1 percent of gross domestic product (GDP) and output by 10.3 percent during the first (lagged) year. But in the subsequent three years, booms led to a sharp reduction in investment efficiency and a drop in output of 18 percent. They conclude,

The overall effect of the typical positive shock in this sample is eventually substantially to reduce output, despite the effect being strongly positive at the time of the shock. . . . Clearly, a positive shock to which the response is a high savings rate should be capable of augmenting output. That it appears not to have done so on average in our sample suggests that either the initial policy regime or the policy response is often problematic. (Collier and Gunning 1999: 36)

The findings of Collier and Gunning were broadly consistent with an earlier, ten-country multisector study by Cuddington (1989). Two of the states in his study (Colombia and Cameroon) adopted sound windfall policies; but in general, he noted,

There has been a tendency to overspend during and following export booms, which has considerably reduced realizable welfare gains. Overspending may be the result of excessive increases in consumption by either the private or the public sector, or overly ambitious and inefficient capital investment programs. The ratchet effect of increased government spending during booms, which proves difficult to reduce once the booms subside, is common. (1989: 154–5)

---

10 The countries with positive shocks were: Bangladesh, Botswana, Cameroon, Colombia, Costa Rica, Côte D'Ivoire, Egypt, Ghana, Indonesia, Kenya, Malawi, Malaysia, Mauritius, Mexico, Niger, Nigeria, the Philippines, Senegal, and Zambia. In sixteen cases, these shocks were caused by commodity booms. The study also covered four states that experienced negative shocks.

Similar results were also reported by Sachs and Warner (1999), who examined the economic impact of natural resource booms in seven Latin American states between 1965 and 1988. In one case (Ecuador), the boom appeared to have a positive effect on per capita GDP; in two cases (Chile and Colombia), the boom had no major effect; and in four cases (Bolivia, Mexico, Peru, and Venezuela), the boom led to a drop in per capita GDP.

Petroleum

The most carefully studied resource windfalls are those that accrued to petroleum exporters following the 1973–4 and 1978–9 oil shocks. The largest single study, authored by Gelb and Associates (1988), tracked the performances of six states: Algeria, Ecuador, Indonesia, Nigeria, Trinidad and Tobago, and Venezuela. All controlled their petroleum sectors through state-owned enterprises and marketing organizations. All had relatively modest petroleum reserves, and hence should have found the careful deployment of their windfalls exceptionally important. Yet the Gelb study found – and Auty (1990) later confirmed – that these states spent their windfalls so quickly that they eventually nullified their initial gains from the oil boom.

Following the 1973–4 oil shock, each of the six states quickly boosted their current spending, subsidies, transfers, and investments. Following the second oil shock, three of the four states for which data were available boosted their spending rates further still. Over the course of the two oil windfalls, spending rose faster than revenues in five of the six states, leaving their governments with higher debt loads than before (Tables 2.2 and 2.3).[11]

Although each of these states used much of their windfalls for "investment," the pace of these investments was too rapid for their economies to absorb without a sharp drop in investment efficiency. Many investments took the form of concessional loans to loss-making firms; in Venezuela, for example, government loans were dispersed "with almost no assurance of project completion and repayment" (Gelb and Associates 1988: 323). A group of ten major oil exporters saw their gross Incremental Output/Capital Ratio (IOCR) – a measure of investment

11 Only Trinidad and Tobago reduced its debt load.

Table 2.2. *Elasticity of Government Spending with Respect to Nonmining Output, Following the First Oil Boom (1974–8/1970–2)*

	Current Spending	Subsidies and Transfers	Investment
Algeria	1.36	2.19	2.15
Indonesia	1.43	1.02	1.53
Nigeria	1.63	3.78	4.96
Trinidad and Tobago	1.34	n.a.	2.89
Iran	1.98	2.67	1.74
Venezuela	1.11	1.38	1.83
UNWEIGHTED MEAN	1.48	2.21	2.52

Note: These figures measure changes in government spending patterns over time. A figure of 1.00 would indicate no change in the government's propensity to spend its revenue during the years 1974–8, compared with 1970–2. Figures above 1.00 suggest increasingly expansionary fiscal policies.

Source: Adapted from Gelb and Associates (1988).

Table 2.3. *Elasticity of Government Spending with Respect to Nonmining Output, Following the Second Oil Boom (1979–81/1974–8)*

	Current Spending	Subsidies and Transfers	Investment
Algeria	0.99	0.80	1.04
Indonesia	1.15	1.42	1.46
Trinidad and Tobago	1.23	3.10	1.10
Venezuela	1.13	1.16	0.68
UNWEIGHTED MEAN	1.13	1.62	1.07

Note: This table represents changes in spending patterns from the period of the second oil shock to the first; the baseline is now 1974–8, when spending elasticities had already been raised. Due to political turmoil, further data on Nigeria and Iran became unavailable.

Source: Gelb and Associates (1988).

productivity – drop by two-thirds following the oil boom, compared with the previous decade (Table 2.4).

Auty's (1990) analysis of windfall investments in an overlapping group of oil exporters (Nigeria, Indonesia, Trinidad and Tobago, and Venezuela) found that all had performed dismally; their investments were so poor that in all but one case (Indonesia), "competitive structural

Table 2.4. *Gross Incremental Output/Capital Ratios Among Mineral and Nonmineral Exporters*

	1960–71	1971–83
Hard-Rock Mineral Exporters	0.28	0.07
Oil Exporters	0.34	0.12
Other Middle-Income States	0.32	0.17
Other Low-Income States	0.26	0.17

Source: Gelb and Associates (1988).

diversification decelerated or even regressed" (131). Auty also noted that Malaysia and Cameroon – states that otherwise enjoyed reputations for prudent economic management – performed just as poorly, even though the delayed timing of their windfalls gave them each an opportunity to learn from the mistakes of others. Auty concluded gloomily, "The inability of governments to fulfill a dominant role in windfall deployment is clear" (1990: 132).[12]

The policy failures of the oil states were in part attributable to a widespread and mistaken belief that oil prices would remain high indefinitely. In at least some cases, however, policymakers were fully aware of the need to conserve their windfalls. Some even designed institutions for this purpose, but with little success.

In Ecuador, for example, the government's planning board (Junta de Planificación) noted that in the country's past,

The periods of relative bonanza [export windfalls] were translated in a short time into economic instability manifested in balance of payments problems and a fiscal deficit of even greater magnitude than prevailed prior to the period of prosperity. (cited in Gelb and Marshall-Silva 1988: 179)

The board crafted a detailed plan whose main objective was to avoid a similar fate. Yet the farsighted "Plan of Transformation and Development" for 1973–7 was largely ignored; so was the 1980–4 plan, which was designed to manage the second oil boom. Instead, Gelb and

12 Auty also found that Saudi Arabia and Bahrain, states with small domestic populations and large oil revenues, were more likely to place a fraction of their windfalls into savings, in part because their economies were tiny compared to the size of their windfalls. Even so, he noted that Saudi Arabia spent more than two-thirds of its 1974–81 oil revenues domestically, much of it on public infrastructure that "could scarcely generate sufficient revenues to service the capital invested, let alone recoup the massive outlays on the large complementary infrastructure investments they required" (112).

Marshall-Silva (1988) found, "Many [budgetary] decisions were made on the spur of the moment in the face of political pressures" (181).

Even more striking was the case of Venezuela. Following the first oil shock, the government established the Fondo de Inversiónes de Venezuela, a financial institution whose chief purpose was to prevent the windfall from overrapidly entering the economy. The fund was charged with placing half of Venezuela's oil revenues, over a five-year period, in foreign investments. Yet in 1975, the plan collapsed and the government instead spent the windfall on a costly investment program, which produced high inflation, an overvalued currency, and a massive foreign debt (Urrutia 1988; Karl 1997).

The proclivity of the oil states to overrapidly liquidate their 1973–4 and 1978–9 windfalls helps explain their subsequent economic stagnation. After conducting economic simulations, Gelb and Associates (1988) concluded,

> It is indeed possible to make the case that oil exporters ended the period worse off than they would have been with a far lower, more predictable rate of increase in oil prices, or, indeed, with constant real prices. (143)[13]

Even though the oil states collectively grew at an annual per capita rate of 2.9 percent before the windfall (1960–71), their growth rates slipped to 1.9 percent during the 1971–83 boom years.

Hard-Rock Minerals

Many exporters of hard-rock minerals enjoyed booming resource prices in the mid-1970s; many also spent their windfalls overrapidly, and suffered from economic stagnation.

Nankani (1980) found indirect evidence of overrapid windfall use among a group of thirteen hard rock mineral exporters between 1960 and 1976.[14] The thirteen mineral states accrued more export revenue and more tax revenue (as a fraction of GDP) than a group of comparable nonmineral states (Table 2.5); yet their marginal savings rates were markedly lower (Table 2.6). Moreover, the external debt ratios of the

---

13 For a compelling account of how the state of Alaska squandered much of its own oil windfall, see Strohmeyer (1993).

14 The mineral exporters in the study were chosen because of their dependence on exports of eight major hard-rock minerals: bauxite, copper, iron ore, lead, manganese ore, phosphate rock, tin, and zinc. The thirteen states were Bolivia, Chile, Guinea, Guyana, Jamaica, Liberia, Mauritania, Morocco, Peru, Sierra Leone, Togo, Zaire, and Zambia.

Table 2.5. *Tax Revenue/GDP Ratios,*
Mineral and Nonmineral States

	1960–70	1971–3
Hard-Rock Mineral Exporters	16.8	17.0
Nonmineral Exporters	13.0	13.5

Source: Nankani (1980).

Table 2.6. *Marginal Gross National Savings Rates,*
Mineral and Nonmineral States (percent of GDP)

	1968–73	1973–6
Hard-Rock Mineral Exporters	5.7	4.1
Nonmineral Exporters	23.6	13.8

Source: Nankani (1980).

Table 2.7. *External Debt/GDP Ratios,*
Mineral and Nonmineral States

	1970	1976
Hard-Rock Mineral Exporters	27.2	45.7
Nonmineral Exporters	13.2	19.2

Source: Nankani (1980).

mineral states were more than twice as large those in a control group of nonmineral states. From 1970 to 1976, their debts also grew more quickly, despite booming mineral prices (Table 2.7).

Further work by Gelb found that the investment productivity of the hard-rock mineral states was exceptionally low, implying that they invested their windfalls too quickly (Table 2.3). Lewis's (1984) survey of research on hard-rock mineral exporters concluded that the "form and pace of use of mineral rents" by these governments was so poor that export booms have led to higher levels of external indebtedness, and less diversification, than before. Several studies have shown that that mineral-exporting states have grown more slowly than their nonmineral counterparts (Nankani 1980; Wheeler 1984; Gelb and Associates 1988; Auty 1993).

Some case studies suggest that large windfalls have placed exceptional pressure on the resource institutions of the mineral-exporting states. Lim (1988) notes that the Papua New Guinea government raided its Mineral Resources Stabilization Fund, and used the revenues to boost current spending, when copper prices were high between 1978 and 1982. According to Auty (1991), when the price of copper rose in the early 1970s, Zambia discarded its Mineral Stabilization Fund; Shafer (1983, 1994) suggests the Zambian government subsequently drained the copper parastatal of its rents, leading to the industry's subsequent decline.

By contrast, the Botswanan government managed its diamond windfall in the 1970s exceptionally well, although it required unusual measures: The government initially disguised the windfall in its budget; it later conducted an education campaign within the government to emphasize the importance of delayed windfall use (Hill 1991; Bevan, Collier, and Gunning 1993). Thanks in part to careful windfall deployment, Botswana sustained a remarkable GDP growth rate of 10.3 percent annually from 1980 to 1990 – the highest in the world.

Agriculture[15]

The agricultural institutions of developing states have been the subject of many studies. There is widespread agreement that they often suffer from a range of ailments, including conflicting policy objectives, urban bias, inefficiency, and corruption. There is also evidence that when they receive windfalls, they have difficulty protecting them from political pressures for overrapid spending.

Bates (1981) notes that when agricultural marketing boards in Africa have accumulated surpluses, central governments have "sought, and won, control over the revenues of the marketing agencies" (14). According to Lele and Christiansen (1989), Africa's agricultural parastatals often suffer from indirect political pressures, that force them to dissipate their reserves:

---

15 All unprocessed agricultural goods are considered primary commodities, but not all are equally likely to produce large windfalls. Agricultural commodities that take longer to cultivate, and require special growing conditions – such as coffee, cocoa, and tea – have more inelastic supply curves and are hence more likely to generate windfalls.

Although there is a tendency to assume that the failure of many parastatals is due to their inherent inefficiencies, the sources of these inefficiencies often lie beyond the control of the parastatals themselves – e.g., in pressure from the government to overstaff as a form of political patronage or to perform development functions without remuneration. (24)

A 1992 World Bank study of eighteen states over a twenty-five-year span produced similar findings, reporting that stabilization funds were used by governments to facilitate "enormous transfers" of wealth from the rural sector to urban consumers, industry, and the state itself. The net effect was to reduce the real income of the poor (Schiff and Valdes 1992).

The most carefully studied agricultural resource boom was the beverage price shock of 1976–8, which affected coffee, tea, and cocoa exporters. The shock was triggered by the July 1975 frost in Brazil, which ruined one-third of the world's coffee crop. Tea and cocoa prices rose as well, as consumers used them as substitutes. Because the shock was widely recognized as transitory, states had a clear incentive to use their windfalls slowly. Davis studied the windfall policies of ten leading exporters of coffee, tea, and cocoa from 1975 to 1978.[16] All received large windfalls, as coffee prices peaked in 1977 at between 200 percent and 515 percent of their 1975 export values. All had institutions designed to protect these windfalls from misuse. In five of the eight states with complete data, however, government expenditures rose faster than revenues, producing higher debt loads at the end of the boom than the beginning (see Table 2.8).

A later World Bank study of five coffee exporters (Cameroon, Colombia, Costa Rica, Côte D'Ivoire, and Kenya) showed similar results: Although government revenues roughly doubled from 1975 to 1978, rising expenditures overtook rising revenues in Cameroon, Costa Rica, Côte D'Ivoire, and Kenya. Colombia was the only state to avoid overspending (Little, Cooper, Corden, and Rajapatirana 1993).

The most worrisome case was Côte D'Ivoire. Before the 1975–8 resource boom, Côte D'Ivoire was one of the most economically successful states in West Africa. Yet during the coffee and cocoa boom, the central government appropriated the large windfall held by the agricultural marketing board (*Caisse de Stabilisation*) and transferred it to the state investment budget. The subsequent spree in government invest-

16 The ten states were Burundi, Cameroon, Colombia, El Salvador, Ethiopia, Haiti, Côte D'Ivoire, Kenya, Rwanda, and Uganda.

Table 2.8. *Fiscal Responses to the Beverage Price Shock, 1975–8*

	Share Exports[a]	1975 D/S[b]	1976 D/S	1977 D/S	1978 D/S
Burundi	91.1	−1.2	−0.2	2.5	−2.7
Cameroon	49	−1.2	−1.1	−1.0	−0.5
Colombia	49.1	−0.2	0.9	0.9	0.9
Côte D'Ivoire	46.9	−4.5	−6.1	−4.1	−8.2
El Salvador	43.4	−1.6	−1.7	2.5	−2.1
Ethiopia	37.7	−4.1	−5.4	−3.2	n.a.
Haiti	35.1	−1.5	−1.9	−2.8	−3.1
Kenya	38.7	−5.3	−6.6	−4.1	−6.8
Rwanda	69.6	n.a.	1.5	1.5	0.2
Uganda	82.1	−5.3	−6.9	−4.7	−0.8
Unweighted Mean	54.3	−2.8	−2.8	−1.3	−2.6

[a] Share of coffee, tea, and cocoa in total exports, averaged for 1974–6.
[b] Overall budget surplus or deficit as a percentage of GDP.
Source: Derived from Davis (1983).

ment was so wasteful that by the early 1980s, the earnings foregone due to the relaxation of preboom investment criteria was equal to 5 percent of GDP (Mitra 1994). By 1983, Côte D'Ivoire's growth rate had dropped to −4.3 percent, the most rapid economic collapse in Africa (Ridler 1988).

Guano

Most studies of resource booms look at recent crises. But the problems caused by commodity windfalls are much older. In the mid-nineteenth century, the government of Peru, then the world's monopoly supplier of guano (dried seabird excrement), received a huge resource windfall. Much like resource exporters a century later, it soon spent itself into debt.

From 1840 to 1879, a handful of tiny islands off the Peruvian coast provided the world with virtually its only supply of guano, which was a valuable commercial fertilizer. In many ways, the Peruvian government enjoyed ideal conditions for a resource boom. As a monopolist, the Peruvian government could collect enormous rents, even while maintaining a slow, deliberate extraction rate.[17] Moreover, production costs were negligible: The guano was shoveled off of cliffs and tossed into chutes, which dumped it directly into the holds of waiting ships.[18]

Thanks to booming guano exports, between 1846 and 1873 government revenues rose fivefold; yet over the same period, government expenditures rose eightfold. Foreign debts gradually became unsustainable, and in 1876 – with guano supplies close to exhaustion – the Peruvian government declared bankruptcy[19] (Levin 1960; Hunt 1985). Once again, a large resource windfall was followed by an even larger rise in government spending.

CONCLUSION

Close to one hundred developing states rely heavily on their natural resource wealth to generate export income. Many of these states have grown increasingly vulnerable to international market shocks; most rely on a variety of state institutions to buffer them against these shocks. There is no simple way to determine how well these institutions perform. But there is strong evidence that these institutions often fail to protect resource windfalls from pressures to quickly boost spending and investment.

It is easy to understand why state institutions might be harmed by negative shocks: States with fewer resources may be less able to finance popular subsidies, to retain competent bureaucracies, and to purchase the support of unhappy constituencies. But it is harder to explain why

17 The optimal depletion rate for exhaustible resources was not worked out, however, until Gray (1914) and Hotelling (1931).

18 Contractors nonetheless refused to pay guano workers a market wage. Instead they relied on unfree labor, including slaves, prisoners, army deserters, and Chinese "coolies" imported under slavelike conditions. Labor conditions were so onerous that, according to a 1853 government report, hardly a day passed without an attempted suicide among workers. To rectify a labor shortage in 1862, contractors launched an armed kidnapping raid of Easter Island, seizing about one thousand of the island's three thousand natives. Although the French and British governments forced the Peruvian government to return the Easter Islanders in 1863, only fifteen survived the ordeal and returned home alive (Levin 1960).

19 Hunt (1985) emphasizes the government's wasteful investment choices.

states may be harmed by *positive* shocks. Positive shocks often are followed by ill-advised spending and investment booms. Why do these
policy failures occur? And why do resource institutions so often fail to
prevent them?

3

Explaining Institutional Breakdown

Why do windfalls lead to policy failures? Since the 1950s, scholars have offered two types of explanations: cognitive explanations, which suggest that windfalls induce either laziness or euphoria among policymakers; and societal explanations, which suggest that windfalls encourage non-state actors – such as interest groups, political clients, and rent seekers – to demand a share of the windfall from the state.

This chapter begins by summarizing these two approaches. It then describes my own explanation, which is that resource booms lead to rent seizing by state actors. It explains some of the assumptions behind the concept of rent seizing, how it may hurt institutions, how it differs from other types of rent seeking, and how it is influenced by a state's regime type. The chapter concludes by explaining how and why I use the cases of the Philippine, Malaysian, and Indonesian timber sectors to illustrate my argument.

COGNITIVE EXPLANATIONS FOR WINDFALL POLICY FAILURES

Cognitive approaches suggest that windfalls produce a type of myopia among public or private actors, which in turn leads to institutional or policy failures.[1] Some observers imply that windfalls lead to myopic

---

1 Pieces of the cognitive argument – that an abundance of natural resource wealth can make citizens lazy or short-sighted – can be found in the major works of Machiavelli, Montesquieu, Adam Smith, and John Stuart Mill. Perhaps this view was stated most pungently by Jean Bodin in *Six Books of a Commonwealth*, who explains that

> men of a fat and fertile soil, are most commonly effeminate and cowards; whereas contrariwise a barren country makes men temperate by necessity, and by consequence careful, vigilant, and industrious. (Bodin 1967 [1606], V:I)

sloth; others argue that windfalls produce myopic exuberance. Wallich (1960) and Levin (1960), for example, argued that periodic commodity booms in sugar-exporting states led to careless economic planning, which inhibited export diversification. Nurske (1958) and Watkins (1963), by contrast, suggested that resource rents lead to irrational exuberance, producing a "get-rich-quick mentality" among businessmen and a "boom-and-bust" psychology among policymakers, marked by bouts of excessive optimism and frantic retrenchments. Although the cognitive argument was made more explicitly in the 1950s and 1960s than it is today, it still has adherents: Karl (1997), for example, claims that Venezuelan policymakers responded poorly to the oil windfalls of the 1970s, in part due to bouts of "petromania" and other cognitive failures.[2]

A similar type of cognitive argument appears in some applications of the "rentier state" concept. Proponents of the "rentier state" argument suggest that large oil windfalls have produced poor economic governance in some Middle Eastern states. Mahdavy (1970), who popularized the "rentier state" concept, contended that resource windfalls produce an oddly risk-averse type of myopia among Middle Eastern policymakers, who grow irrationally optimistic about future revenues, yet simultaneously "devote the greater part of their resources to jealously guarding the status quo" instead of promoting development (443).[3]

Because the cognitive argument is often made in an ad hoc or implicit manner, it is difficult to test. But in one important way, it is inconsistent with a large body of research on commodity windfalls.[4]

If commodity windfalls produced myopic disorders among a wide variety of otherwise intelligent policymakers, we might expect it to

2 For other recent examples of the cognitive argument, see Auty (1993); Mitra (1994); Krause (1995).
3 The "rentier state" argument comes in different forms; not all of them rely on cognitive mechanisms. See, for example, Beblawi and Luciani (1987), Bellin (1994), Shambayati (1994), and Chaudhry (1994).
4 It is important to note that policymakers who are unprepared to manage their new-found wealth are typically blanketed with advice from the World Bank and other international organizations. For recent examples, see Salant (1995); Varangis, Akiyama, and Mitchell (1995).

An older example can be found in Machiavelli's *Discourses,* which prescribes measures to counteract the hazards of wealth-induced sloth:

as for that idleness which (an exceptionally fertile) site invites, one should organize the laws in such a way that they force upon the city those necessities which the location does not impose. (Machiavelli 1979 [1531], 173–4)

produce similar disorders among private actors. Yet there have been many studies of how private actors respond to commodity windfalls, virtually all of which suggest they react with admirable prudence: Even in impoverished states, private actors save a large fraction of their windfalls to buffer themselves against future market downturns, and to "smooth" out their income (MacBean 1966; Knudsen and Parnes 1975; Morduch 1995; Townsend 1995). A notable study of Kenya's 1976–9 coffee export boom compared the windfall responses of private actors to that of their own government. It showed that Kenya's coffee farmers – many of them poor and illiterate – had a remarkably high windfall savings rate of 70 percent; the Kenyan government had a windfall savings rate of just 20 percent (Bevan, Collier, and Gunning 1993).[5] Collier and Gunning found a similar pattern in other developing states, noting that "as far as the evidence permits, it suggests that private agents respond in a cautious and far-sighted way to shocks as long as they have uncontaminated information" (1999: 21).

Societal Explanations for Windfall Policy Failures

The second explanation for windfall policy failures is that on receiving windfalls, states are overwhelmed by distributional pressures from influential classes, sectors, client networks, or other interest groups. These distributional pressures lead to a breakdown of state institutions and policies, and the overrapid expenditure of any windfall on patronage, corruption, and pork barrel projects.

According to Wheeler (1984: 9), states in Sub-Saharan Africa overspent their commodity windfalls in the 1970s, because the governments were "pressured politically into 'sharing the wealth' by expanding patronage in ways which [were] difficult to reverse." Ranis and Mahmood (1992: 223) argue that the more a state accrues resource rents, "the more animated the struggle among various contending parties to appropriate these rents on their own behalf." Studies of timber booms in Indonesia, Malaysia, and the Philippines commonly suggest that the clients or cronies of leading politicians used their influence to capture most of the forest rents, producing ruinous government policies.[6]

One version of this argument has been developed in a formal model

---

5 When they tracked the repercussions of the coffee boom to the early 1980s, they found the government's savings rate had turned negative.
6 See, for example, Hurst (1990); Nectoux and Kuroda (1990); Rush (1991); Broad (1995); Dauvergne (1997); and Barr (1998).

by Tornell and Lane (1999), who refer to it as the "voracity effect." They suggest that when a country has weak legal and political institutions, and powerful private actors have open access to the economy's aggregate capital stock, that a windfall can lead to a reduction in growth, as "each group attempts to grab a greater share of national wealth by demanding more transfers." The severity of the effect is determined by the concentration of power in the private sector, the absence of institutional barriers that limit the ability of these groups to acquire government transfers, and the difference between the rates of return in the formal and informal sectors.

Societal arguments have some advantages over cognitive ones. They maintain the rational choice assumptions that many analysts prefer; they use well-established analytical frameworks, such as interest group theory, rent seeking, and clientelism; and they can explain why states handle windfalls less well than private actors, who face no comparable distributive pressures. Societal explanations are also consistent with a number of case studies that show that privileged individuals and groups have profited disproportionately from commodity booms.[7]

Still, the societal argument tells us little about how governments themselves respond to windfalls – a central concern for both political scientists and policymakers. Most societal arguments assume that the state is institutionally weak before the windfall arrives, enabling rent seekers to strip the state of its resources. But do windfalls *make* the state weaker? Should not windfalls make the state institutionally *stronger*, and hence better able to protect itself against rent-seeking groups? Should not windfalls make it easier for the state to pursue relatively "autonomous" economic policies, by financing payoffs to government opponents, buffering important constituencies against the impact of painful adjustments, and funding a more competent bureaucracy?

Societal arguments can plausibly explain why nonstate actors attempt to capture commodity windfalls; yet this is only part of the story.

A THEORY OF RENT SEIZING

In this section, I develop an alternative explanation for the influence of windfalls on government policies and institutions. Unlike cognitive

---

7 See, for example, studies of the Peruvian guano boom (Levin 1960; Hunt 1985), the Zambian copper boom (Shafer 1983; Auty 1991); the Indonesian oil booms (Bresnan 1993; Winters 1995; Ascher 1998), and the Venezuelan oil boom (Karl 1997).

approaches, it assumes that policymakers act rationally; and unlike societal approaches, it focuses on the choices and constraints that face policymakers, not private actors. My argument, in brief, is that windfalls trigger a type of rent-seeking behavior by politicians, who attempt to capture the right to allocate the windfall to others; in the course of their efforts they dismantle the institutions and policies that constrain them. The concept of *rent seizing* can complement societal arguments, to form a more complete model of how windfalls lead to policy failures.

Rent seeking is sometimes defined as any effort by private actors to capture economic rents, in a manner that is socially unproductive.[8] One of the central insights of the rent-seeking literature is that when a state has the ability to distribute supranormal profits (rents), private actors will make supranormal efforts to obtain them, for example, through lobbying or bribery. The larger the rents, the more that rent seekers should be willing to spend – and the greater the risks they should be willing to incur – to capture them.

Most studies of rent seeking assume that rents are "artificially" created by governments – for example, through restrictions on trade – in response to, or in anticipation of, lobbying by firms. But resource booms can provide governments with a "natural" source of rents, one that need not depend on any socially suboptimal market interventions.

Scholars in the Public Choice tradition commonly recognize two types of rent seeking. The first is "rent creation," in which private actors seek rents created by the state, by bribing politicians and bureaucrats; the second is "rent extraction," in which politicians and bureaucrats seek rents held by private actors, typically by threatening them with costly regulations.[9]

Rent seizing is a third type of rent seeking, which occurs wholly within the state, when public officials seek the right to allocate rents that are held by a branch of the government.[10] Since the rent seekers in this case are public officials, they may use their rule-making or rule-enforcing powers to remove institutional constraints that stand in their way.

A theory of rent seizing can be built on a simple cost-benefit analysis, in which a windfall raises the benefits (to politicians) of allocating state

---

8 On the definition of "rent seeking" see Buchanan (1980); Bhagwati (1982); Colander (1984); Lee (1985); DiLorenzo (1988).

9 See Chapter 1, footnote 2.

10 This is not a "right" in the moral sense, but in the social sense: an actor has the "right" to use an asset in certain ways when her authority is implicitly or explicitly recognized by those who have the ability to impede her.

assets, while the costs lag behind. I first assume that politicians seek to maximize their influence over the allocation of state assets, subject to costs; and that among state assets, the ability to distribute rents to private actors is exceptionally valuable. Politicians may use this influence for a wide range of purposes, which may be legal (such as funding favored social projects), illegal (obtaining personal wealth), or somewhere in between (distributing patronage and pork barrel funding).

I also assume that in pursuing this influence, politicians face rising marginal costs and declining marginal benefits, and that they make cost-benefit calculations about fulfilling their goals. These assumptions imply that politicians will attempt to gain control of state assets when it becomes cost-effective – that is, when the marginal benefits are above the marginal costs. The benefits of gaining influence over state assets include political influence and personal wealth. The costs are the risks of being apprehended and punished.

Now consider the impact of a windfall. A windfall will raise the value of state assets in the natural resource sector, and hence the benefits to politicians of gaining the ability to distribute them. If the costs rose quickly and commensurately, the gap between costs and benefits would remain the same, producing no change in the behavior of politicians. But if the costs adjust more slowly (or not at all), a windfall would lift the benefits above the costs, setting off an effort by politicians to gain influence over the windfall.

A key assumption in this model is that in the event of a windfall, the costs of gaining influence will lag behind the benefits. Is this assumption reasonable?

Let us assume that a politician seeks the costliest type of political influence – the ability to use state assets for corrupt personal gain – and that this carries a heavy penalty. The likelihood that a politician will be apprehended and punished for corruption is largely determined by variables that change slowly, and are unlikely to respond much to a windfall. These include anticorruption laws and regulations; the ability of the judiciary or bureaucracy to enforce them; the level of government transparency, which determines how well third parties can monitor illicit activities; the freedom of the press, which can report corruption; and the ability of civil society to organize against, and oppose, corrupt politicians. Many of these factors are determined by a state's regime type. All but the first change slowly over time. None seem likely to change quickly in response to a windfall.

How Does Rent Seizing Effect Institutions?

The theory of rent seizing implies that much of a windfall will be spent on patronage, corruption, and pork barrel projects.[11] Yet rent seeking produces the same result, making it difficult to distinguish between these two processes. When we look at state institutions, however, we find important differences. Rent seeking may produce no visible changes in state institutions, save for a higher incidence of corruption as politicians and bureaucrats succumb to bribes. Rent seizing, however, should produce distinctive types of institutional change.

Politicians who wish to use state assets for patronage and corruption must first gain *allocation rights* – the formal or informal ability to distribute economic rents to themselves or others. They should also strive to make these allocation rights *direct, exclusive, and discretionary.*

Politicians may obtain allocation rights that are either indirect or direct; direct allocation rights are more valuable. Distributing rents through intermediaries creates principal-agent problems. The more direct their authority, the lower the cost of these problems. Since natural resource institutions are often constituted as independent, self-governing agencies, a politician who seeks direct allocation rights must dilute or dismantle the agency's autonomy.

Rent-seizing politicians should also seek to make their allocation rights exclusive, by preventing others from holding similar rights. Like any supplier of goods or services, a politician who supplies state assets to his clients or friends can benefit from being a monopolist. If other politicians also hold allocation rights, each will have fewer assets to distribute. Multiple allocators also may create common pool problems, giving each allocator an incentive to use state assets more quickly than they would otherwise prefer. To make their rights exclusive, politicians may need to change any institutions that give others the right to influence allocation decisions.

Finally, politicians also can gain by making their allocation rights discretionary, to maximize their bargaining leverage with recipients. When officials have heightened discretionary powers, they can create new costs

---

[11] By "patronage," I mean a politician's distribution of selective benefits to clients, in exchange for political support; by "corruption," I mean a politician's appropriation of state assets for personal or familial gain; and by "pork barrel projects," I mean a politician's distribution of collective benefits to constituent groups, in exchange for support.

and benefits – such as burdensome regulations or spurious delays – in order to extract a larger quid pro quo from their recipients; they also can enforce the recipient's ongoing fealty and ward off the danger of postcontractual defection.[12] To gain this discretion, politicians may need to further dismantle institutional constraints on the asset's use.

Consider the example of a commodity stabilization fund, which has just received a large windfall. If it is the target of rent seekers, we might observe rising levels of corruption but no institutional change. If it is the target of rent seizers we should observe politicians altering institutions to give themselves the right to directly allocate the fund's assets, to flexibly assign and rescind these assets, and to exclude others from holding similar powers. These institutional changes should create a trail of observable evidence that can help us distinguish rent seizing from rent seeking.[13]

How is Rent Seizing Different from Rent Seeking?

Rent seizing differs from other forms of rent seeking in four ways.

First, rent seekers seek rents; rent seizers seek the right to allocate rents to others.[14] Rent-seizing politicians can also be seen as rent suppliers: When private actors seek to acquire rents, state officials seek to supply them.

Second, rent seizing damages state institutions, as public officials reconfigure these institutions to give themselves allocation rights to state assets, and to make these rights direct, exclusive, and discretionary.

Third, rent seizing is socially unproductive for different reasons than rent seeking. Rent seeking is socially unproductive when firms spend

---

12 The relationship between a patron and his client can be seen as a type of implicit contract. Like other types of contracts, the patron-client contract can easily break down: the interests of the two parties may diverge over time; their exchange of goods and services is not simultaneous, giving the party who benefits first an incentive to defect; the client may be given incentives by rival politicians to break the contract and switch his loyalty; and there is no independent third party to enforce the contract. Politicians who gain discretionary rights to an asset improve their ability to penalize any client who breaks the contract.

For a discussion of the value of discretionary influence for corrupt officials, see Rose-Ackerman (1978); Klitgaard (1988).

13 Although I explain here that rent seizing should lead to changes in state institutions, it may also effect nonstate institutions that restrict rent seekers. Chapter 7 includes an example.

14 They may, of course, allocate these rents to themselves.

their resources on bribes and lobbying costs; and when the prospect of blackmailing firms encourages state actors to intervene in markets to create rents (Appelbaum and Katz 1987; Kurer 1993).

Rent-seizing politicians need not spend money on lobbying, but their behavior is socially unproductive in other ways. Rent seizing diverts state assets into patronage, corruption, and pork barrel funding. Assets used for patronage and corruption are not transferred to the actors who would use them most productively and pork barrel projects tend to be less productive than other public investments. Moreover, as I argue below in greater detail, corruption and patronage tend to lead to the overly rapid dissipation of commodity windfalls.

Finally, once they have gained influence over a resource sector, public officials may find it easier to adopt new, socially unproductive regulations. Rent-seizing politicians may initially seek out preexisting state assets, like resource windfalls; but once they hold the ability to reshape resource institutions to their advantage, they may use the opportunity to create additional, allocable rents to meet their patronage and corruption needs. The rent seizers can become rent setters.[15]

Consider once more the example of a commodity sector. After gaining control of a state's commodity institutions, politicians may create additional rents by speeding the pace of natural resource extraction and externalizing any environmental costs – fouling the air, soil, and waters. If the commodity is extracted or produced by a state-owned enterprise, they may underfund routine maintenance and capital costs, and neglect the costs of worker safety.[16] All of these rent-creating regulations are socially unproductive. To distinguish these "endogenous" rents from the "exogenous" rents of the initial windfall, I refer to them as "ransack rents."

Figure 3.1 illustrates this argument. Under normal conditions, firms have supply curve S^1. At the normal commodity price P^1 they produce quantity q^1. When the price rises to P^2, firms wish to supply quantity q^2. Before the price shock, the sector generated profits A, which are sub-marginal rents; after the price shock, it generates profits A and B, a much larger sum of rents. The increase in the rents creates a powerful incentive for rent-seizing – and institution-busting – behavior by politicians.

If rent-seizing politicians wish to create ransack rents, they can allow firms to externalize the social and environmental costs of resource

---

15 A similar point is made by Appelbaum and Katz (1987).
16 In an earlier era, the returns to labor could be held down by the use of unfree workers. See the example in Chapter 2 of the nineteenth-century Peruvian guano boom.

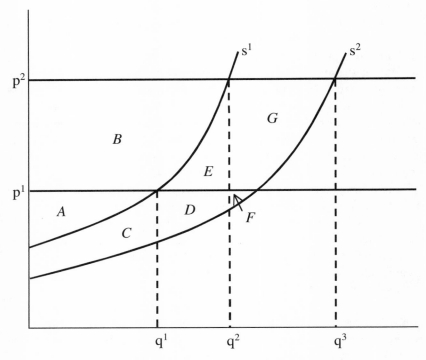

Figure 3.1. The Incentive for Ransack Rents.

extraction, which will shift the supply curve to S^2 and create rents represented by areas C, D, and E. The shift in the supply curve also gives firms an incentive to increase resource extraction. If politicians allow firms to extract quantity q^3, they can create an additional sum of rents (represented by F and G) to seize and allocate.

How Quickly Is the Windfall "Spent" on Patronage and Corruption?

Most studies of patronage and corruption conflate a politician's efforts to *acquire* personal influence over state assets and their decision to *spend* them. Plainly, the two processes are distinct: A politician may gain the ability to allocate rents yet spend them quickly or slowly. I have already suggested that state officials seek to maximize their allocation rights, subject to costs. What variables influence their subsequent spending decisions?

The spending decisions of politicians will always be influenced by idiosyncratic, case-specific factors. But two variables should have systematic effects: a politician's ability to establish exclusion rights, and his security in office.

Politicians should prefer to have exclusive allocation rights. Yet they may be forced to share allocation rights with other state officials – for example, from other branches of a central government, other levels of a federal government, or other parties or factions in a coalition government or legislative committee. If several actors simultaneously hold nonexclusive allocation rights, and each can make independent spending decisions about the windfall, the result will be a "common pool" problem: Each actor will have an incentive to use the windfall more quickly than they would otherwise prefer, lest another actor use it first.[17] The common pool problem may be avoided, but only if the actors can come to a binding agreement on mutual restraint.[18]

The second factor is the politician's security in office.[19] Secure officeholders, such as strong authoritarian leaders, can spend their patronage assets more slowly, reflecting their longer time horizons. Insecure officeholders – such as weak authoritarian rulers, or politicians in democratic states who face competitive elections – are likely to spend their resources more quickly, both to ward off imminent defeat and to use their allocation rights before they lose them.[20]

---

17 A similar argument about corruption is made by Rose-Ackerman (1978), and Shleifer and Vishny (1993).
18 Cooperation to limit windfall spending may be easy or difficult depending on a wide range of factors, including the number of actors, their private discount rates, their ability to monitor each others' behavior, and the relative payoffs of cooperation and defection. Libecap (1989) finds that in the private sector efforts to resolve common pool problems are often impeded by disputes among claimants about the distribution of future gains.
    If several actors share allocation rights, but each can block the other's independent spending decisions, then we should expect a much slower spending rate. The parties now must cooperate in order to *increase* their windfall expenditures. For a formal treatment of this scenario, see Persson, Roland, and Tabellini (1997).
19 For a discussion of variables that may influence a politician's time horizon, and hence her preferred spending rate, see Levi (1988).
20 A similar argument – that politicians with longer time horizons will exercise more restraint when tempted by corruption – was made by Alexander Hamilton in *The Federalist* (No. 72) to justify the principle of reelection for the president:

An avaricious man, who might happen to fill the office [of president], looking forward to the time when he must at all events yield up the emoluments he enjoyed, would feel a propensity, not easy to be resisted by such a man, to make the best use of the oppor-

The quickest spending should occur during competitive election campaigns. Imagine that the holder of an elected office has gained exclusive allocation rights to a commodity windfall; that he faces a serious electoral challenger; and that each candidate's chance of victory is a function of their campaign expenditures in bribes, patronage, pork barrel funding, and promises of the same. The incumbent should be willing to spend all of the windfall, discounted by his chances of losing, in order to remain in office; the challenger should be willing to make a similar bid, if not in present expenditures then in promises of future patronage.[21] The result should be the joint expenditure of a sum that is equal to a large fraction of windfall.[22]

How Does a State's Regime Type Influence Rent Seizing?

The theory of rent seizing implies that a state's regime type will have a contradictory impact on its response to a windfall.

The costs of gaining allocation rights should generally be higher in democracies than in authoritarian states. Democracies are more likely to have institutions – like a politically independent judiciary, a transparent government, a free press, and a politically mobilized civil society – that make it easier for third parties to monitor and penalize government

tunity he enjoyed while it lasted, and might not scruple to have recourse to the most corrupt expedients to make the harvest as abundant as it was transitory; though the same man, probably, with a different prospect before him, might content himself with the regular perquisites of his situation, and might even be unwilling to risk the consequences of an abuse of his opportunities. . . . But with the prospect before him of approaching an inevitable annihilation, his avarice would be likely to get the victory over his caution, his vanity, or his ambition.

21 Note that even if there are meaningful limits on campaign spending, candidates can nonetheless "bid" for support with promises of patronage once elected. Ames (1987), finds that on gaining office, politicians in Latin America used fiscal measures to pay off their patronage debts, producing a sudden rise in spending.

22 By adjusting our assumptions about this electoral contest – including assumptions about the number of rent seekers engaged in bidding, the marginal returns each one receives on his investment in the bidding process, the secrecy of the bidding process, the existence of incumbency advantages, the risk profiles of rent seekers, the ability of players to correctly estimate the bids of others, and the winner's level of certainty that he will have secure exclusion rights – we can construct scenarios in which the level of campaign spending is below, above, or equal to the size of the windfall. See the analyses of rent-seeking contests in Tullock (1980, 1995); Blomqvist and Mohammad (1986); Wenders (1987); Hillman and Samet (1987); Michaels (1988); Dougan and Snyder (1993); and Paul and Wilhite (1994).

corruption. Authoritarian leaders are hence more likely than their democratic counterparts to gain allocation rights to a windfall, and to make
these rights direct, discretionary, and exclusive. Rent-seizing authoritarian leaders should cause greater damage to commodity institutions than
rent-seizing democratic leaders.

Yet when it comes to the spending rate, authoritarian states should be
better off. Authoritarian leaders are more likely to hold exclusion rights
to a windfall, and to be politically secure. As a result, they should have
the luxury of allocating rents at a slower pace. In democratic states,
politicians should find it harder to gain exclusion rights, particularly
when the government's formal powers are divided between executive and
legislative branches, or between local, state, and federal levels. They also
face competitive elections, and are hence less secure in office. Democratic politicians may capture fewer state assets for patronage and corruption, but they are likely to spend them more quickly. Authoritarian
leaders may cause more harm to resource institutions but, paradoxically,
they face less pressure to spend their assets quickly.

The notion of rent seizing holds a further, even gloomier implication:
that democracies put proreform politicians at a disadvantage. To illustrate this implication, let us loosen our initial assumption that all politicians are patronage maximizers, and instead imagine that their
corruption and patronage preferences vary. Now we have both "good"
politicians, who exercise modest self-restraint in the pursuit of patronage, and "bad" ones who are patronage maximizers.[23] The electoral
contest can be likened to a bidding war for public office between good
and bad politicians. Each candidate makes a bid that reflects the expected
value of winning. Since bad politicians anticipate a larger payoff (in
allocation rights) from victory, they should consistently outbid good
politicians.

The result is that bad politicians will drive the good ones out of office,
or force them to adopt "bad" policies. When campaign spending (in
patronage, bribes, and pork barrel funding) is correlated with electoral
success, bad policies will be rewarded and reform will be difficult.[24]

---

23 Good politicians can be defined here as politicians who choose not to gain allocation rights to state assets; or who use their allocation rights more slowly.

24 This mechanism is a simple application of the so-called Coase Theorem. Coase
(1960) suggests that when there is a market for property rights, and transaction
costs are negligible, the rights will be purchased by the actor who will use them
most efficiently – since this is the actor who assigns these rights the highest value,
and who is therefore willing to pay the highest price for them. In the application

Summary

Windfalls tend to harm state institutions and policies by causing rent seizing, which are efforts by state actors to gain the right to allocate economic rents. The argument can be expressed as a series of hypotheses:

1. When a state receives an economic windfall, public officials will seek the right to allocate the windfall, in the form of economic rents, to others.
2. They will also seek to make these rights
   a. direct,
   b. exclusive,
   c. and discretionary – that is, to gain the ability to impose additional costs and benefits on recipients.
3. These efforts will weaken institutions that restrict windfall use.
4. The rate at which public officials allocate these rents will be influenced by:
   a. their ability to make their allocation rights exclusive. A politician with exclusive allocation rights will spend the rents more slowly than one with nonexclusive rights.
   b. the politician's security in office. A secure politician – one who believes he will remain in office for a long time – will spend the rents more slowly than a less secure politician.

CASE SELECTION AND THE COMPARATIVE METHOD

Since the early 1990s, there has been a renewed appreciation in political science of the "comparative method" – the careful and systematic use of a small number of cases to examine a conceptual puzzle.[25] For exploring the problem of windfall politics, the comparative method has several notable virtues. My independent variable (resource revenues) can be measured, but my causal mechanism (rent seizing) and dependent variable (resource institutions and policies) often cannot, at least in ways that can be meaningfully aggregated across different cases. The problems

---

here, the actor who assigns the highest value to the windfall, and is willing to pay the highest price for it, is the worst of the "bad" politicians.

For speculation on a similar effect in U.S. electoral politics, see Parker (1996).

25 See, for example, Collier (1993, 1998); Dogan (1994); Laitin et al. (1995); Mohr (1996); Dion (1998).

of quantification are compounded in developing states, where data tend to be scarce and have varying degrees of accuracy. Qualitative case studies also have special value in the earlier stages of theory building, since they give scholars a chance to explore the validity of their claims before investigating their generality.

Choosing a Narrow Set of Cases

When selecting cases, the comparative method usually forces scholars to make tradeoffs between validity and generality. More precise explanations are typically valid for smaller sets of cases; less precise explanations are commonly needed for larger sets of cases. At some point, explanations can become so imprecise and heavily qualified that they are conceptually "overstretched" and lose much of their utility (Sartori 1970).

If I wished to maximize my argument's generality, I could select a set of cases that represented the broadest possible range of commodity exporters, varying by commodity, region, and level of development. This approach may be well suited to studies that are part of a mature research program, in which the validity of a causal mechanism has already been established and scholars wish to know how broadly it can be applied. But when an argument's validity has not been established, and the causal mechanisms are still poorly understood, an overly broad set of cases is inappropriate and courts the problem of conceptual overstretch.

I have hence chosen a more cautious strategy, using a narrowly clustered set of cases, comprised of states from the same region (Southeast Asia) that received windfalls from the same commodity (hardwood timber). This "narrow cluster" strategy makes it easier to demonstrate my argument's validity, since I can have greater confidence that I am comparing "like with like" and observing similar phenomena in all four cases. The disadvantage of this approach is its lack of generality: I cannot make strong claims about the applicability of my explanation to a broad set of states or a wide range of commodities. Still, I hope that future studies will test my arguments in a larger domain of cases.

Even within the narrow domain of Southeast Asian forestry institutions, it is difficult to measure institutional quality in ways that facilitate useful cross-case comparisons; it is even harder to do so while controlling for other variables that influence institutional quality, including colonial history, legal and judicial systems, national income, and population pressures. As a result, the most analytically valid comparisons I make are within each of the cases over time. I examine each country's forestry institutions over three to five decades and observe how changes in the independent variable (timber revenues) led to the causal mechanism (rent seizing), which produced changes in the dependent variable (forestry institutions and policies); at the same time I try to account for other variables that influenced the dependent variable along the way. Together, the four cases constitute what Skocpol and Somers (1980) call a "parallel demonstration of theory," which illustrates that the same causal mechanism is at work in settings that vary.

The Case of Hardwood Timber

The study of windfalls produced by timber exports has two important virtues.

First, it can cast light on the widespread policy failures of the timber-exporting states. Tropical countries have been exporting wood for centuries.[26] Before World War II, this trade was limited to special, exotic hardwoods that were used for decorative purposes, and to the naturally durable "heavy hardwoods" (such as teak), which were well suited for a limited number of outdoor uses, such as railway ties. The richly forested countries of the tropics (most of which were then European colonies) were net timber importers during this period.

After World War II, the international market for tropical timber developed rapidly for a number of reasons. On the demand side, the developed countries needed timber for postwar reconstruction, and later, to satisfy growing consumer needs. During the 1960s and early 1970s, much of this demand came from Japan – the result of a Japanese construction boom, a thriving plywood export industry, and the rising cost of logging in Japan's own native forests. In 1962, Japan imported 10.4 million cubic meters of logs, 26 percent of world trade; by 1973, it imported 57.4 million cubic meters, 51 percent of world trade. After oil, timber was Japan's second largest commodity import.

---

26 So have the temperate countries. In the *Critias*, Plato laments the deforestation of ancient Attica, which bared the landscape like "the bones of the wasted body ...all the richer and softer parts of the soil having fallen away, and the mere skeleton of the land being left" (Jowett 1892, 530). Much of the Mediterranean was deforested in biblical and Roman times, while the great forests of Western and Central Europe were felled in the sixteenth and seventeenth centuries.

On the supply side, newly independent states in the tropics needed exportable commodities, while technological developments in logging, wood preservation, and plywood and veneer manufacturing made it possible for tropical timber to compete with temperate timber in international markets. Gradually, timber – which used to stand alongside other tropical forest exports like rubber, gums and latex, waxes, fibers, oil, fruit, bird's nests, aromatic woods, reptile skins, and medicinal plants – became the most valuable commodity in the forest. Between 1961 and 1993, tropical timber exports rose from $546 million to $17.992 billion in value.

Although both Africa and Latin America have larger forests, Southeast Asia quickly came to dominate the international trade in tropical hardwoods because its forests were more densely stocked with trees that had commercially desirable properties.[27] By 1991, Southeast Asian countries supplied 75 percent of all hardwood logs, 73 percent of all sawn hardwood, and 82 percent of all wood-based hardwood panels (plywood, veneer sheets, particle board, and fiberboard) entering international markets.

From an economic view, tropical timber could be an ideal commodity for developing states: It grows naturally in the forest and need not be cultivated; it can be harvested by workers with minimal training; and when logged at sustainable rates, it can provide a source of income in perpetuity. Yet in practice, almost all governments in the tropics have mismanaged their commercial forests. A landmark study by Poore, Burgess, Palmer, Rietbergen, and Synnott (1989) covered seventeen states that collectively harbored more than 70 percent of the world's tropical forests; it found that fewer than 0.2 percent of these forests were under some form of sustainable management.[28] Cross-national studies by Repetto and Gillis (1988), Schmidt (1990), Williams (1990), Vincent (1992), Grut, Gray, and Egli (1991), and Johnson and Cabarle (1993)

---

27 The average volume of commercial timber extracted from the forests in Latin America is eight cubic meters per hectare, in Africa fourteen cubic meters per hectare, and in Asia thirty-three cubic meters per hectare (World Resources Institute 1994: 134). This not only means that the Asian forests are more valuable commercially; it also means that logging there is more intensive and has more severe environmental and social consequences.

28 The countries included in the study were Cameroon, the Congo, Côte D'Ivoire, Gabon, Ghana, Liberia, Indonesia, Malaysia, the Philippines, Papua New Guinea, Thailand, Bolivia, Brazil, Ecuador, Honduras, Peru, and Trinidad and Tobago.

all found that tropical governments have failed to carry out even the weakest forms of sustained-yield management.

It is not obvious why these governments manage their forests so badly. Some scholars have used cross-country regressions to search for variables that are linked to these policy failures. Hobbled by a paucity of reliable data, most have produced weak or negative results. According to a survey by Bilsborrow and Geores (1994),

> This type of analysis is extremely frustrating, with suspicious or extremely poor quality data and missing data omnipresent. Problems also exist in determining how to measure some of the concepts, and what measures of what variable (ratios, percentage changes, absolute changes) should be compared with what measures of another. And what is appropriate for one comparison is often not for another. (131)[29]

One advantage of this book's focus on timber booms is that it can cast light on the policy failures that have contributed to the loss of tropical forests.

The second virtue of studying the timber sector is methodological: The exceptional duration of most timber booms makes them easier to study. Most other resource booms are relatively brief, since they are caused by the temporary disruption of supplies from one or more major exporters, typically due to war (the 1973–4 oil shock), revolution (the 1978–9 oil shock), or crop failure (the 1976–8 coffee shock). Within one to three years, most windfalls are over.

The brevity of these windfalls makes them difficult to analyze, for two reasons. First, when a windfall is brief, all of the ailments it may trigger are compressed into a short span of time. Rent seizing, if it occurs, may be more difficult to separate from other sources of policy failure, such as those caused by inexperience, myopia, bureaucratic overload, or poor information.

Second, short-term windfalls may produce just a single point of data for comparative analysis – a single instance of policy failure or success. When we study more enduring phenomena, we can observe the responses of a succession of politicians and governments, and use variations over

---

29 A similar problem has plagued the broader study of tropical deforestation. Deacon (1995: 2), for example, noted that "the empirical basis for identifying sources of deforestation is exceedingly thin; thus conclusions depend heavily on a priori reasoning." A survey by Angelsen and Kaimowitz (1999: 73) concurred, noting that "Although the boom in deforestation modeling has yielded new insights, weak methodology and poor-quality data make the results of many models questionable."

time to draw causal inferences within a single case; when we study a brief, infrequent event like a resource windfall, within-case comparisons are harder. While we can turn to other states for cross-country comparisons, we then lose our ability to control for many potentially important variables, leaving us less confident about the validity of our findings.

These problems can be circumvented by the study of timber windfalls, thanks to their exceptional duration. Timber booms are rarely caused by short-term supply shocks; more commonly, they reflect the steady rise in tropical timber prices since World War II, due to both the rise in global demand and the dwindling forests of many former exporters.[30] As a result, large timber rents are available in many tropical timber-producing states.[31] The duration of these windfalls provides us with many usable observations, within the controlled environment of a single state. In the four cases in this study, different politicians, different governments, and even different types of political regimes responded to the steady rise of forest rents, making it possible to draw stronger causal inferences within each case.

The Philippines, Indonesia, Sabah and Sarawak

Between 1950 and 1995, four states dominated the international trade in tropical timber: the Philippines, Indonesia, and the Malaysian states of Sabah and Sarawak (Figure 3.2).[32] These four states form a good cluster of cases for the study of commodity booms: They are similar enough to give us confidence we are comparing like with like; at the same time, there is substantial variation both within and among the cases in many important variables (Table 3.1). Because I derived the theory of rent seizing, in part, from these cases, I cannot use them to test my hypotheses. Still, they allow me to show how the concept of rent seizing can help account for policy failures that might otherwise be puzzling; and to compare my own theory's explanatory power with that of other approaches.

---

30 Hardwood timber is one of the only commodities exported by developing states whose real price has *risen* over the course of the twentieth century (Grilli and Yang 1988; Cuddington 1992; Bleaney and Greenaway 1993).
31 Vincent and Gillis (1998) provide a more detailed explanation of the sources of timber rents. They note that some of these rents are inframarginal rents, which are sometimes available even when timber prices are relatively low.
32 Although other states had larger forests, these four had forests that were more densely stocked with trees that had valuable commercial properties.

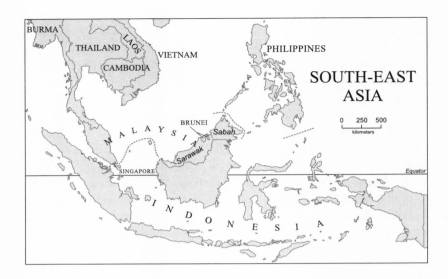

Table 3.1. *Major Indicators for Indonesia, the Philippines, Sarawak, and Sabah*

	Indonesia	Philippines	Sarawak	Sabah
Colonial History	Dutch	US, Spain	British	British
Population, 1995 (million)	200	70	1.8	1.7
Area (1,000 sq km)	1,905	300	124	74
Beginning of Timber Boom	1967	1951	1976	1956
GNP per Capita, 1995 (US$)[a]	980	1,050	3,890	3,890
Original Forest (% of land area)	100	95.3	99.5	99.5
Forests, 1995 (% of original)	64.6	6.0	N.A.	59[b]

[a] Figures for Sabah and Sarawak are for Malaysia as a whole.
[b] Figure is for 1992.
Sources: Ministry of Primary Industries (1993); Awang (1994); World Resources Institute (1998).

The cases illustrate my first, second, and third hypotheses – that resource windfalls lead to rent seizing, which in turn weakens state institutions – by making longitudinal comparisons within each case. Each of the four states received large timber windfalls; in each case, politicians fought for the right to allocate timber licenses. In the three states that had relatively autonomous forestry departments before their timber boom (the Philippines, Sabah, and Sarawak), the pursuit of allocation rights led to the dismantling of this autonomy. Politicians also sought to

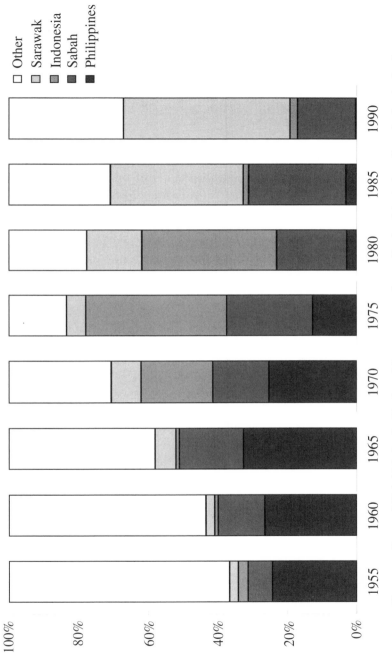

Figure 3.2. Shares of Global Market for Hardwood Logs, 1955–90. *Source:* Food and Agriculture Organization (various).

Legend:
- Other
- Sarawak
- Indonesia
- Sabah
- Philippines

49

make their allocation rights direct, exclusive, and discretionary; whenever they succeeded, they further weakened the laws and regulations that had previously kept the forests under sustained-yield management. In the two states that had previously recognized the traditional property rights of forest dwellers (Sabah and Indonesia), politicians rescinded or diluted these rights after the timber boom, to create ransack rents. In each case, rent seizing weakened the institutions that protected the forests from overuse.

Illustrating my fourth argument is more difficult. I claim that variations in two factors (the exclusiveness of allocation rights, and the security in office of rent-seeking politicians) will produce variations in the rate at which politicians spend the windfall. These politically induced variations, however, must be filtered out from variations caused by other, nonpolitical factors, including changes in timber prices, weather, and the harvesting technology available to loggers. Still, the political factors can help explain variations that might otherwise be puzzling. Three of the four states went through changes in regime type during their windfalls: the Philippines moved from democratic to authoritarian rule, while both Sabah and Sarawak went from colonial rule to transitional governments and, later, to parliamentary democracies. Each of these three also experienced repeated changes in government, as parties and leaders rose and fell. Indonesia remained under a single authoritarian ruler during the period I examine, though the regime grew more consolidated over time. Many of these shifts produced changes in the security of politicians, and in the exclusiveness of their allocation rights; these in turn can help explain changes in the rate at which the forests were harvested, and used for patronage and corruption.

Besides illustrating my own argument, I wish to compare its explanatory power with that of two alternative arguments for the policy failures of these four states. To assess the claim that policy failures were caused by poor information or short-sightedness, I use contemporaneous documents – many of them previously confidential – to determine how well informed policymakers actually were. I also consider the role of distributive pressures, which varied over time and across the four cases.

In addition to their analytical merits, the four cases also raise special policy concerns. Asia has already lost over two-thirds of its original forests. Southeast Asia has had the highest deforestation rate in Asia, and one of the highest rates in the world. Southeast Asia's forests also have unusual ecological importance. The Philippines, Indonesia, Sarawak, and Sabah are part of a distinct floristic region called *Malesia*, which stretches

south and east of the Asian land mass toward Australia. While all tropical forests are ecologically important, island habitats tend to support a
greater number of unique species than continental habitats. The islands
of Malesia, heavily forested and lying astride the equator, have forests
that are "exceedingly rich and varied" in species (Potter 1993: 103).[33]
Any progress toward protecting these forests will have ecological consequences that reach far beyond the region.

The Case Study Format

The four case studies follow a similar format. The first part of each
chapter is a brief introduction to the state's political institutions. I pay
special attention to the role of political patronage, to set developments
in the timber sector in a broader context.

The second part of each chapter is organized chronologically. It begins
with a description of the state's forestry institutions before the timber
boom; succeeding sections describe the timber boom's impact on these
institutions. The Appendix has a chronology of key events from each
chapter.

The ways I operationalize three variables – forestry institutions, the
timber windfall, and the windfall spending rate – bear some explanation.

By *forestry institutions*, I mean the forestry laws, forestry regulations,
and forestry departments (and related organizations) in each state. The
institutions I am most concerned with are those that protected the ecological health of the state's commercial forests, and limited logging to
sustained-yield levels. Before their respective timber booms these institutions were relatively strong in Sabah, moderately strong in the Philippines and Sarawak, and virtually nonexistent in Indonesia.

By *timber windfall*, I mean the windfall profits that became available
when export prices rose above extraction costs. Although states often
receive windfalls in the form of revenues, they may also receive windfalls when the value of an unliquidated asset, such as a forest, rises
sharply in value. When states receive windfalls in the form of revenues,

33 The Philippines, Indonesia, and East Malaysia (Sarawak and Sabah) have been
classified as three of the world's ten biodiversity "hotspots," areas with high biodiversity, high endemism, and rapid rates of habitat depletion. Malaysia and
Indonesia are also considered two of the world's twelve "megadiversity" countries, which are states with the greatest biological diversity and species endemism
(Abramovitz 1991; Myers 1988; Mittermeier and Werner 1990).

politicians can allocate the windfall through government spending. When they receive windfalls from an unliquidated asset, they can allocate the windfall by allocating exploitation rights, such as logging permits. In each of the four cases, politicians used undertaxed logging permits to allocate the windfall to their supporters and family members.

Finally, by the *windfall spending rate*, I mean the rate at which the government allowed licenseholders to log their concessions. To facilitate comparisons across the four cases – and to specify when this logging rate is "overrapid" – I compare this authorized logging rate to the maximum permissible logging rate set out by the state's forestry institutions. Three of the four states (the Philippines, Sabah, and Sarawak) set this limit as the maximum sustainable yield (MSY) that their forests could bear – that is, the maximum rate at which a constant flow of timber could be extracted from the forests indefinitely.[34] When politicians authorized logging at rates that they knew – or plausibly should have known – would exceed this limit, I consider it a sign of policy failure. I treat these high logging rates as policy failures not because they are unsustainable, but because they violate the government's own forestry policies. By measuring how far each state's authorized logging rate deviated from its own guidelines, I generate a rough comparative measure of windfall spending rates.

The incentives that timber-exporting states have to harvest their forests at sustainable rates are similar to the incentives that any resource exporter has to conserve a commodity windfall. Both the standing forest and the cash windfall are exhaustible, but potentially renewable

---

34 The MSY estimates I use apply only to commercial forest land, not to land set aside for agricultural conversion or other nonforest use (which is to be permanently deforested), and not to forests set aside for conservation or recreation (where all logging is prohibited). Only the remainder of the forest, which is explicitly set aside for sustained-yield logging, is subject to these MSY limits.

There are considerable economic, social, and environmental benefits to adhering to this limit: it produces a long-term stream of government revenue and foreign exchange; it can serve as the basis for a wood-processing industry that progressively adds value to forest products; it provides stable employment in rural areas; and it can help safeguard the forests' natural ability to moderate floods and droughts, protect fragile soils, and supply rural peoples with a wide range of game, fruit, resins, and other nontimber forest products.

Still, a policy of maximum sustainable yield is neither necessary nor sufficient for the sustainable management of tropical forests. Most observers now advocate more comprehensive definitions of sustainability that include other measures of forest health. The minimal definition I use is meant only as a benchmark – a lowest common denominator that the Philippine, Sabah, and Sarawak governments had each adopted by the 1950s.

resources that, if conserved, can produce a permanent income stream for the government. For timber exporters, this revenue stream comes from the revenues generated by a sustained-yield timber harvest; for other commodity exporters, it comes from the yield on any investments they make with their windfall. In both cases, a future income stream is assured only if the principal remains wisely managed and unspent.

4

The Philippines

The Legal Slaughter of the Forests

The combined effects of kaiñgin [swidden] *farming and the "legal" slaughter of the forest include widespread erosion and a reported deterioration in climatic conditions. Every recent study of forestry has stressed this alarming and irresponsible destruction . . . The public should be shocked into a realization of the consequences of continued suicidal forest destruction.*

(World Bank 1962: 16)

In 1951, the Philippines became the world's leading exporter of hardwood logs. Though heavily damaged by the war, the Philippine forest sector was in an admirable position. Almost half the nation was forested, and the logging industry used some of the most advanced harvesting practices in the tropics. Most important, the timber industry was governed by a forestry bureau with a well-trained staff, a considerable degree of political independence, a policy of promoting sustained-yield forestry, and a reputation for avoiding the corruption and patronage that plagued many other government agencies. Yet, by the 1960s, the forestry bureau had lost its political independence; its policy of sustained-yield logging was all but abandoned; and the nation's forests were on their way to being badly overlogged.

This chapter shows how the timber windfall of the early 1950s led to rent seizing, which in turn led to the deterioration of the institutions and policies that protected the forests. Between 1901 and 1951, Philippine forest policies and institutions were relatively sound; yet once windfall profits became available in the early 1950s, the forestry bureau gradually lost control of timber licensing to members of congress and the executive branch, along with the ability to keep logging to sustainable levels. These politicians used their allocation rights to grant undertaxed logging permits to their political

54

clients and family members, collectively sanctioning logging at unsustainable rates. It also shows how rent seizing changed in important ways under Ferdinand Marcos, who was the elected president from 1965 to 1972, and an authoritarian ruler from 1972 to 1986.

POLITICS AND PATRONAGE IN THE PHILIPPINES

Between 1946, the year of independence, and 1972, when President Marcos declared martial law, the Philippine government looked much like a U.S.-style democracy, with two major political parties, an elected president, and a bicameral legislature with strong fiscal authority. These formal institutions, however, were heavily shaped by informal networks of patrons and their clients.

Under Spanish and American colonial rule, Filipino society was dominated by a class of urban and rural elites, who stood at the apex of extensive networks of personal loyalty and obligation. As the Philippines gained its own political institutions under U.S. rule, these elites quickly colonized both the state and the two major parties. According to Carl Landé's classic analysis,

> The two rival parties in each province are structured by vertical chains of dyadic patron-client relationships extending from great and wealthy political leaders in each province down to lesser gentry politicians in the towns, down further to petty leaders in each village, and down finally to the clients of the latter: the ordinary peasantry. . . . The existence of competing but identical multiclass structures of this sort in every province largely explains why the national parties also are identical (ideologically). It also explains in part why there is so little basis for intraparty solidarity (Landé 1965: 2).

As longstanding patron-client bonds in rural areas deteriorated, local party leaders became less able to mobilize electoral support by using traditional ties of kinship and loyalty; they instead grew reliant on the distribution of cash, or in-kind payments, to win votes. When traditional oligarchs and their family members moved into politics, they sought out state resources to fund their client networks.

The Philippines' formal institutions – with a president and bicameral congress sharing fiscal authority – gave a wide range of national politicians, from both major parties, the ability to force bureau directors and division chiefs to grant them access to patronage in exchange for approval of the budget. This ability to use state resources for patronage can be seen as a type of allocation right. Since these allocation rights were nonexclusive, and Philippine politicians were politically insecure (because they faced regular, competitive elections), they were generally inclined to spend their patronage and corruption resources as quickly as possible.[1]

While the benefits of patronage and corruption were high, the costs remained moderate. As a democracy with a vigorous free press, corruption – when uncovered – could be subject to public criticism and even sanctions from voters; yet the weakness of the judiciary and bureaucracy, and the widespread acceptance of patronage as part of the electoral process, kept the costs of patronage and corruption relatively low, at least for many state assets. Moreover, Philippine voters came to expect gifts or favors in exchange for their votes. Stauffer (1975) describes a 1959 gubernatorial candidate, for example, who gave out T-shirts, shawls, handkerchiefs, sacks of rice, sardines, pencils, soft drinks, calendars, ballpoint pens, combs, cigarette lighters, religious items, and cash payments, to mobilize support – even though this type of vote buying was forbidden by the election code.

Indeed, in the 1950s and 1960s, the benefits of patronage so greatly exceeded the costs that members of congress grew preoccupied with using their offices to engage in "institutionalized looting" to finance their own survival (Nowak and Snyder 1974). Moreover, at election time, rival patronage networks bid up the cost of votes: By the election of 1969, the pressure for patronage and pork barrel funding was so great that "Congress appropriated more than the amount of the total gross national product of the Philippines, and reportedly typically passed a budget three times the size of revenues" (Stauffer 1975: 16).

The 1965 election of Ferdinand Marcos as president marked a watershed in Philippine politics. Marcos shifted the locus of federal patronage from the legislative to the executive branch, and within the executive branch, toward the president's office. He gained more exclusive influence over state resources that had partially been controlled by congress; he found new, more efficient ways to distribute patronage; and he tapped new sources of patronage by borrowing heavily on international markets. Indeed, Marcos's ability to extend his influence over state assets, and to distribute them more directly and efficiently, helped him win the 1969 election – making him the first and only president to ever be reelected.

---

1 Party discipline, which might have forced officeholders to spend their patronage resources more slowly, was almost entirely lacking (Landé 1965).

Upon declaring martial law in September 1972, Marcos adopted a new set of strategies to give his government the patina of legitimation: He supervised the drafting of a new constitution, established rigged procedures for elections and referenda, and used the police and military to mute the opposition. He also used martial law to establish more direct, exclusive, and discretionary property rights to a widening range of public assets, allowing him to become a "superpatron" with exceptionally broad client networks. As Marcos grew more reliant on the use of force to remain in office, he began to establish client networks in the military.

In declaring martial law, Marcos was able to make his allocation rights more exclusive; he also became more secure in office. The result, ironically, was that in the early years of martial law, the dissipation of state assets into patronage and corruption appeared to slow, as Marcos replaced the haphazard pillage of the state with a more deliberate and unified system of patronage and corruption (Nowak 1977). In the later years of his rule, however, Marcos's security in office began to diminish, due both to heightened political challenges and his own illness. As he grew less secure, his spending on patronage and corruption rose commensurately (Aquino 1987; Thomson 1995).

GOVERNING THE FORESTS, 1901–51

The Philippine Bureau of Forestry had its origins in the *Inspeccion General de Montes*, which was set up by the Spanish colonial government in 1863. Shortly after the U.S. takeover of the Philippines in 1898, Captain George P. Ahern was assigned to create a new forestry administration to replace the Spanish system. Ahern was an explorer, geologist, and hunter, who had once been a translator for Chief Sitting Bull; he was also a friend and protege of Gifford Pinchot, the head of the U.S. Forest Service and a leading figure in the American conservation movement.

Ahern and Pinchot together toured the Philippines in 1901. Ahern was impressed by the quality of the Spanish forestry laws, which he pronounced were "excellent, practicable, and in line with similar laws and regulations of Europe, where the science of forestry has reached such a high state of perfection" (Ahern 1901: 11). But he and Pinchot were appalled at how poorly these laws were enforced, and how ecologically damaging unregulated logging in the tropics could be.

Backed by President Theodore Roosevelt and Governor General William Howard Taft, the two men set out to organize a new Bureau of Forestry that had the legal authority, bureaucratic independence, and professional training to properly supervise commercial logging, and to protect the forests from overexploitation. In 1904, the two men drafted the Philippine Forest Act, which created a legal framework for forest management that would last until 1975.

The 1904 Forest Act adopted a key provision of its Spanish precedent by declaring all forest land – which at the time constituted about 70 percent of the archipelago – to be government property. It also gave the bureau sweeping authority to govern the forests, and to issue licenses for commercial logging.[2]

The first timber concession under U.S. jurisdiction opened in 1904 on the island of Negros. A few years later, the leading American forester and ecologist Barrington Moore[3] – a strong backer of the conservation ethic – wrote, "In utilizing the forests the most astounding progress has been made from a lumbering point of view" (cited in Tucker 2000). By the 1920s, the Philippines had become Asia's largest timber supplier, a position it would hold for almost fifty years.

The U.S. administration soon began to train Filipino foresters and turn the bureau's management over to them. In 1910, the United States opened a forestry school in Los Baños, near Manila; leading graduates were sent to the Yale Forestry School for advanced training. As historian Richard Tucker notes,

By the mid-1920s nearly all foresters in the islands were Filipino: the entire 500-man hierarchy of guards, rangers and foresters, except for five Americans at the top. In 1936 Arthur Fischer, the last American chief of the Bureau, turned his office over to his Yale-seasoned protege and friend, Florencio Tamesis. From that time onward Americans were only consultants in the exploitation of the Philippines' forest wealth ... (the Filipino foresters) had adopted the skills, values, and perspectives of the forestry fraternity. (2000: 42)

By the eve of World War II, the Philippine forest industry had become a major economic force. In capital investment, it was the nation's fifth largest industry; in the value of its production, the fourth largest; in the size of its labor force, the second largest. The Philippine Bureau of

---

2 In 1909, a decision by the U.S. Supreme Court in *Cariño v. Insular Government* created an important exception to the bureau's authority, ruling that the nation's people who had occupied the Philippine forests since "time immemorial" had rights to the land. The *Cariño* decision remained unenforced.
3 And father of the sociologist, Barrington Moore Jr.

Forestry was considered a model of professionalism, and widely admired by other foresters in the region (Egerton 1953). At the same time, timber production remained at roughly sustainable levels.

World War II and the Japanese occupation brought heavy damage to many of the nation's forests, and to the forestry bureau itself.[4] Less than a year after the war's end, the forestry bureau's resolve was tested when the secretary of Agriculture and Natural Resources – who oversaw the bureau's operations – ordered the bureau to increase the annual timber harvest to two and a half times the maximum allowable cut, in order to meet the overwhelming demand for lumber for national reconstruction.[5] The bureau objected to even this temporary permission to overcut the forests; after a month of negotiations the secretary relented, and agreed to only a slight increase in the maximum allowable cut.

Even this temporary loosening of the harvesting limits brought strong protests from within the bureau. In July 1946, the bureau's Committee on Matters Pertaining to the Division of Forest Concessions – composed of district foresters and foresters from the Manila headquarters – passed a resolution declaring

> The Committee desires to be on record that the Bureau should adhere strictly to the basic principle of forestry that only the growth of our forest should be cut and leave the principal or capital stock unimpaired. In times of emergency or national necessity, a slight deviation from the basic principle may be followed, but after such emergency or national necessity, the adherence to said basic principle be made. (Foresters' Conference 1947)

To facilitate postwar reconstruction, log and lumber exports were banned until 1949. Once export restrictions were lifted production grew quickly, thanks to the enormous demand for lumber in Japan and the United States.

In 1950, the bureau celebrated its fiftieth year. At a commemorative conference, prominent foresters and leading politicians stressed the need to reforest the lands denuded by wartime damage, to conserve existing

---

4 Among the many assets lost were the bureau's forestry records, which were burned by the Japanese in 1945. It was the second time that the nation's forestry records had been destroyed by fire; the first time was in 1897, in Manila.

5 The secretary's motivation appears to have been genuine. Since the secretary at the time had little or no influence over the allocation of licenses he had little opportunity to profit from this order. Moreover, there was great demand in the Philippines for timber after the war's end. All timber exports had been temporarily banned to help make lumber available for local use.

forests, and to stop the spread of *kaiñgineros*.[6] A message from President Elpidio Quirino emphasized,

We must, therefore, do everything within our power to bring back the forests on our denuded hills and mountains. But above all, we must conserve through prudent use the remaining forests we still have. (Bureau of Forestry 1950: 29)

The foresters also heard an address from Marcelo Adduru, a former congressman, governor, and secretary of labor, who reminded them of their reputation as one of the government's least-corrupt institutions:

At this momentous period in the history of our nation wherein due, perhaps, to the effect of war or what not, moral values of government service has regretfully been depressed as manifested by rampant grafts and corruptions and abuses of power and favoritism daily exposed in our newspapers, it is a satisfaction to know that the Bureau of Forestry stands among the few bureaus unaffected by the devaluation of moral values. (Bureau of Forestry 1950: 12)

At the beginning of the 1950s, the Philippine government had in place a set of institutions designed to protect the nation's forests in perpetuity. They included a forestry bureau with a well-trained staff and a strong professional ethic; a formal commitment to sustainable forestry; a forestry college with close ties to similar institutions in the United States; a legal ruling protecting the rights of longstanding forest dwellers; and a policy of placing key decisions on the allocation of timber licenses, and the release of forest land for agricultural conversion, in the hands of a trained forester – the bureau's director.[7]

In retrospect, it is easy to find flaws in these institutions. The policy of sustainability relied too heavily on the decisions of a single figure, the director of forestry; forestry taxes and royalties were set in pesos, and hence eroded by rising timber prices; there were no mechanisms to enforce the rights of forest dwellers; and the bureau had little protection

---

6 In the Philippines, the practice of swidden agriculture is commonly referred to as making *kaiñgin*; those who make *kaiñgin* are referred to as *kaiñgeros* or *kaiñgineros*, often derisively.

7 The formal commitment to the principal of sustainability was enunciated in the Forest Law, Section 1824, Chapter 47:

Principle governing administration of forests. The public forests of the Philippines shall be held and administered for the protection of the public interests, the utility and safety of the forests, and the perpetuation thereof in productive condition by wise use.

from pressures for favors from congressmen and senators. Still, in 1951, the Philippines had a functioning network of institutions that were designed to continue the policy of sustainable forest use – alongside the prudent release of suitable lands for agricultural conversion – regardless of the price of timber.

THE TIMBER WINDFALL AND RENT SEIZING, 1951–65

The lifting of export restrictions in 1949 soon produced a windfall for Philippine loggers. Loggers could now receive export prices, instead of domestic prices, for their products; moreover, from 1949 to 1956, the export price rose in real terms by 38 percent (Figure 4.1).

Had taxes and royalties risen along with timber prices, the state – not the loggers – would have collected this windfall. But taxes and royalties remained exceptionally low; they were also fixed in pesos and hence eroded by both inflation and rising real timber prices. As a consequence, the holders of logging permits could receive resource rents. The forestry bureau, which had sole authority to distribute these permits, was suddenly besieged on two sides: on one side by citizens who began to shower the bureau with applications,[8] on the other, by rent-seizing politicians who sought allocation rights to these licenses.[9]

Until 1955, the director of forestry – a position traditionally held by a professional forester – had sole legal authority to issue timber licenses. But in March 1955, President Magsaysay ordered Juan Rodriguez, who headed the Department of Agriculture and Natural Resources (DANR, which held jurisdiction over the forestry bureau), to issue an administrative order removing the director of forestry's authority to issue licenses.[10] The order transferred this power to a committee of three, composed of the director of forestry and two political appointees – the DANR legal advisor, and the DANR undersecretary, who chaired

8 By 1956, the Forestry Bureau reported a backlog of nine hundred applications, some pending since 1945. About two hundred licenses had been issued (*Philippine Lumberman* 1956; Golay 1961). On the rush for applications, also see Bedard (1957).
9 Although I focus here on federal politicians, there is abundant evidence that local politicians made similar efforts.
10 DANR later became the Ministry of Natural Resources under President Marcos, and the Department of Environment and Natural Resources (DENR) under President Aquino. Similarly, the Forestry Bureau became the Bureau of Forest Development in the 1970s and 1980s, and the Forest Management Bureau under Aquino.

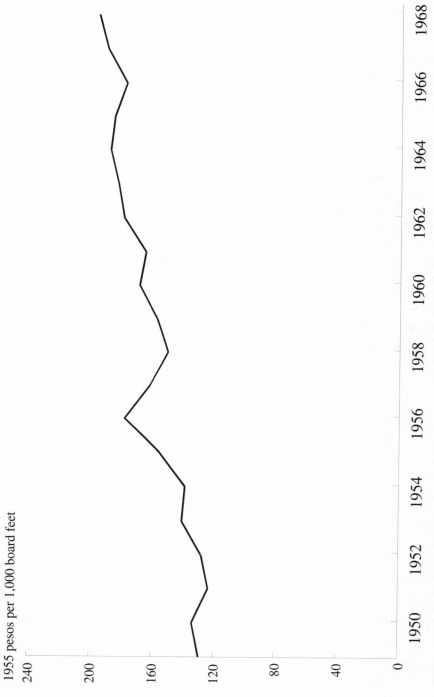

1955 pesos per 1,000 board feet

Figure 4.1. Wholesale Price of Philippine Logs, 1949–68 (1955 Pesos per 1000 board feet). *Source*: Office of Statistical Coordination and Standards (1968).

the committee. The order also gave the president the authority to review the committee's decisions.

Although DANR Secretary Rodriguez had just issued an administrative order stipulating that all forest concessions were to be awarded through public bidding, on February 15, 1955, the cabinet voted to exclude all concessions smaller than 6,000 hectares from the regulation. At the time, a 6,000 hectare concession was larger than the vast majority of existing concessions. These two measures gave President Magsaysay an indirect type of allocation right – an ability to assign rent-bearing licenses on a preferential basis. These moves may have reflected changes in the price of timber: between 1951 and 1955, export prices rose 26.4 percent in real terms.

From 1955 to 1956, timber prices rose another 12.4 percent in real pesos; evidence began to emerge that leading politicians and their clients were acquiring valuable logging permits. At the end of 1956, a group of logging firms, armed with evidence from the Bureau of Internal Revenue, claimed that the Magsaysay government was discriminating against "legitimate" lumberman and favoring "'fly-by-night' operators backed up by influential politicians." Politically backed concession holders, they charged, had been given higher annual allowable cuts, de facto permission to smuggle timber abroad, and exemption from paying standard forestry fees and penalties. The critics gained support from an independent industry journal, the *Philippine Lumberman*, which lamented

Forestry men in the field are being persecuted and blackmailed by politicians. Gone were the days when decisions of forestry men in the field were final. Now, decisions and policies cow at the whim and caprices of Malacañang.[11] (*Philippine Lumberman* 1957: 5)

Philippine political institutions gave fiscal power to both the executive and legislative branches of government, and within the congress, to both majority and minority parties; as a result, a large number of national politicians held at least some sway over the forestry bureau's annual budget, which they could use to influence the allocation and regulation of timber licenses. Conversely, this dispersal of influence made it hard for any one branch of government, or political party, to gain exclusive allocation rights to these licenses.

In December 1956, Senate President Eulogio Rodriguez Sr. – hoping to clamp down on the patronage available to the opposition Liberal party

---

11 "Malacañang" is the Philippine presidential palace.

– asked the forestry bureau for a list of liberal congressmen and senators holding timber concessions. Forestry Director Felipe Amos instead released a list of *all* members of congress holding logging permits – four liberals and seven nacionalistas. Three of the eleven held multiple concessions. Other members of congress were alleged to hold licenses through "dummies" or "fronts." All but one had obtained their concessions while serving in congress, even though holding a timber license while serving in public office was a violation of Section 17, Article VI of the Constitution. The list of concession holders contained a number of congress's rising stars, including a future chairman of the house committee on forests (Guillermo Sanchez); a future director of forestry in the Macapagal administration (Mateo Pecson); and a future president, Ferdinand Marcos.[12]

Paul Bedard, a U.S. forest management advisor stationed in the Philippines from 1952 to 1957, warned his superiors there was now heavy competition for logging permits, and that "[p]olitical pressure has entered into this matter (license distribution) to an extremely undesirable degree" (Bedard 1957: 16). Moreover, due to "political interference," the bureau was being forced to grant timber concessions to forest land that it had already set aside for watershed protection, and for national parks.

The shift toward political use of timber licenses under President Magsaysay set a pattern that persisted through the Garcia (1957–61) and Macapagal administrations (1961–5), while timber prices flattened out. Like Magsaysay, both Garcia and Macapagal shared their influence over timber licensing with influential members of congress from both parties. With no single figure holding exclusive allocation rights to the timber windfall – and all politicians facing regular challenges at the polls – officeholders held incentives to exploit their influence, and spend the windfall, as quickly as possible.

The Rise in Logging Rates

In 1954, loggers removed 3.6 million cubic meters of wood from the forests – a harvest that foresters believed was close to the

---

12 Marcos was the only one on the list to have received his concession before entering congress. He did, however, have it renewed yearly after arriving in congress, an arrangement of doubtful constitutionality (see Liwag 1963). Marcos claimed in late 1956 that he no longer held title to the concession and had legally abandoned it "some time ago"; but contemporary records from the Bureau of Forestry showed the concession still listed in his name (*Philippine Lumberman* 1957).

MSY.[13] Yet by 1964 the government was authorizing a cut of 11.4 million cubic meters, roughly three times the MSY (Figure 4.2). The rapid escalation in logging rates provoked a stream of protests in the 1950s and early 1960s from prominent public figures (see Table 4.1). Their objections had no discernible effect on policy; yet they are important to record, to refute both the claim that the Philippine public was indifferent, and the claim that policymakers were acting out of ignorance.

In 1955, as President Magsaysay began to dismantle the forestry bureau's restrictions on license allocation, the bureau's Luis Reyes – considered the nation's foremost authority on forest use – published an impassioned article that asked,

"Are we overcutting our forests?" Alarmed at the rate at which the forests are being cut down . . . people continually ask this question of us foresters . . . it seems *imperative that a revision of our forest policy should be made* insofar as it pertains to the administration of timber licensees. . . . In the first place a *reduction of the annual cut is in order*. (Reyes 1955; emphasis in original)

Reyes's plea came at a time when loggers were cutting 3.6 million cubic meters of timber a year.[14] His recommendation was consistent with the bureau's internal estimate that the MSY of the Philippine forests was 4.7 million cubic meters a year – and that due to losses from "pilferage" and *kaiñgin*, the annual allowable cut should be considerably lower (Gooch 1953).[15]

One year later, a report by the U.N. Food and Agriculture Organization warned that to "maintain actual production on a sustained yield basis," the government should not raise the annual allowable cut above the current level of production – 4.3 million cubic meters (quoted in Gill 1959: 9).

13 A substantial proportion of Philippine log exports were sent illegally to avoid forest charges. The figures used in this chapter, whenever possible, are not taken from government reports, but independent sources that attempt to correct for illegal exports (principally the FAO). For details on the illegal export of Philippine timber, see Nectoux and Kuroda (1990); Callister (1992); and Hicks and McNicoll (1971).
14 The log production figure is for 1954. Reyes's article was published in the February–March 1955 issue of the *Philippine Lumberman.*
15 Gooch states the bureau's internal MSY was roughly two billion board feet a year; the bureau's conversion rate was 424 board feet to one cubic meter. This figure is also consistent with the 1956 recommendation of Keith that logging be restricted to fewer than 46,000 hectares per year (Gill 1959: 9).

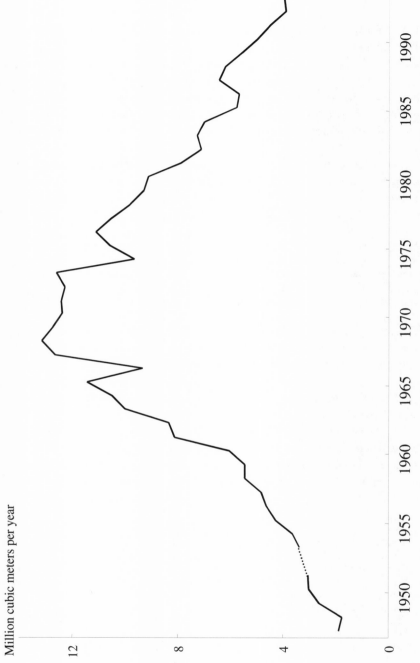

Figure 4.2. Philippine Timber Harvest, 1947–93 (million cubic meters per year). *Source:* Food and Agricultural Organization (various).

Million cubic meters per year

Table 4.1. *Evaluations of Philippine Logging Rates, 1955–71*

Year	Source	Evaluation
1953	Bureau of Forestry	States that maximum sustainable yield is 4.7 million cubic meters a year (Gooch 1953).
1955	Luis Reyes, Bureau of Forestry; considered the "father of Philippine forestry"	" 'Are we overcutting our forests?' Alarmed at the rate at which the forests are being cut down . . . people continually ask this question of us foresters . . . it seems *imperative that a revision of our forest policy should be made* insofar as it pertains to the administration of timber licensees. . . . In the first place a *reduction of the annual cut is in order*" (Reyes 1955) (emphasis in original).
1956	H.G. Keith, U.N. Food and Agriculture Organization	In theory, 46,000 hectares of forest can be cut annually (roughly 4.6 million cubic meters of wood); but such a high cut leaves no room for error and is ill-advised (Gill 1959).
1956	Gaudencio Mañalac, Philippine Lumber Producer's Association	"There is apprehension, even from those directly connected with the industry, that the timber stand of the country is not as vast as official statistics may want us to believe. In off-the-record conversations, this is not only grimly recognized by some of our leading lumbermen but, ironically enough, even by direct official sources. Some quarters even consider the situation so bad that the present drain on the timber reserves even exceeds the replacement" (Mañalac 1956: 6).
1959	National Economic Council (NEC)	Government report expresses alarm at deforestation rate (Kummer 1992: 47).
1959	Senator Emmanuel Pelaez	Cites government data that thirty-one provinces have already lost the forest resources needed to maintain adequate soil cover; introduces bill to phase out log exports (*Philippine Lumberman* 1959).
1959	Tom Gill, leading US forester, consultant to the NEC and the US International Cooperation Agency (ICA)	"The Philippines is well on the way of devastating her forest resources . . . forest lands have been released not because of agricultural suitability but the deciding factor seems to be the political strength of the demand . . . (at) the present rate of timber removal, disastrous inroads are being made on the forest capital" (Gill 1959: 5).
1959	Society of Filipino Foresters	Votes to support restrictions on log exports to "more reasonable levels," as the "timber drain has become so excessive that deforestation is very alarming" (*Daily Mirror* 1959).

Table 4.1. *(continued)*

Year	Source	Evaluation
1960	Segundo Fernandez, Chief, Forest Reserves Section, Forest Management Division, Forestry Bureau	"There was never in the history of the Philippines (a time) where alarming and wanton destruction of forest had so much caught public attention and condemnation as it is today due to attributed catastrophic occurrences like flood, drought resulting to shortage of power and 'brownouts,' soil erosion, landslides, etc." (Fernandez 1960: 36).
1961	Paul Zehngraff, ICA forestry advisor	"At the rate Philippine forests are being denuded, the nation stands to lose its valuable timber industry if indiscriminate destruction of forests continues unabated" (*Daily Mirror* 1961).
1961	Philippine Forest Conservation Association	Group is founded by major timber firms to "generate national interest in preserving the country's forest resources" (*Manila Times* 1961).
1962	Godofredo Neric, Boy Scouts National Director	"At this rate (of deforestation), there will be a time when the country will be comparable to some countries in the Middle East"; urges legislation to protect forests; begins tree-planting program (*Manila Times* 1962).
1962	World Bank	"The combined effects of *kaingin* farming and the 'legal' slaughter of the forest include widespread erosion and a reported deterioration in climatic conditions. Every recent study of forestry has stressed this alarming and irresponsible destruction ellipisis. . . . The public should be shocked into a realization of the consequences of continued suicidal forest destruction" (World Bank 1962: 20).
1967	Juan Utleg, Assistant Director, Bureau of Forestry	"Everybody sees the handwriting in the wall that unless there is applied a restraint on the policy of forest liquidation . . . we shall soon have no forest to convey as a legacy to the next generation" (Utleg 1967: 8).
1971	United Nations and Presidential Committee on Wood Industries	Report finds that if forest loss continues at the current pace, the Philippines will face an "irreversible descent" in timber production and forest cover and be forced to import wood (Mercado 1971).

Perhaps the most widely publicized plea came from Tom Gill, the most prominent tropical forester in the United States. In 1959, acting as a consultant to the National Economic Council, Gill issued a study that warned

The Philippines is well on the way of devastating her forest resources . . . forest lands have been released (for logging and subsequent agricultural use) not because of agricultural suitability but the deciding factor seems to be the political strength of the demand . . . (at) the present rate of timber removal, disastrous inroads are being made on the forest capital. (Gill 1959: 5)

The Gill report had a catalytic effect on public opinion; between 1959 and 1962, the trickle of public concern turned into a torrent. In 1959, the Society of Filipino Foresters voted to support restrictions on log exports, noting that "the timber drain has become so excessive that deforestation is very alarming" (*Daily Mirror* 1959). In 1961, a group of timber firms tried to raise public support for forest conservation, while in 1962 the Philippine Boy Scouts began a nationwide tree-planting program and urged congress to adopt legislation to protect the forests.

Even the World Bank – at the time, a major advocate of commercial logging in the tropics – urged the government to take action. A 1962 report stressed,

The combined effects of *kaiñgin* farming and the "legal" slaughter of the forest include widespread erosion and a reported deterioration in climatic conditions. Every recent study of forestry has stressed this alarming and irresponsible destruction. . . . The public should be shocked into a realization of the consequences of continued suicidal forest destruction. (World Bank 1962: 16)

The authorization of high logging rates would have been less harmful, had loggers been forced to comply with the bureau's harvesting regulations. The regulations stipulated that loggers leave a certain number of trees on each plot, and refrain from harvesting smaller, younger trees; these restrictions were designed to help the forests regenerate, and to discourage agricultural settlements on logged-over land. But politicians often prevented the forestry bureau from enforcing these regulations on the concessions of their clients, allowing them to use more profitable, and reckless, harvesting practices.

There are no reliable quantitative data on the bureau's attempts to enforce harvesting regulations. But between 1955 and 1966, every independent analysis of the Philippine timber industry lamented the weak enforcement of these critical regulations.[16] Many linked the problem to political interference. Perhaps the bluntest assessment came from Gill:

> In the Philippines, nothing has so completely served to discredit the (Forestry) Bureau in the eyes of the public as has the impunity with which legal and political authorities, high and low, thwart its every attempt to protect the nation's property. (Gill 1959: 5–6)

Eufresina Boado, writing about forest practices in the 1950s and 1960s, concurs:

> Because a significant number of timber operators were politicians, it was almost impossible to enforce policies that would reduce the operators' profit margins. Concessions that belonged to these influential people became almost untouchable by mere foresters. (Boado 1988: 186)

Top officials in the forestry bureau sometimes complained bitterly about the political pressures they faced to overlook regulatory violations:

> (Assistant Forestry Director Juan) Utleg decried that political interference has been setting back the bureau's campaign against illegal logging and *kaiñgin*. In the past, many forest officers prosecuting forest violators found themselves persecuted and prosecuted instead, he said. He expressed hopes that politicians, who usually used pressure for the dismissal of criminal cases filed against their constituents or followers for violation of forestry rules, would help boost the bureau's protection and conservation program. (*Manila Times* 1965)

The arrival of a timber windfall in the early 1950s led to rent seizing by both members of congress and the executive branch; this in turn led to a sharp decline in the institutional autonomy of the forestry bureau. The efforts of politicians to gain allocation rights thwarted the bureau's efforts to award licenses impartially, to limit the number of licenses issued and their annual allowable cut, and to enforce logging regulations. Until 1965, a wide range of politicians held allocation rights to the windfall, though none had been able to make these rights direct, or exclusive, or discretionary. With the election of Ferdinand Marcos that would change.

---

16 See, for example, U.S. Bureau of Foreign Commerce (1955); Bedard (1957); Gill (1959); World Bank (1962); Landgrebe (1966). Bedard also notes that congress refused to fund the bureau's enforcement activities.

PRESIDENT MARCOS AND THE FORESTS, 1965–72

By 1965, timber production had become one of the nation's leading industries, accounting for over 6 percent of GNP. The industry's growth had made it an important employer in many rural areas, and a leading source of foreign exchange for the nation (Figure 4.3). But it also provoked greater public concern about the depletion of the forests. Although no figures were released at the time, by 1964 the government was authorizing logging at roughly three times the sustainable rate.

In 1965 Ferdinand Marcos was elected president. Over the next seven years, he established a type of influence over the forestry bureau that was more direct, and more exclusive, than any president before him. His efforts may have been influenced by the rising benefits of acquiring patronage: The price of Philippine timber rose 22 percent in real pesos between 1959 and 1965; at the same time the cost of campaigning for president was also rising, and would reach record levels in 1969. His efforts may have also reflected his exceptional skills as a politician, who found new ways to use state resources to advance his career. In any case, Marcos showed himself willing to bear political costs that his predecessors were not, in order to gain allocation rights that were more direct and exclusive than his predecessors had enjoyed.

Within days of taking office, Marcos embarked on a strategy to increase the directness and exclusivity of his authority over timber licensing. In January 1966, he suspended the distribution of all timber licenses "until such time when (1) the Bureau of Forestry shall have been reorganized, (2) the boundaries of licenses shall have been relocated, and (3) the records of licensees examined." Marcos personally reviewed the list of licensees; permits held by some of defeated President Macapagal's supporters were cancelled. For the first time since the war, timber production dropped significantly (see Figure 4.1).

While Magsaysay, Garcia, and Macapagal had worked through DANR to influence the forestry bureau, Marcos preferred more direct control. He had appointed Fernando Lopez, his vice president and a member of the country's richest family, as DANR secretary. But his alliance with Lopez was one of convenience.[17] As DANR

---

17 Under martial law, Marcos would drop Lopez from his government and dismantle the business empire of the Lopez clan, while leaving alone most of the nation's other wealthy families. For more on the Lopez clan, see McCoy (1993).

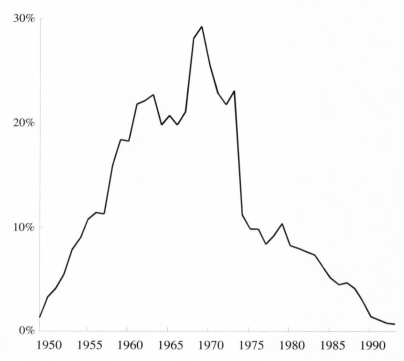

Figure 4.3. Philippine Timber Export Revenues as a Fraction of Total Export Revenues, 1949–93. *Sources*: Baldwin (1975); Food and Agricultural Organization (various).

secretary, Lopez gained authority over the nation's sugar, banana, and coconut sectors, which gave him considerable influence over the business empires of the country's economic elite. But Marcos kept personal control over the forestry bureau by appointing a series of close allies to direct it, and granting them the authority to bypass Lopez on key decisions.

Marcos selected Antonio Quejado as his first director of forestry. Unlike past directors, Quejado had no training as a forester; his only qualification seemed to be his relationship with Marcos.[18] Quejado quickly established a reputation for malfeasance, granting favored

18 Indeed, Quejado falsified his curriculum vitae, fraudulently claiming he had a B.S. degree in industrial chemistry from Quisumbing College.

applicants permission to overcut their concessions, or to harvest timber without a valid license. He regularly overrode the decisions of his subordinates, citing Marcos's verbal instructions.

Quejado's actions – and Marcos's efforts to trim the bureau's authority – was politically costly for Marcos. The Quejado nomination brought protests throughout 1966 and 1967 from the Society of Filipino Foresters, senior civil servants in the forestry bureau, the *Philippine Lumberman*, and newspaper columnists in the general press. In July 1967, students and faculty from the University of the Philippines College of Forestry staged an anti-Quejado rally at Malacañang Palace, Marcos's official residence.

The congress also fought Quejado's appointment, either out of respect for the bureau's remaining autonomy, or out of fear that Marcos was threatening their access to the timber windfall. Marcos submitted Quejado's nomination to the Senate three times; each time it was rejected. Frustrated by Marcos's obstinance, Representative Eladio Caliwara introduced a bill to curtail the powers of the Forestry Director, who he said was "the most powerful director in the entire Philippine bureaucracy" (*Daily Mirror* 1967).

Marcos's relationship with Quejado eventually led to a rift with Vice President and DANR Secretary Lopez. In January 1968, Marcos gave Quejado new powers to grant licenses without Lopez's approval. In protest, Lopez threatened to resign his DANR post; Marcos finally fired Quejado and replaced him with Teofilo Santos, a trained forester. But Marcos kept the appointment of Santos temporary and chose not to submit his name to the senate for confirmation, so Marcos could monitor "what he's going to do" – thus retaining the power to fire him on a moment's notice.

Closely watched by the president, Acting Director Santos reshuffled the forestry bureau's top managers, disbanded the legal staff, and issued a series of permits for logging in national parks – violating both bureau regulations and the recommendations of his own staff. Like Quejado, Santos was soon in trouble with both congress and the press (*Philippine Lumberman* 1968b, 1968c).

Unable to stop their loss of influence, professional foresters in the forestry bureau sometimes complained bitterly to the press. In 1967, Juan Utleg, the bureau's assistant director, admitted,

Everybody sees the handwriting on the wall that unless there is applied a restraint on the policy of forest liquidation . . . we shall soon have no forest to convey as a legacy to the next generation. (Utleg 1967: 8)

As the 1969 election approached, Marcos faced a dilemma. He no doubt wished to benefit from his unprecedented influence over timber licenses; but he also had to minimize the concomitant costs of public dismay. His solution was to campaign as a conservationist, but quietly use timber patronage at an unprecedented rate.

In 1967, Marcos issued an administrative order to gradually reduce log exports. He also delivered a well-publicized speech declaring his dedication to forest protection:

> I have flown over Mindanao several times now and every time I did I felt like crying. I felt like crying because we have denuded the area, and before long it is going to be a wasteland ... (describes corruption in Forest Bureau) ... I would rather resign as President if we cannot remove this stigma. (Marcos 1968: 18)

But a month before the election, Marcos quietly suspended his order to reduce log exports. Around the same time, the forestry bureau suddenly issued 969 minor forest product licenses covering a remarkable 775,592 hectares of land;[19] the annual allowable cut for fiscal year 1969–70 jumped 14 percent from fiscal year 1968–9, to a new record level. Grateful for these favors, most concession holders reportedly backed the Marcos reelection campaign (*Daily Mirror* 1969a; *Philippine Lumberman* 1969).

After first taking office, Marcos had reduced the annual allowable cut by canceling licenses associated with his rivals; in a single year it dropped from 11.0 to 6.1 million cubic meters. Over the next four years he increased the annual allowable cut from 6.1 to 15.5 million cubic meters, roughly four times the sustainable rate.

After winning the November 1969 election, Marcos focused once again on reducing the political costs of liquidating the nation's forests. A few days after his victory, he announced a plan to shut down the logging industry over a ten-year period, to prevent further deforestation, soil erosion, and flooding; he also blamed "millionaire loggers" in congress for the ruin of the forests (*Daily Mirror* 1969b). The annual allowable cut, the total number of licenses, and the area of forest under concession all leveled off, albeit at the record levels they hit on the eve of the election. In February 1972, Marcos's new DANR secretary, Arturo

---

19 Minor forest product licenses gave their holders the right to collect a range of nontimber forest products. They were widely used by state officials and loggers, however, as informal short-term logging permits.

Tanco, warned in a speech of the "grave implications of a denuded Philippines" and announced a series of measures to better protect the forests, including the suspension of 124 of the 131 "Special Timber Licenses," a type of permit that had been particularly prone to abuse[20] (Tanco 1972).

It is unclear whether the public was reassured by Marcos's gestures; but concern about protecting the forests remained strong. A 1971 United Nations study found that if forest loss continued at the current pace, the Philippines would face an "irreversible descent" in timber production and be forced to import wood; the report received wide and favorable publicity in the national press (Mercado 1971). Most delegates to the 1971–2 Constitutional Convention appeared to favor a constitutional provision that would virtually close down the timber industry, in order to "preserve the national patrimony"[21] (*Manila Times* 1971). In September 1972 Marcos declared martial law, before the convention could complete its work.

PRESIDENT MARCOS UNDER AUTHORITARIAN RULE, 1972–86

From September 1972 to February 1986, the Philippines continued to be governed by President Marcos, but under authoritarian rule. Because the country's *regime* changed, while the *president* did not, it gives us a rare opportunity to study the influence of regime type on the governance of a commodity windfall, while holding constant many other factors – including the preferences of the ruler himself, President Marcos.

Previous studies of Philippine forest policies have suggested that Marcos destroyed much of the nation's forest estate while the country was under authoritarian rule.[22] These accounts are only partially correct. Marcos did retain abysmal forest policies under his authoritarian

20 Vitug states that in 1972, on the eve of martial law, the Forestry Bureau issued a remarkable 12,000 special timber licenses, whose use had supposedly been suspended by Secretary Tanco at the beginning of the year (Vitug 1993: 15). The records of the Forestry Bureau – which are notoriously incomplete – contain no information about these licenses. On the problems of recordkeeping at the Forestry Bureau, see Kummer (1995).
21 Marcos gave logging permits to at least five delegates to the Constitutional Convention, which he hoped would produce a new constitution enabling him to stay in office (Vitug 1993: 99).
22 Cf. Boyce (1993); Broad and Cavanaugh (1993); Vitug (1993); Dauvergne (1997).

government. But as bad as these policies were, in some ways they were *better* than his own policies, and the policies of previous Philippine governments, under democratic rule.

Marcos used his authoritarian powers to make his allocation rights more direct, more exclusive, and more discretionary. At the same time, Marcos became a more secure office holder. Under the democratic constitution, presidents were limited to two four-year terms in office; moreover, reelection after the first term was unprecedented, leaving Marcos perpetually insecure, with only a short time horizon. By declaring martial law, Marcos gave himself a longer time horizon, and an incentive to spend his patronage resources at a more measured pace. Authoritarian rule damaged the nation's forestry institutions, but gave the forests themselves a brief reprieve.

After 1972, no new timber licenses were issued without Marcos's approval and the bureau lost all real influence over his clients in the industry. After keeping on Santos, and later Jose Viado, as "acting" directors of forestry, in 1975 Marcos appointed Edmundo Cortes to fill the position. He would remain director until Marcos was ousted in 1986. Cortes had been Marcos's channel to the forestry bureau since 1971, when he was named Forestry Division Chief.[23] As director, Cortes assumed unprecedented authority over the bureau, working closely with Malacañang and often bypassing the Ministry of Natural Resources altogether (Vitug 1993).

With his control of the bureau more direct and exclusive than ever before, Marcos took three measures to slow the pace of logging, and to heighten his discretion over the allocation of timber rents.

The first was to move the industry from short-term to long-term timber licenses. Even though timber concessions could legally be issued for as long as twenty-five years, before 1972 long-term licenses were rare; almost all licenses were issued for four years or fewer. There was good reason for this: under the 1935 Constitution, a president could only be reelected once. With a weak party system, presidents had no incentive to buy support that would last beyond a single four-year term. But once he was freed from the election cycle, Marcos began to distribute long-term licenses. The move was both good for the forests, since longer concessions gave licensees an incentive to harvest their timber

---

23 Cortes's 1971 promotion had been pushed through the Civil Service Commission with unusual haste and secrecy. His appointment triggered protests from many of the bureau's senior foresters (*Philippine Lumberman* 1971).

more slowly; and good for Marcos, who now preferred a slower pace of forest loss.

In fiscal years 1970–71 and 1971–2, the forestry bureau had issued a total of six Timber License Agreements (TLAs), the type of license with the longest duration (usually twenty-five years). In the first year of martial law, fifty-six new TLAs were granted; in 1973–4, fifty-one more.

Marcos's second measure was to restrict the export of unprocessed ("raw") logs. Forestry experts had recommended these restrictions – and ultimately a ban on raw log exports – since the late 1950s. Advocates believed such a policy could slow the pace of logging and boost the domestic wood-processing industry. But before martial law, all attempts to enact these restrictions had failed, including Marcos's own disingenuous 1967 plan.

After martial law was in place, however, Marcos found that log export restrictions were not only possible but politically useful. The move toward long-term licenses could diminish Marcos's leverage over his clients, who no longer had to regularly apply for license renewals. But by forcing licensees to obtain export permits – which were issued monthly – Marcos could place finely graded sanctions on his clients; conversely, the monthly quotas would force licensees to perpetually demonstrate their fealty to him. Marcos and his top deputies compiled the list of approved exporters themselves, and often made last-minute adjustments in the quotas (Vitug 1993: 35). Some concessionaires became so anxious to show their loyalty to the president – and win a lucrative quota – that they placed his silhouette in their company logo.[24]

At the same time, the quota system also gave Marcos a tool to reduce the logging rate. By distributing long-term licenses, Marcos had raised the annual allowable cut 24 percent to a new record level and raised the area of land under concession from 8.5 million hectares to 10.3 million hectares. But the export quotas had a countervailing effect, limiting the number of trees that could profitably be harvested.[25] From 1967 to 1973,

24 Concessionaires obtained their permits using a combination of bribes and political clientage; the two were apparently fungible. Several loggers report being forced to deposit a fee in a Hong Kong bank account before getting their export quota. The fee was based on the quality of the applicant's political connections; it also rose over time as permits grew more scarce. Well-connected firms might pay less than $10 per cubic meter; poorly connected ones, as much as $20 per cubic meter.
25 The bribes and political favors needed to purchase export quotas acted as an export tax, reducing the number of trees that were profitable to cut.

the annual timber cut remained virtually unchanged. With the quotas in place, timber production dropped by 55 percent over Marcos's remaining twelve years in office. Much or all of this drop might be explained by the growing scarcity of timber; it is difficult to know whether the quotas actually helped slow the pace of logging. Still, under authoritarian rule, Marcos made more significant efforts to reduce the logging rate than he or his predecessors had under democratic rule.

For Marcos, the export quotas were a valuable political device: they allowed him to place finely-graded costs and benefits on licensees; they burnished his image as the guardian of the nation's forests; and they enabled him to make the remaining forests last longer. But they also had an awkward drawback. The annual quotas were supposed to drop each year, until the export of raw logs was completely banned. Yet a ban, if enacted, would nullify the political advantages of the quota system. Rather than lose such a valuable tool, Marcos repeatedly postponed the ban. In February 1973, Marcos had announced that the export of unprocessed logs would be phased out by January 1, 1976. But three days before the ban was to take effect, he issued another order allowing exports to continue until 1982. The 1982 ban was also rescinded at the last moment. Until he fell from power in 1986, Marcos continued to issue export permits.

The third measure was a far-reaching reform of the Forestry Code – the first since 1904 – which Marcos issued as Presidential Decree No. 705 in May 1975. The new code had many provisions to promote forest conservation: It prohibited logging on steep slopes, in critical watersheds, and in other fragile areas; it required greater attention to the ecological limits of the forests; and it promoted the reforestation of degraded areas.[26] But it simultaneously gave the president far greater legal

---

26 It is impossible to know how much of the new code was enforced; and whether regulatory enforcement was worse under authoritarian than under democratic rule. In the 1950s and 1960s, the Philippine government solicited – and received – frank advice from the U.S. government, and international organizations; these reports offer a rough basis for independent evaluations of enforcement. But under martial law, foreign evaluations were rarely solicited, and typically confined to noncontroversial topics. Only one independent report from this period touched on enforcement. A 1976 FAO study reported,

According to various sources, for the time being, the Bureau of Forestry does not seem to have possibilities to protect reserved or protected forests. Even if the Government declares an area as reserved forest, local politicians can dispose of it for agricultural purposes in pursuit of party or personal politics (Food and Agriculture Organization 1976: 88).

authority to interfere with the allocation and use of forest licenses, stating in Section 20 that "when the national interest so requires, the President may amend, modify, replace or rescind any contract, concession, permit, license, or any other form of privilege granted herein."

Firmly in control of the timber industry, Marcos gave logging rights to many members of his own family. Marcos's sister (Fortuna Marcos-Barba) and her husband (Colonel Marcelino Barba) received permits to log almost 200,000 hectares of forest in Nueva Vizcaya, Quirino, Aurora, and Quezon. Other relatives – including Marcos's mother (Josefa Edralin Marcos), brother (Pacifico Marcos), and two uncles (Simeon Valdez and Judge Pio Marcos) – joined the boards of logging firms (Vitug 1993: 20–2).

The bulk of the industry, however, was placed in the hands of clients who Marcos believed would buttress his regime's political foundation. As Gary Hawes notes,

His loyal followers (in exchange for Marcos's patronage) were expected to control their own followings, so as to maintain a hierarchical political coalition based on personal patronage, not on common causes or sectoral economic interests. Promoting those close to him was one way of breaking the power of business and political interests opposed to his rule. (Hawes 1992: 156)

No single Marcos client dominated the timber industry. Instead, valuable concessions were granted to a range of important clients, including:

- Alfonso Lim, a Marcos backer since the early 1960s, who had at least partial control over 600,000 hectares of forest through Taggat Industries and Veterans Woodworks (Manapat 1991);
- Herminio Disini, who ran Cellophil, a 197,000 hectare joint venture with several Japanese firms, established shortly after martial law (Nectoux and Kuroda 1990: 84–5);
- Felipe Ysmael Jr., a major contributor to Marcos's 1965 campaign, who held 150,000 hectares of forests in Quirino and Palawan;
- the Philippine Veteran's Investment and Development Corporation (Phividec), a logging company established by Marcos to provide

An even harsher assessment came in 1986 from Ernesto Maceda, the Aquino government's new minister of natural resources. Several weeks after taking office, he estimated that 90 percent of the nation's 170 concession holders were violating forestry regulations, particularly the provisions on reforestation (Malaya 1986). Still, this does not tell us whether enforcement was any worse under authoritarian rule than under democratic rule.

pensions to military officers on their retirement – giving active military officers an enduring incentive to keep him in office (Vitug 1993: 19, 31);

- Juan Ponce Enrile, Marcos's longtime defense secretary, who owned Dolores Timber, San Jose Corporation, and JJ Tirador Lumber Corporation, and had links to other timber and timber processing firms in Bukidnon, Butuan, Palawan, and Cebu[27] (Manapat 1991);
- General Fidel Ramos, armed forces vice chief of staff, who (along with his father and daughter) largely controlled Greenbelt Wood Products, which received a timber license in 1977; and who served as chairman of the board of Phividec[28] (Vitug 1993: 170–1);
- Jose Alvarez, who was closely tied to Teodoro Pena, a local oligarch and Marcos cabinet member, and received 168,000 hectares of concessions in Palawan[29] (Clad and Vitug 1988).

The change in regime had one final effect: it helped Marcos lower the political costs of forest misuse, by suppressing information. The 1973 edition of *Philippine Forestry Statistics*, which contained embarrassing data on deforestation rates, was quietly removed from all forestry libraries and official archives (Kummer 1992: 49). Government forestry reports were increasingly fabricated. On the eve of martial law, independent estimates of the deforestation rate were about 20 percent higher than the forestry bureau's official rate. By 1987, independent estimates were 2,100 percent above the official rate (see Figure 4.4) (Kummer 1995).[30]

---

27 Enrile defected to the opposition in the waning hours of the Marcos government, and was able to retain his position as defense secretary in the Aquino government.
28 Ramos also defected and became Aquino's armed forces chief of staff, and, later, defense secretary. He was elected president in 1992.
29 Alvarez switched loyalties in 1986, backing Ramon Mitra, who became Aquino's minister of agriculture, and later, a congressman and speaker of the house. He was able to retain his concessions.
30 Though it worsened drastically under martial law, the falsification of forestry data dates back to at least the beginning of the timber boom. According to government reports, during the first five years of the timber boom – 1955 to 1960 – the Philippine forests actually *expanded* from 14 million hectares to 16.5 million hectares; by 1968, the year of peak production, they had grown further still, to 16.7 million hectares! An independent estimate in 1964 put the figure closer to 10.5 million hectares, and the deforestation rate at about 2 percent a year (Zafra 1955; Zafra 1960; Kummer 1992).

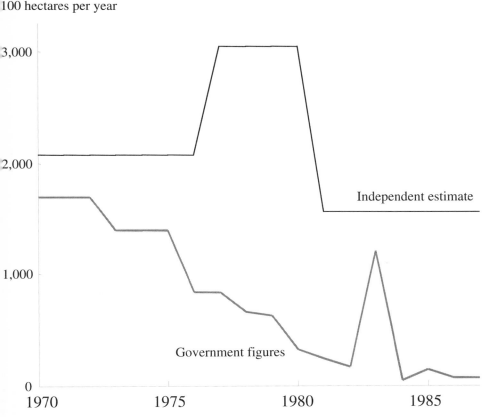

100 hectares per year

Figure 4.4. Independent and Government Estimates of Philippine Deforestation Rates, 1970–87 (100 hectares per year). *Source*: Kummer (1992).

THE UNDERTAXATION OF TIMBER LICENSES

Timber licenses became vehicles for distributing the timber windfall only because they were egregiously undertaxed. The problem of undertaxation can be traced to 1904, when the U.S. colonial government adopted a new set of timber royalties, to replace the Spanish system. The new charges ranged from .50 to 6 Philippine pesos per cubic meter (depending on the species of wood), equivalent in 1905 to a sales tax of between 6.6 and 15.7 percent. Barrington Moore, the prominent U.S. forester, denounced these fees as "ruinously favorable" to loggers. But given the government's determination to attract new investors to the timber sector, the low charges may have been justified – at least initially.

Table 4.2. *Ratio of Implicit Forest Charge to*
Domestic Log Prices in the Philippines, 1903–90

	Group One	Group Two	Group Three
1903	6.6–7.8	4.2–7.1	4.3–4.6
1904	8.4–11.2	5.7–9.2	3.7–5.5
1905	11.0–15.7	9.2–10.9	6.6–10.0
1946–9	5.6	3.5	n.a.
1965–8	1.8	2.0	1.6
1969–71	1.4	1.8	1.4
1972	2.9	3.2	3.3
1973	2.0	2.9	2.8
1974–9	1.0	1.7	1.9
1980	1.9	2.9	2.2
1981	2.1	4.0	3.0
1982–9	0.9	1.6	1.0

Source: Bautista (1992).

Remarkably, between 1904 and 1980, these fees were raised just once – in 1939, and then by an average of less than 22 percent. A series of Philippine administrations tried to boost the royalty rates, but were invariably frustrated by congress.[31] Three times – in 1934, 1949, and 1968 – the forestry bureau managed to raise forestry revenues without congressional approval by reclassifying wood species from less expensive to more expensive tax categories. The government also created a series of new fees, including a license fee, a grading fee, a reforestation charge, a public education fee, and a silvicultural fee. But the net impact of the new fees was small, due to their low rates, their erosion by inflation, and sometimes, the failure of the government to actually collect them. In 1970, for example, the Marcos administration raised the silvicultural fee by 300 percent; the move was cosmetic, however, since the silvicultural fee was never collected.

Between 1905 and 1989, the net tax burden on the timber industry, for domestic log sales, dropped by almost 90 percent (see Table 4.2). Levies on wood exports also declined: Between 1956 (when the earliest figures are available) and 1989, fees dropped from 7.7 to 1.35 percent of the export price. After 1976, the forestry bureau was no longer able to cover its operating costs from forestry revenues (Bautista 1992).

31 Even before independence in 1946, royalty rates came under the jurisdiction of the Philippine legislature, which was established in 1907.

Three studies have tried to determine how much of the forest windfall was captured by the government, and how much went to licensees. Bautista found that the government collected between 4 and 30 percent of the rents before 1981 (depending on the timber product) and slightly more thereafter (Bautista 1992). Boado suggests that between 1979 and 1982 – when tax rates peaked – the government collected an average of 11.4 percent of all timber rents (Boado 1988: 184). A 1989 World Bank study estimated rent capture in the 1960s at approximately 5 percent, rising to 14 percent in the 1970s (World Bank 1989: 18). By any measure, the vast majority of the windfall was transferred to concession holders.

The undertaxation of licenses cannot be explained by ignorance: It was widely denounced in the 1960s and early 1970s by both Filipino and foreign experts. The World Bank complained in 1962 that the low fees constituted "a bargain sale of the Filipino birthright" (World Bank 1962: 16). Armed with data from the commissioner of internal revenue, in 1963 Representative Manuel Cases noted that lumbermen paid only 3 million pesos in taxes on 700 million pesos of exports. "I realize that several of these big lumbermen are members of the Senate and lower house, and the cabinet," said Cases, "but that does not mean they should pay less taxes than the small common man" (*Philippine Lumberman* 1963).

The Marcos government tried to capitalize on public disgust with low logging royalties, while doing little to raise them. On the eve of martial law, DANR Secretary Arturo Tanco vowed to "remove the excess profits from the logging industry" by increasing forest charges and allocating timber licenses through competitive bidding. "Much of the rapacious destruction of our forests," he charged, "may be traced to the excessive, extravagant profits derived from logging" (Tanco 1972: 6). Yet even after declaring martial law, the Marcos administration was slow to raise timber royalties. In 1980 and 1981, after fifteen years in office and eight years of martial law, Marcos finally boosted royalties. Yet with timber prices soaring, the industry's net tax burden still declined under authoritarian law.

CONCLUSION

Thirty years of rent seizing had a calamitous impact on both the nation's forestry institutions, and the forests themselves: Between 1951 and 1986, the Philippines lost 55 percent of its forest cover, one of the fastest deforestation rates in the tropics (Kummer 1992). The deforestation led to the extinction of 40 percent of the archipelago's endemic flora; it also produced extensive soil degradation, the loss of arable land, the siltation of rivers and streams, disastrous flooding during the rainy season, diminished water flow in dry seasons, and the destruction of coral reefs (Porter and Ganapin 1988; World Bank 1989). The incursions of logging firms into the forests also displaced the indigenous cultural communities that had long managed these areas for their own use. Unlike in Sabah, Sarawak, and Indonesia, the state took few legal measures to usurp indigenous land rights; instead it simply ignored them.[32]

Philippine forest policies were influenced by many factors in addition to rent seizing. Three that deserve special mention are the government's need for revenue, pressures from U.S. or Japanese firms, and rent seeking from private actors.

Since independence, the Philippine government has been chronically short of funds. If high logging rates were strongly influenced by the government's demand for revenues, however, we might expect the government to make reasonable efforts to impose and collect taxes on the timber industry. Yet between 1901 and 1990, the industry's tax burden was remarkably light, and declined in real terms. By allowing licensees to capture 70 to 95 percent of the timber windfall, the government gave up a vast source of revenue. The government's desire to spur economic growth and bring in foreign exchange must have created some pressures to keep logging rates high; still, this economic need was rarely, if ever, offered as a rationale for high logging rates. And economic pressures cannot explain the forestry bureau's loss of authority.

Some analysts have blamed Philippine deforestation on foreign firms and governments, particularly Japan. This view may reflect the presence of foreign firms in the Philippine timber industry, and the export of most of the nation's timber harvest. Still, there is little evidence that foreign firms or governments received any type of preferential treatment, or that they had a harmful influence on Philippine forest policies or institutions. For three decades, bureau officials and other foresters loudly complained

---

32 This occurred despite the 1909 ruling by the U.S. Supreme Court in *Cariño v. Insular Government* that people who had occupied the Philippine forests "since time immemorial" had rights to the land. The decision was never enforced, and both the colonial government and the Philippine government treated forest dwellers as unlawful occupants of public land. The 1987 Constitution explicitly recognized the land rights of indigenous cultural communities; the implementation of this provision is still a matter of dispute.

about pressure from the congress, the secretary of agriculture and natural resources, Malacañang Palace, and from Philippine lumbermen. Newspapers, forestry journals, and conference records reveal no complaints about pressure on the bureau from foreign firms or governments. Indeed, the deterioration of forest policies and institutions coincided with a decline in the presence of foreign timber firms.[33]

Even in the 1950s and 1960s, most timber concessions were small and owned by Filipinos. By 1966, 14 percent of the land under forest concession was held by American firms, 28 percent by joint American-Filipino companies, and 58 percent by Filipino firms (Hicks and McNicoll 1971). By the time U.S. privileges under the Bell Trade Act expired in 1974, the United States had only a small presence in the industry, and Japan took over as the industry's main source of foreign capital. There is no evidence that Japanese investors received favorable treatment.

The process of rent seizing ran parallel to strong rent-seeking pressures from outside the state. Private actors not only sought the right to cut timber; they also tried to gain land rights to logged-over forest land, to use it for cultivation.[34] The rapid growth in the Philippine population, and the unevenness of land distribution, made the search for cultivable

33 There can be no dispute that until the 1950s, the Philippine timber sector was heavily shaped by the United States. The first American concession opened in 1904; by the early 1920s, U.S. and Filipino firms each accounted for one-third of timber exports, with the remainder controlled by a mix of Western and Asian firms (Roth 1983).

When the Philippines gained independence in 1946, its forest policies took a nationalist turn. Article XIII, Section I of the Philippine Constitution limited the "disposition, exploitation and development, or utilization" of timber and other natural resources to Philippine citizens, or corporations with at least 60 percent Philippine ownership. But the Bell Trade Act, passed by the U.S. Congress in 1946, tied $620 million in postwar reconstruction aid to an agreement by the Philippine government to grant U.S. citizens access to Philippine natural resources on the same terms as its own citizens until 1974. The result was a bitter fight in the Philippine Congress, a national plebiscite, and ultimately a "Parity Amendment" to the Constitution acceding to the U.S. demand. To win the requisite votes in congress, President Manuel Roxas disqualified opposition congressmen on charges of terrorism and electoral fraud. The Parity Amendment gave U.S. firms an important place in the Philippine timber industry in the 1950s, helping finance the mechanization of logging practices and capturing a fraction of the timber windfall.

34 Swidden farmers in the Philippines typically prefer to cultivate land whose forest cover has recently been removed by loggers. Logged-over land in the Philippine dipterocarp forests, when left undisturbed, will regenerate in sixty to eighty years. When *kaingineiros* cultivate this land, they block the process of regeneration and hence are a proximate cause of deforestation.

land – through legal or illegal measures – exceptionally urgent. There is also evidence that politicians distributed squatting or settlement rights to deforested land the same way they distributed timber rights, through patronage and corruption.[35] This rent seeking went hand-in-hand with rent seizing: Private demand made allocation rights valuable to politicians; politicians then profited by dismantling the nation's forestry institutions.

35 See, for example, Gill (1959); World Bank (1962).

5

Sabah, Malaysia

A New State of Affairs

Qui Hing tells me he has contracted with Andy Goroo's people, the orang semoonals, to buy 500 planks for export. The dawn of a new state of affairs.
    Diary of Sandakan founder William Pryer, August 1879 (John 1974: 56)

In 1963, the British colonies of North Borneo, Sarawak, and Singapore joined the Federation of Malaya to create a new state, the Federation of Malaysia.[1] Yet the former colony of North Borneo – now called Sabah – retained many of the powers of a sovereign state, including special control over immigration, religion, language, and land use. It also kept control of its forests, which remained exempt from the federal government's national forestry laws and taxes.

The Sabah government had good reasons to retain authority over its forests: they were densely packed with trees from the *Dipterocarpaceae* family – the same type that the Philippines so profusely exported. In 1953, Sabah held 2.7 percent of world hardwood market; by 1973, it had captured 20.1 percent of a much larger international market. Sabah was the world's second largest supplier of hardwood logs from 1959 to 1990 – second to the Philippines, then to Indonesia, and finally to its East Malaysian neighbor, Sarawak.[2] Sabah's tiny city of Sandakan became one of the world's leading timber ports. Locals claimed it had more millionaires per capita than any city in the world.[3]

---

1 Singapore left the Malaysian Federation in 1965 and became independent.
2 Sabah dropped into third place in 1971 for a single year (behind both Indonesia and the Philippines), and was the top hardwood log exporter from 1981 to 1983.
3 Timber, conversely, was Sabah's most lucrative export. By 1964 the timber sector provided the Sabah government with almost a quarter of its revenues; by 1979, over three-quarters.

Sabah's spectacular growth as a timber exporter, however, went hand-in-hand with the deterioration of its forestry institutions. In the 1950s and early 1960s, Sabah had an unusually sound set of forestry institutions, the strongest of the four cases in this study. Yet in the late 1960s and 1970s, the Sabah government dismantled these institutions and began to authorize logging at increasingly unsustainable rates. By 1991, Sabah's forests were so badly overlogged that the World Bank warned the government, in a confidential report, that the state was facing "an abrupt transition to a state of comparative destitution" (World Bank 1991: v).

Like the Philippine case, the case of Sabah illustrates how a commodity windfall can lead to rent seizing and the breakdown of state institutions. Three facets of the Sabah case set it apart from the case of the Philippines. First, Sabah began to receive a timber windfall while the state was under colonial rule. During this period (1953–63) the government faced rent-seeking pressures, but no apparent rent seizing. This chapter treats the events of this period as a natural experiment – examining the impact of rent seeking on state institutions, while rent seizing is controlled for.

Second, although both the Philippines and Sabah had democratic governments during much of their windfalls, the Philippines had a presidential system, in which executive and legislative powers were divided; Sabah had a parliamentary system, in which executive, legislative, and even constitutional powers were fused. One consequence was that Sabah's chief ministers could gain full allocation rights to the windfall, and reshape the state's forestry institutions, as soon as the transition from colonial rule was complete. Philippine presidents, by contrast, were constantly struggling over allocation rights with an independent congress, which slowed their rent-seeking initiatives and impeded their efforts to alter the state's forestry institutions.

Finally, the Sabah case provides a better opportunity to see whether democratic elections can help promote reform. In the Philippines, the democratic process was interrupted by Marcos, at a time when public concern about forest loss was rising and might have become an important political force. Sabah continued to hold competitive elections as the forests dwindled and public concern became intense. The results, however, are discouraging. Patronage played a central role in Sabah's elections. High-spending politicians tended to defeat their underfunded competitors; and when advocates of forest reform were elected, they soon reversed themselves and adopted the patronage practices, and unsustainable forest policies, of their predecessors. The Sabah case illustrates how difficult it may be to curtail rent seizing in democratic states, when candidates rely heavily on patronage to sway votes.

POLITICS IN SABAH

From 1881 to the beginning of World War II, British North Borneo was ruled by a British syndicate, the British North Borneo (Chartered) Company; from 1946 to 1963, it came under direct British rule.[4]

The Chartered Company's principal mission was to turn British North Borneo into a source of commercial profits. While the company showed little interest in building popular support, it believed that the most cost-effective way to govern the colony was to purchase the acquiescence of local elites. Yet the company's efforts to do so were initially frustrated by what it saw as the "anarchy" of Sabah's ethnic groups: Village headmen often had little authority and were chosen in seemingly haphazard ways; even worse, the headmen were not organized in any clear or hierarchical manner.

The company set out to rectify these problems by strengthening the position of the headmen within their own villages, organizing the headmen into a kind of federation, and using this federation to both distribute goods and enforce colonial policies. Still, by 1946, the territory's many ethnic groups had only loose and poorly institutionalized chains of patron-client relationships, unlike the highly institutionalized patronage networks in colonial Indonesia and the Philippines.

When the British government established direct colonial rule in 1946, few Sabahans participated in state-level politics. The colony was run by a British governor and a bureaucracy staffed largely by expatriates. A handful of Sabahans were appointed to the new executive and legislative councils, but neither body had any independent authority: both councils were chaired by the governor, who could appoint and suspend members at will. As a consequence, under colonial rule, Sabahans had virtually no opportunities to capture the spoils of office; nor would doing so help them advance politically.

With the end of colonial rule in September 1963, politics in Sabah quickly changed. As a member of the Malaysian Federation, Sabah gained its own state constitution and parliamentary government; and like

---

4 British North Borneo was the last British colony to be ruled by a chartered company.

the neighboring state of Sarawak, Sabah received an unusual degree of independence from the federal government in Kuala Lumpur over matters of immigration, religion, language, land use, and forestry.

Sabah's political institutions are heavily majoritarian – or more precisely, supermajoritarian, since they grant legislative, executive, and constitutional powers to any government that controls two-thirds of the seats in the assembly. Sabah's electoral laws also have a majoritarian tilt, since legislators are elected by pluralities from single-member districts.

The state's majoritarian features are based on those of the British government. But they were modified – like the institutions of the Malaysian federal government – to help forge coalitions among a population that was ethnically and linguistically fragmented.[5] At the end of colonial rule, 37 percent of Sabah's population was classed as "non-Muslim native," 36 percent as "Muslim native," and 23 percent as ethnic "Chinese." The state's political parties have largely followed these cleavages.[6]

From 1963 to 1967, Sabah was ruled by a transitional government, in which all the major parties – under pressure from both Kuala Lumpur and London – held seats in the cabinet. Both the British government and the Malaysian federal government were anxious to foster a smooth transition from colonial rule. Both were concerned about the objections of the Philippine and Indonesian governments to the incorporation of Sabah and Sarawak, on the island of Borneo, into the relatively distant Malaysian Federation.[7]

---

5 Sabah has some thirty to forty ethnic and linguistic groups, which can be divided into three broad categories: non-Muslim "natives," principally the Dusun, Kadazan, and Murut; Muslim "natives," a grouping that includes a variety of coastal peoples, including the Bajau, Sulut, Illanun, Kedayan, and the Brunei Malays; and the ethnic "Chinese," who fall into many dialect groups, including Hakka, Cantonese, Hokkien, Teochew, and Hainanese.

6 At the beginning of the transitional government, most of the Chinese population backed the Sabah Chinese Association (SCA); the Muslims largely supported the United Sabah National Organization (USNO); and the non-Muslim natives were divided, with the Kadazan and Dusun backing the United National Kadazan Organization (UNKO) and the Murut backing the Pasok-Momogun ("Sons of the Soil") party. Each of these parties would later split, collapse, or merge with others; but the parties that replaced them tended to remain divided along ethnic lines.

Until the 1994 state elections, Malaysia's national parties – which are also organized along ethnic lines – consistently failed to win seats in the Sabah state assembly.

7 The Philippines claimed sovereignty over Sabah; and Indonesia's Sukarno pursued a policy of *konfrontasi* (armed confrontation) with Malaysia to protest the incorporation of Sabah, Sarawak, and Singapore into Malaysia.

Table 5.1. *The Governments of Sabah, 1963–96*

Year	Chief Minister	Party
1963–7	Donald (Fuad) Stephens (1963–4) Peter Lo (1965–7)	USNO, UPKO, SCA
1967–76	Mustapha Harun (1967–75) Mohd. Said Keruak (1975–6)	USNO, SCA
1976–85	Donald (Fuad) Stephens (1976) Harris Salleh (1976–85)	Berjaya
1985–94	Joseph Pairin Kitingin	PBS
1994–6	Sakaran Dandai (1994) Salleh Said Keruak (1995–6) Yong Teck Lee (1996)	UMNO, PDS, SAPP, PBRS, LDP, AKAR

Note: the following abbreviations are used for party names: United Sabah National Organization (USNO); United Pasok-Momogun Kadazan Organization (UPKO); Sabah Chinese Association (SCA); Bersatu Baryat Jelata Sabah (Berjaya); Parti Bersatu Sabah (PBS); United Malays National Organization (UMNO); Parti Demokratik Sabah (PDS); Sabah Progressive Party (SAPP); Parti Bersatu Rakyat Sabah (PBRS); Liberal Democratic Party (LDP); Angkatan Keadilan Rakyat (Akar).

Parliamentary governments come in many forms, and can be classified according to the relative influence of the prime minister, the ministers (acting individually), the cabinet (acting collectively), the legislature, and the bureaucracy (Laver and Shepsle 1994). The 1963–7 "Sabah Alliance" functioned in part as a ministerial government, and in part as a cabinet government: some matters were decided by individual cabinet ministers, others by the cabinet as a whole. Both the chief minister (Sabah's "Prime Minister") and the assembly had limited authority; even the ability of the cabinet to take decisive action was limited by the presence of rival parties, who spent much of their time jockeying for advantage in the upcoming elections.

After the first direct elections were held in 1967, most of the cabinet's power shifted to the chief minister, who was no longer compelled to maintain an all-party coalition, and hence could appoint and dismiss cabinet ministers more freely.[8] After 1967, each of Sabah's Chief Ministers used his authority to establish control over a wide range of state

8 By 1967, Indonesia's policy of *konfrontasi* had ended, following President Sukarno's removal from power in 1965–6. The more secure international setting gave the Sabah chief minister a freer hand to engage in partisan politics.

assets – most importantly, timber licenses. Each also maintained a two-thirds majority in the assembly, and, hence, simultaneously held executive, legislative, and constitutional powers.

In fact, Sabah's chief ministers used these two prerogatives – their control over patronage, and their fusion of executive, legislative, and constitutional authority – to create a positive feedback loop: they used patronage to put together a two-thirds majority coalition, and used the coalition to strengthen their hold on patronage, making their allocation rights more direct, exclusive, and discretionary.[9]

This self-reinforcing link between patronage and constitutional control has given incumbent parties a large advantage over the opposition. Opposition parties have only defeated incumbents – in 1976, 1985, and 1994 – with the intervention of the ruling party in Kuala Lumpur (UMNO).[10]

Political patronage, and promises of patronage, have played a decisive role in Sabah's state elections. Since the winning coalition gains exclusive access to government patronage, and there are no meaningful restrictions on campaign spending, state elections tend to resemble auctions, with rival parties bidding for control of the spoils of office. Under a simple rent-seeking model with perfect competition, each bidder should be willing to spend on patronage a sum equal to the expected net present value of the spoils of office, discounted by the likelihood they will succeed.[11] As the value of government spoils has grown – largely due to the timber windfall – so have the amounts spent by rival parties.

During the first direct elections in 1967, the major parties disbursed an estimated $1.5 million to influence an election in which just 163,000 votes were cast. The sum was over $9 per vote; at the time, Sabah's per capita GDP was about $350[12] (Milne 1973; Roff 1974). In the 1976 contest over $10 million was used to sway just two hundred thousand voters, a cost of $50 per vote. Toward the end of the campaign, major party contributors – principally ethnic Chinese loggers – left the state to elude political candidates who were demanding further contributions (Ross-Larson 1976).

---

9 Malaysia's central government has followed a similar pattern.
10 In 1976 and 1994, UMNO gave the opposition enough campaign resources to counterbalance the incumbent party's control of patronage; in 1985, UMNO officials blocked the incumbent from nullifying the election results.
11 There are many more complex models of rent-seeking games; see Chapter 3.
12 Unless otherwise noted, all sums are in U.S. dollars.

During campaigns dominated by the incumbent party (1970, 1981, and 1990) spending was apparently modest;[13] and the 1985 election, though bitterly fought, was also less expensive since the opposition PBS lacked the financial resources to compete with the incumbent Berjaya party. But the 1994 contest saw record-breaking spending once again, as the main opposition party (UMNO-Sabah) received tens – perhaps hundreds – of millions of dollars from Kuala Lumpur, in an effort to displace the incumbent PBS. One experienced observer calculated that $230 million was spent by the winning coalition alone – including $100 million to influence the state's 436,000 voters, and $130 million to induce opposition legislators to switch parties. These figures suggest an expenditure of over $500 per vote by the winning side.[14]

No matter how large the sums, political leaders have found it difficult to buy a two-thirds majority with campaign patronage, since most Sabahans vote for ethnically based parties and are reluctant to switch. Hence party leaders often use some of their funds after elections are over, to persuade elected legislators to switch parties. Following the 1967 election, the victorious Mustapha offered the twelve opposition assemblymen timber concessions, cabinet positions, and other inducements to switch sides and give him a two-thirds majority; after two defections, the opposition party dissolved altogether.[15] Following the 1976 vote, the winning Berjaya party offered $175,000 to each of the first two defectors, whose votes would gain them a two-thirds majority: Nine opposition legislators soon switched over (Ross-Larson 1976). During the prolonged postelection struggle of 1985 and 1986, the winning PBS

---

13 For the 1981 election, however, Chief Minister Harris Salleh used 200 million ringgit – about $80 million – in state funds. Part of this money was used to purchase television sets for every village headman in Sabah; in villages without electricity, the headmen also received solar power cells to run them. Since the Berjaya party controlled the local television station, and used television news programs and advertisements to tout its achievements, it was an effective tactic (Raffaele 1986).

14 Gomez and Jomo (1997) cite reports that UMNO manipulated the Kuala Lumpur Stock Exchange to raise these funds for the Sabah campaign.

   Sabah's election campaigns have ironically taken on an important redistributive function, forcing politicians and their backers to transfer enormous resources to the voting population at election time. The redistributive effect of Southeast Asian elections was first noted by James C. Scott (1972).

15 Once the critical number of members has defected, a "tipping" effect can occur, since the remaining assemblymen lose any incentive to stay in the opposition, which has little access to the spoils of office.

gained three defectors; but they subsequently lost six legislators to the opposition, who were reportedly lured by money and promises of high appointments (Means 1991).

Assemblymen who defect generally move from a minority party to a majority party, since the latter is usually wealthier, thanks to their access to the spoils of office. But after the 1994 vote, the richer party was UMNO-Sabah, which had virtually unlimited backing from the national UMNO party. After election day the victorious PBS held thirty-one seats, while the remaining twenty-three were held by UMNO-Sabah and its allies.[16] But within weeks, twenty-six of PBS's thirty-one legislators defected to the UMNO-Sabah coalition, which then formed a new government. There were many reports that the earliest defectors had been offered large sums – $1 million or more – to switch parties (Chin 1994; *Asiaweek* 1994a, 1994b).[17]

THE GOVERNANCE OF THE FORESTS UNDER COLONIAL RULE, 1920–63

Between 1920 and 1963, the governance of Sabah's forests passed through two phases: From 1920 to 1952, all commercial logging was controlled by a private monopoly, the British Borneo Timber Company (BBT); from 1952 to 1963, the BBT monopoly was replaced by a system of long-term concessions.

Beginning in 1952, the colonial government established an exceptionally sound set of forestry institutions, designed to restrict logging to sustainable levels in perpetuity, while safeguarding the rights of forest

---

16 PBS won twenty-five of the forty-eight elected seats, and Chief Minister Pairin quickly filled the six appointed seats with PBS candidates.
17 Party leaders have used a wide variety of strategies to prevent the defection of their legislators. Both Mustapha and Harris forced their own legislators to submit undated letters of resignation from the assembly; if they left the party, the party could retaliate by forcing them to resign their seats. Mustapha and Pairin both tried to sequester their legislators during critical junctures, to prevent them from receiving bids from rival parties. The wealthy Mustapha hastily arranged expenses-paid "fact-finding" tours abroad for vulnerable party members during political upheavals in 1971 and 1975; following the 1976 election, Mustapha hid his legislators in a "safe haven" in Kuala Lumpur. The less wealthy Pairin sequestered legislators in his own house following the 1985 and 1994 elections, to prevent them from receiving inducements to defect.
   Pairin also pushed an "antihopping" law through the assembly after the 1986 elections, to establish legal penalties for defectors. But the law was struck down by the Supreme Court in 1993; the ruling opened the door to the defections that ended nine years of PBS rule in 1994 (Kahin 1992).

dwellers. Between 1954 and 1963, these institutions came under pressure from rent seekers; the resilience of these institutions implies that rent seeking – without rent seizing – could only do limited damage to Sabah's forestry institutions and forests.

The British Borneo Timber Company, 1920–52

The goal of the British North Borneo (Chartered) Company was to turn a commercial profit. Yet for the first three decades after its 1881 founding, the company struggled to survive.

The company recognized North Borneo's potential as a major wood exporter, but its efforts to develop a timber industry were hampered by the absence of a large domestic market, a dearth of capital, and in at least one case, the presence of headhunters.[18] In 1920, the company finally was able to attract the capital it sought by granting the BBT a twenty-five year monopoly on all timber production in the state. The monopoly would be renewable for two ten-year periods, ending in 1965.

Although the international log market was small in the interwar period, the BBT's exports expanded steadily until the company was forced to close its operations by World War II. Spurred by the British empire's postwar timber shortage, exports began to rise again after 1950.

But the BBT's postwar renewal was short-lived. The sovereign rights and assets of the British North Borneo (Chartered) Company were transferred to British Crown in 1946, which administered North Borneo directly as a colony. The new colonial administration disliked the BBT's monopoly on log production and sought to end it. The administration realized that a monopoly was no longer needed to attract investment to the timber industry; it also chafed at the BBT's low royalties – fixed in 1920 at three farthings per cubic foot – and criticized its negligent management of the forests[19] (Baker 1965). In 1952 the colonial government bought out the monopoly, and began to establish a new set of institutions to govern the forests.

---

18 To stave off bankruptcy, the company relied on the export of a wide range of nontimber forest products, including edible birds' nests, rattan, kapok, illipe nuts, camphor, elephant tusks, and tree resins.

19 By 1952 this was worth just 2.1 U.S. cents per cubic foot, about $0.74 per cubic meter (Baker 1965). At the time, Sabah timber sold for close to $20.00 per cubic meter.

The Institutions of Sustained-Yield Forestry, 1952–63

After breaking up the BBT monopoly, the colonial government set out to build a new array of forest institutions. Like the BBT, the government sought to exploit the forests' commercial value; but it also wished to protect the ecological value of the forests, and restrict logging to sustainable levels. The government's objectives were spelled out in the Forest Ordinance and Forest Rules of 1954:

a. To reserve permanently for the benefit of the present and future inhabitants of the country land sufficient:
    i.   for the maintenance of the climate and physical condition of the country, the safe-guarding of water supplies and the prevention of damage to rivers and agricultural land by flooding and erosion;
    ii. for the supply in perpetuity at reasonable rates of all forms of forest produce required by the people for agricultural, domestic and industrial purposes.
b. To manage the Forest Estate with the object of obtaining the highest revenue compatible with sustained yield, in so far as this is consistent with the two primary objects set out above.

The government's new forestry institutions had five key components. The first was the conferral of broad powers to protect and manage the forests upon the state's chief forestry official, the conservator of forests. The conservator was also the head of a newly invigorated forest department. The Sabah Forest Department had been established in 1914, and was modeled on the Philippine Forestry Bureau.[20] But during the 43-year BBT monopoly, the department had virtually no influence over the management of the forests, which was left almost entirely to the BBT (Fyfe 1964). The new forest ordinance both restored the department's role in forest management and gave the conservator a considerable degree of autonomy from outside pressures – including the exclusive authority to allocate timber licenses.

The second component was a system of large, long-term concessions, which were designed to be logged sustainably in eighty-year cycles. Four British firms and one U.S. firm initially received these concessions. Because no accurate forest surveys had been carried out, the department

---

20 The Sabah Forest Department's first two top officers – D. M. Matthews and the aptly named D. D. Wood – both had Philippine experience, and until 1941 almost all forest rangers were Filipino.

had little idea how much commercial timber was in the forests; it was hence unable to tell these firms how much timber could be annually harvested. So to ensure that the forests were cut sustainably, the department limited the *area* to be cut each year, rather than the volume of timber. Figuring it would take eighty years for the forests to regenerate after logging, the department allowed each concessionaire to log 1 percent of its land every year.[21] By the time the British departed in 1963, 70 percent of Sabah's commercial forest land had been set aside for twelve foreign and domestic concession holders, to be harvested in perpetuity according to these eighty-year cycles.

The third component was a comprehensive set of silvicultural regulations, designed to minimize the environmental damage caused by loggers, and to help logged-over forests regenerate. These measures included prefelling inventories of licensed areas, tree marking, postfelling sample inventories, postfelling silvicultural treatments to promote regeneration, postfelling surveys to assess penalties for any regulatory violations, and follow-up inventories to monitor regeneration.

The fourth component was a system of royalties devised to capture any windfall profits and place them in state coffers. After breaking up the BBT monopoly in 1952, the colonial government raised timber royalties from 2.1 cents to over 10 cents per cubic foot (about $3.50 per cubic meter). One of the colony's five concessionaires, Montague L. Meyer, Ltd., realized it was unlikely to turn a profit and abandoned its license. Although the other four began to log their concessions, from 1953 to 1955 their profits were modest at best. By capturing all or most of the resource rents, the government curtailed any incentives for rent seeking: a concession in North Borneo was likely to produce a normal return on any investments, and did not merit any large bribes or rent-seeking expenditures.

The final component was the 1962 Land Ordinance, which protected the rights of forest dwellers. Earlier laws gave land rights to upland natives only under highly restrictive conditions. The 1962 Land Ordinance set out more lenient procedures for granting land titles to natives, recognizing communal rights, and establishing native reserves. Since native land could not be sold to "nonnatives" (including ethnic Chinese

---

21 The department assumed that 20 percent of the concession land would turn out to be unsuitable for logging. It was a primitive method of sustainable harvesting; but its crudeness was justified, given the small size of the forest department and the lack of a proper forest survey. Sabah's first comprehensive forest survey was not completed until 1975.

Sabahans), the new ordinance acted as a brake on the expansion of commercial logging.

Rent Seeking under Colonial Rule, 1953–63

Despite the government's commitment to sustained-yield forestry, these institutions soon came under pressure from rent seekers, who found an important flaw in their design. Under colonial rule, these rent seekers had only limited success; after 1963, however, their fortunes improved markedly.

In 1950 and 1951, the forest department planned to only sanction commercial logging by long-term concessionaires. But in 1952, the department decided to issue several dozen one-year logging permits for small plots of forest, in order to meet the local demand for timber, and to clear land along the coasts and river deltas that was suitable for agriculture. Because the land given to the holders of these annual licenses was slated for agricultural conversion, and production was expected to be negligible, the department saw no need to restrict felling to sustainable levels; nor were the annual licenseholders required to meet the same silvicultural standards as the long-term concessionaires.

The department's decision to issue annual licenses turned out to be a terrible mistake. Because annual licenses came with lax silvicultural standards, and were issued for areas that could be logged cheaply – without building roads or railways into Sabah's hilly interior – they became highly profitable and were soon in great demand. By 1954, the annual licensees were cutting more timber than the concessionaires; alarmed, the forest conservator stopped issuing new annual licenses.

The annual licensees – most of them ethnic Chinese Sabahans – were angered by the forest conservator's decision, and appealed first to the colonial government, then to the British parliament. In a compromise, the conservator agreed to continue issuing annual licenses to their current holders. He also offered the largest licensees either long-term concessions, or – as a transitional arrangement – a new, temporary class of licenses that sanctioned logging in mid-sized tracts of upland forests for five to ten years. Like the annual licenses, these "special licenses" were not part of the department's design for long-term sustainable forest management. Rather, they were seen as temporary measures to give more secure tenure to a handful of qualified annual licensees, who after accumulating sufficient capital, would apply for long-term concessions and become part of the state plan for sustainable forest management. By

1963, eight annual licensees had completed this cycle – first taking special licenses, then full concessions. Five other firms held special licenses (Milne and Ratnam 1974; Lee 1976).

After the forest department reached an accord with the annual licensees, Sabah's forest institutions remained intact until 1963, despite rising logging rates and rising profits. From 1952 to 1956, commercial logging rose from 275,000 cubic meters to 779,000 cubic meters, mostly due to the rise of annual licenses (Figure 5.1). Yet export prices declined sharply from their 1951 peak: At the end of 1957, the governor reported to the legislative council that the timber industry was neither stable nor entirely healthy. He also noted that the government had abandoned its hopes of "great profits quickly reaped," and that future profits were unlikely to be extravagant.

But from 1956 to 1963, the average export price for Sabahan timber rose 46 percent, while the volume of exports jumped 446 percent (Figure 5.2). Most of these exports were produced by the large concession holders, who were now using mechanized equipment, and were fully logging their annual coupes. At the same time, the government continued to limit the number of annual licenses to the 1955 levels. The 1963 commercial timber harvest of 3.478 million cubic meters was well within the forests' maximum sustainable yield.

From 1952 to 1963 the colonial government built an array of institutions designed to protect the sustainability of the forests. They included the system of long-term concessions; the harvesting regulations; the high royalties, which dampened incentives for rent seeking; and the recognition of native land rights, which set limits on the expansion of commercial logging. The integrity of these institutions was guarded by a fifth: the forest conservator's wide discretionary powers and political autonomy.

Sabah's forest policies also had an unsustainable component: the annual and special licenses. As British rule drew to a close in 1963, the department hoped to phase out these short-term licenses and return to the original plan of relying solely on long-term concessions (Fyfe 1964). While both the annual and special licenses authorized "unsustainable" logging, they were seen as temporary measures; and besides, they covered only small tracts of forest that would eventually be used for agriculture, and thus could be harmlessly cleared of trees. Had these temporary classes of permits been phased out as planned, Sabah's forest estate would have soon returned to a simple form of sustainable management.

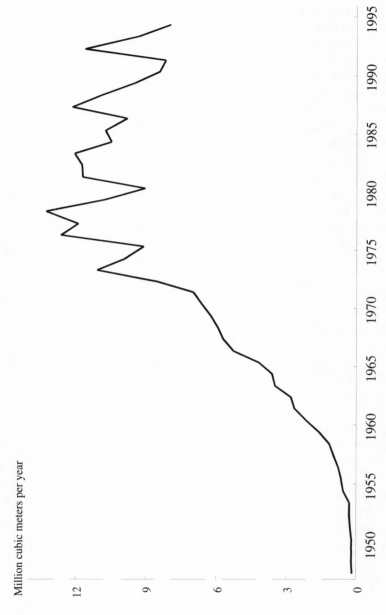

Million cubic meters per year

Figure 5.1. Sabah Timber Harvest, 1947–94 (million cubic meters per year). *Sources*: Food and Agriculture Organization (various); Ministry of Primary Industries (1993).

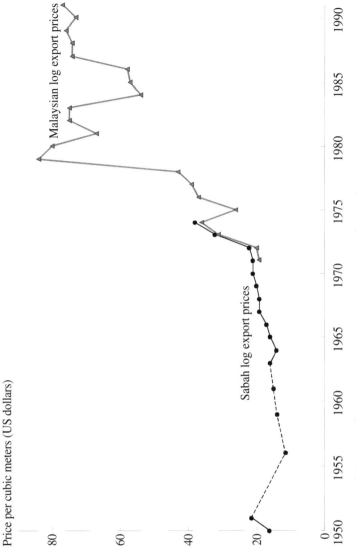

Price per cubic meters (US dollars)

Figure 5.2. Sabah and Malaysian Log Export Prices, 1950–91 (US$ per cubic meter). *Source*: Food and Agriculture Organization (various).

Malaysian log export prices

Sabah log export prices

TIMBER POLITICS UNDER THE SABAH ALLIANCE, 1963-7

In September 1963, the colonial government departed, and was replaced by a transitional state government, run by an all-party coalition known as the "Sabah Alliance." The departure of the British and the rising price of timber opened the door to rent seizing. Yet until 1967, this rent seizing was limited by the transitional government's power-sharing arrangements. Cabinet members were able to gain limited allocation rights, and hence issue short-term licenses. But they were unable to dismantle the institutions that kept most of the commercial forests under sustained-yield management, lest they fracture the all-party coalition and bring down the government.

The 1963-7 period illustrates the proposition briefly discussed in Chapter 3: that "bad" politicians who prefer to spend patronage at a high rate tend to triumph over "good" politicians who use patronage with more restraint. The proposition is difficult to test, in part, because matchups between "good" and "bad" politicians – whose political assets are otherwise similar, and hence can be controlled for – are rare; and in part because it is hard to know when politicians are truly "good," since they may adopt pro-restraint rhetoric but covertly deploy (or promise to deploy) patronage just as readily as "bad" politicians.

This brief four-year span provides a way to mitigate both problems. Between 1963 and 1967, the state's two largest parties were closely matched: each represented about one-third of the electorate; each drew upon similar financial resources; and each ran one of the state's major newspapers.

Moreover, since each was part of the 1963-7 Sabah Alliance coalition, each revealed its patronage preferences to the electorate in advance of the 1967 election. In this case, the high-spending party triumphed over the one that favored restraint.

The Strategies of USNO and UNKO

Between 1963 and 1967, Sabah's two largest parties were the United Sabah National Organization (USNO), which was supported by the coastal Muslim population; and the United National Kadazan Organization (UNKO, later UPKO), which was backed by non-Muslim, upland natives. Each party was built around a strong central figure: USNO was led by Tun Mustapha Harun, a British-educated Muslim leader who claimed hereditary links to the Sulu Sultanate; UNKO was headed by Donald Stephens, the Roman Catholic son of an Australian father and Kadazan mother, who was a popular advocate of Kadazan rights. Both had become prominent communal leaders under British rule, and both owned major newspapers, which they used as unofficial organs of their parties.

Under the Sabah Alliance government, both Stephens and Mustapha sought to use logging permits to reward their own party backers, and build coalitions with other parties for the upcoming election. Stephens favored the issuance of a modest number of new Special Licenses, for non-Muslim native cooperatives in the hilly interior – providing his Kadazan constituents with jobs and helping them clear land for permanent, settled agriculture.[22]

Stephens also tried to use Special Licenses to unite Sabah's non-Muslim indigenes under the banner of his UNKO party. His own Kadazan peoples (along with the closely related Dusuns) constituted 32 percent of the population. The Muslim groups along the coast that generally supported Mustapha's USNO made up 36 percent. In the balance were a second non-Muslim group from Sabah's far interior, the Muruts (4.9 percent of the population), and the ethnic Chinese (23 percent). Stephens hoped to merge UNKO with the Pasok-Momogun party of the Muruts and thus match USNO in size; he could then seek out Chinese support. To win the backing of the Muruts, Stephens used his influence in the Sabah Alliance government to issue special licenses to Murut cooperatives in Sabah's upland forests.[23]

Yet on balance, Stephens backed a more restrained forest policy than Mustapha. While Stephens favored a modest rise in the number of special licenses, he tried first to ban then freeze, the distribution of annual licenses – even though this position alienated Sabah's main Chinese political party, the Sabah Chinese Association, which was dominated by timbermen. While serving as chief minister in 1963–4, Stephens complained that the great majority of those who came to see him requested timber licenses, and described Sabah's timber wealth as the state's "biggest political curse" (Milne and Ratnam 1974: 316, 377).

22 Like the British, Stephens believed that swidden farming should be replaced by permanent cultivation.
23 The UNKO-Pasok Momogun merger was consummated after the June 1964 indirect elections. UNKO (United National Kadazan Organization) henceforth became known as UPKO (United Pasok-Momogun Kadazan Organization). It remained under Stephens' leadership.

Mustapha, by contrast, favored a large increase in the number of annual licenses. Annual licenses provided jobs for the coastal groups that USNO largely represented; they were also highly profitable for the ethnic Chinese timbermen who dominated the Sabah Chinese Association (SCA), the main Chinese political party and a member of the government coalition.[24] Mustapha openly courted the Chinese timbermen with promises of patronage; in 1963 they reciprocated, naming him honorary advisor to the North Borneo Timber Producer's Association (Lee 1976). By helping them gain annual licenses, Mustapha was able to forge a partnership between his USNO party and the SCA – a partnership that eventually gave him the upper hand in the Sabah Alliance government, and a source of funding for the 1967 election.

Rent Seizing, 1963–7

From 1963 to 1967, the three main coalition parties engaged in a limited form of rent seizing by fighting for control of the forestry portfolio, and the right to allocate timber licenses.

Rent seizing became possible, and attractive, under the Sabah Alliance government for three reasons. First, the export price of timber was high enough to provide license holders with rents. The holders of annual licenses (whose extraction costs were exceptionally low) were probably earning rents in the mid-1950s, despite the government's high royalties. Moreover, while royalties remained fixed, the price of timber rose from $11 per cubic meter in 1956 to $19 per cubic meter in 1967 (Figure 5.2). These rising prices made both annual and special licenses, and the right to allocate them, valuable.[25]

24 Before March 1965, the core of the SCA was contained in a separate party, the Sabah National Party (SANAP); earlier still SANAP was known as the Borneo Utara National Party (BUNAP).

25 Over the next three decades, royalties lagged well behind timber prices, leaving about half of the timber windfall in the hands of permit holders. According to Vincent (1990), between 1966 and 1985 the government captured just 46 percent of the timber windfall; a 1991 World Bank study put the government's share of the windfall, between 1966 and 1989, at 53 percent (World Bank 1991). Both studies suggest that about half of the state's timber windfall went to permit holders.

  A third study, by Gillis (1988b), suggested that from 1979 to 1983 rent capture may have reached 83 percent, though the author admitted the actual figure was probably smaller. Vincent (1990) found that Gillis underestimated the rents held by licensees by a factor of three.

  The World Bank noted that if the rents accrued by licensees between 1966 and 1989 had been collected by the government and invested at 10 percent interest,

The second reason was the removal of the forest conservator's exclusive right to allocate annual and special licenses, a right established by the 1954 Forest Ordinance and Forest Rules. Before the British departed, Sabah's new parties agreed that the conservator's autonomy should end, and that most of his powers should be transferred to a new minister of forests.[26] Over the next four years, this position would become the object of constant political skirmishes between USNO and UNKO.

Finally, rent seizing was attractive after 1963 because its costs were low. In theory, both Sabah's judicial system and the voting public had the ability to penalize rent seizing, and hence protect the forests. In practice Sabah's judiciary had little power to challenge the government; and during the 1960s, the public showed little concern about rent seizing – in part because the state's major newspapers were owned by USNO and UPKO, in part because Sabah's forests were still abundant, and in part because the state's forestry institutions were associated with colonial rule and had no popular constituency.[27]

Yet during the Sabah Alliance government, rent seizing was constrained in important ways. Whomever gained the minister of forests portfolio would hold only a limited right to allocate annual and special licenses, since the minister could not afford to use his powers in such a partisan way that it ruptured the coalition government, which remained fragile throughout its four-year life span. Moreover, he could only issue annual and special licenses in a limited number of areas, since most of the forests were still protected by two colonial-era institutions: the twelve long-term concessions, which covered 70 percent of Sabah's commercial forests; and the Land Ordinance of 1962, which gave extensive rights to forest-dwelling groups.

by 1990 it would total M$30.5 billion ringgit (close to $11 billion U.S.). For comparison, Sabah's annual state budget was M$1.7 billion. The sum of rent foregone could provide every Sabah citizen with a one-time lump sum payment of M$21,137 – about three times the average yearly income in Malaysia (World Bank 1991: 77–8).
 Most of the government's revenues from the forest sector come from royalties. Other fees include a timber cess (export tax), a special timber extraction charge, a timber development charge, and a set of smaller charges.
26 In some cabinets, the minister of natural resources acquired the forest department portfolio in lieu of a separate minister of forests.
27 Unlike the U.S. administration in the Philippines, the British had been slow to turn the governance of the forests over to native Sabahans, leaving the postcolonial forest department with little public support.

In the months preceding the end of colonial rule, Stephens and Mustapha each sought to become the minister-designate for agriculture, lands, forests, and natural resources – the position that would hold interim authority over logging permits. At first Mustapha prevailed. But when he decided to accept the largely ceremonial post of head of state (*Yang di-Pertua Negara*) the USNO-UNKO fight was reopened, and this time Stephens won.[28] As a concession, the portfolio was divided in two, with Stephens's UNKO retaining control over the forests and natural resources fraction and the rest going to a member of Mustapha's USNO.

When Sabah became a Malaysian state in 1963, Stephens turned the forests and natural resources portfolio over to Richard Yap, one of UNKO's two cabinet members; as the new chief minister, however, Stephens controlled forest policy himself. Stephens first tried to ban all annual licenses. But under pressure from ethnic Chinese timbermen, he agreed to continue issuing them, but at the same "frozen" levels maintained by the colonial government since 1955. He also gave out six special licenses to Murut and Kadazan cooperatives, which provided them with generous incomes[29] (Means 1976).

Disputes within the coalition – largely over timber licensing – led to a pair of cabinet crises in 1964. The first came in June, and was resolved when Stephens agreed to turn the natural resources portfolio over to a "neutral" minister, Thomas Jayasuriya, who belonged to none of the coalition parties. But a second crisis in December forced Stephens to step down as chief minister. To maintain the coalition, USNO agreed to make Natural Resources Minister Jayasuriya a member of Stephens's UPKO; UPKO agreed in turn that all decisions on license allocation would be made by the full cabinet, not the minister. Since the cabinet was dominated by the partnership between USNO and SCA, the two parties gained effective control over the dissemination of licenses.[30]

From 1963 to 1964, Stephens maintained a policy of restraint – holding the number of annual licenses steady, giving out six new special licenses, and allowing timber production to rise just 3 percent. After the

28 Mustapha had made a tactical error, failing to realize that the head of state would have little real authority.
29 The Sabahan Chinese turned out to benefit as well, by working as contractors for the inexperienced cooperatives.
30 Through the various cabinet shifts between 1963 and 1967, USNO and SCA together maintained a slight voting edge over UNKO/UPKO, which was the largest single party.

power to issue timber licenses passed to the full cabinet – and, hence, to the USNO-SCA voting bloc – over the next three years the number of special licenses rose by three, the number of annual licenses jumped from 60 to 184, and the net timber harvest climbed by 59 percent (see Figure 5.1).

With the USNO-SCA partnership boosting the number of annual licenses, Sabah's logging rate exceeded sustainable levels for the first time. Under the assumptions maintained by the forest department, 4.83 million cubic meters of wood could be sustainably removed from the forests each year, including 2.63 million cubic meters by the concessionaires, and 2.2 million cubic meters by the annual and special licensees.[31] In 1967, the government's policies produced a harvest of 5.7 million cubic meters – including 2.11 million cubic meters by concession holders, and 3.59 million cubic meters by the holders of annual and special licenses.

By 1967, the rising pace of logging began to worry some observers; according to the *Far Eastern Economic Review*,

there is alarm (in Sabah's capital) over Kuala Lumpur's failure to prevent excessive exploitation of Sabah's forests. If allowed to continue at present rates for five more years, this practice will so cripple the State's economic development that Sabah will become dependent on handouts from Kuala Lumpur. (*Far Eastern Economic Review* 1967: 714–15)

Over the next thirty years, however, the quality of Sabah's forest policies would deteriorate much further.

The 1967 Election

Both loggers and party leaders realized that the stakes were high in the 1967 vote, Sabah's first direct election for its own government. Since

---

31 The concessionaires were to harvest the commercial forest reserve (2.63 million hectares) at a rate of 1 percent annually (26,300 hectares), assuming an eighty-year rotation, and that 20 percent of the land was unsuitable for harvesting. A generous average yield of one hundred cubic meters per hectare would produce 2.63 million cubic meters annually. This figure may be overly generous: Even with prices at their peak, the twelve concessionaires only harvested 2.11 million cubic meters in 1967 and 2.06 million cubic meters in 1968.

The annual and special licenses were only to be issued for the state land forests, which were to be cleared for agricultural use. The average conversion rate in the state land forests, between 1962 and 1990, was twenty thousand hectares per year. If we assume these lands produced 110 cubic meters of commercial timber per hectare (a higher figure than in the commercial forest reserve, where undersized trees should be left to help the forests regenerate), the annual and

most voting occurred along ethnic lines, patronage could sway a limited number of votes; still, each party engaged in bidding wars for swing constituencies. Collectively the parties spent an estimated $1.5 million to influence just 163,000 votes; at over $9 per vote, it was an extraordinary sum in a state whose per capita income was just $350. For voters who entertained rival bidders, the election was "better than Christmas"; some reportedly had more money in their hands during the election than at any previous time in their lives[32] (Milne and Ratnam 1974: 207).

Some of the campaign funding came from the personal finances of the party leaders, who had received special licenses in the final years of British rule.[33] Much of the rest came from businessmen who sought to acquire or protect their logging permits. Most annual licensees predictably lined up behind USNO and SCA, who had organized an electoral alliance. But the Chinese timber merchants were divided, and several reportedly donated $M1,000,000 ($400,000 U.S.) to UPKO to help defeat USNO's ally, SCA President Khoo Siak Chiew, whom they considered an industry rival (Milne and Ratnam 1974; Ross-Larson 1976).

---

    special licensees could produce an additional 2.2 million cubic meters of wood per year.

32 Toward the end of the campaign some candidates tried to contain costs, and to ward off defections, by promising to pay off their backers only if they won.

33 Just before the end of British rule, the colonial government had given special licenses of close to 2,500 hectares to each of Sabah's three most prominent non-Chinese leaders: Stephens, the founder of UNKO; Mustapha, the founder of USNO; and Murut leader Gunsanad Sundang, who went on to found the Pasok-Momogun party. The permits were meant by the British to narrow the welfare gap between the Chinese and non-Chinese populations. But because the holders of these licenses went on to found three of Sabah's main political parties, the proceeds were used to fill party coffers. Shortly after decolonization, politicians began to treat these special licenses as legitimate components of party politics. After UNKO and Pasok-Momogun merged, USNO was given a second special license to even out party finances. Prominent SCA members also received a special license to provide party funding – even though timber barons already made up much of the party's leadership (Roff 1974; Lee 1976).

    There can be little doubt that up through the 1967 elections, both Stephens and Mustapha – neither of whom came from wealthy families – provided much of their parties' finances through personal contributions; and that these personal contributions came largely from their timber operations. In 1967, Stephens said he gave $M10,000 a month to the party (about $4,000 U.S.), and undoubtedly more during the elections. Mustapha admitted giving millions of ringgit to USNO and its unofficial organ, *The Kinabalu Times*. By the middle of the 1967 election campaign, he had reportedly spent $M1,000,000 (about $400,000 U.S.) on USNO's operations (Ross-Larson 1976; Sta. Maria 1978).

The USNO-SCA alliance won a close victory at the polls. The Assembly had thirty-two seats; on election day, USNO won fourteen, UPKO twelve, and SCA five. Although this gave the USNO-SCA alliance firm control of the Assembly, Mustapha had fallen two seats short of the two-thirds majority he sought. Using logging permits and cabinet positions as inducements, Mustapha persuaded two UPKO members to switch parties. Under heavy pressure from Mustapha, opposition leader Stephens dissolved his party and urged all UPKO members to join USNO.[34]

The single case of Sabah's 1967 election, cannot "test" the claim that bad (high patronage) politicians generally defeat good (low patronage) ones; it can only illustrate its plausibility. Had Stephens been willing to use annual licenses to bid for the support of the SCA leadership, his chances of prevailing within the Sabah Alliance government, and of forming a new government after the election, would have been greater; had Mustapha favored restraint, his success would have been less likely.

RENT SEIZING UNDER TUN MUSTAPHA, 1967–76

In May 1967, Tun Mustapha Harun became Sabah's first elected chief minister. With the end of the transitional government, the chief minister's powers increased substantially. Mustapha had greater influence than his predecessors over the government's executive powers, since he could appoint and remove ministers without fear of bringing down a fragile all-party coalition. The collapse of the rival UPKO party left Mustapha's USNO with a two-thirds majority in the Assembly, giving Mustapha broad legislative and constitutional powers, and a strong hand over SCA, his sole remaining coalition partner.[35]

---

34 Stephens's motives for dissolving UPKO were the subject of much speculation. Stephens had been concerned since the early 1960s that party politics would lead to interethnic strife, and had previously approached Mustapha about merging their parties. But there also is evidence that Mustapha's control over timber licenses had forced Stephens's hand. USNO leaders suggested at the time that more defections were imminent – perhaps due to a "tipping" effect – and that Stephens disbanded UPKO rather than have it collapse around him. Stephens may have also feared that Mustapha would cancel his special license, depriving his party of its main source of income.

35 According to Harris Salleh, Mustapha's finance minister (and successor as chief minister),

As ministers of the USNO government, we hardly had a voice in any decision. We were passed over by Tun Mustapha and Syed Kechik (Mustapha's deputy) without a hearing.

Using this concentration of executive, legislative, and constitutional authority, Mustapha embarked on two parallel efforts to reconfigure Sabah's forestry institutions. The first would enhance his influence over the timber windfall; the second would boost the windfall's size, by creating "ransack rents."

Gaining Direct and Discretionary Allocation Rights

Thanks to his power over the cabinet, the chief minister's allocation rights were now exclusive: No other politician could issue licenses or otherwise gain access to the windfall without his consent. But his authority was neither direct nor discretionary, due to obstacles created by the Forest Ordinance and Forest Rules of 1954. Mustapha quickly revised Sabah's forest laws and regulations to remove these constraints.

On January 1, 1969, the forestry laws and regulations established by the colonial government in 1954 were replaced by a new law, the Forest Enactment 1968, and a new set of regulations, the Forest Rules 1969. The new law and regulations gave the chief minister direct authority, and a remarkable level of discretion, over timber licenses.

After the 1967 election, Chief Minister Mustapha named himself Minister of Natural Resources – gaining the direct authority over licensing that, under colonial rule, had been held by the forest conservator. The new forest enactment helped clear away legal obstacles to this arrangement.[36] Mustapha now absorbed the old ministry of natural resources into the chief minister's department, and appointed a secretary – under his direct supervision – to handle natural resource matters.

The new forest enactment also gave the chief minister wide discretion over the use of the forests, including, in Section 42.d, the ability to make rules

i.   regulating the manner in which, and the conditions upon which, licenses and permits may be issued;

> Mustapha began to make decisions without even giving us the courtesy of consultation. It did not matter what we decided in government committee meetings. (Raffaele 1986: 173)

36 Section I.2 of the enactment gave broad discretionary powers to "the Minister for the time being responsible for matters relating to Natural Resources"; yet it failed to establish either a discrete ministry of natural resources or a minister of natural resources. Every chief minister since 1968 has used this provision to retain control of the natural resources portfolio.

iii. prescribing fees, royalties and payments payable to the Government
on forest produce, and the manner in which, and time at which, they
are to be levied;
iv. providing for the remission or exemption from payment, in
whole or in part of any fees, royalties or payments payable to the
Government.

Neither the forest enactment nor the forest rules set out what the actual
terms of these licenses and fees should be; all such matters were left
to the minister's discretion. Even more striking was a clause in Section
18.2 that gave the minister's licensing powers precedence over the enactment itself – placing the decisions of the chief minister, in effect, above
the law:

... where any provision of such license agreement is inconsistent with any provision of this Enactment, compliance with the provisions of such license agreement shall be deemed to be compliance with the provisions of this Enactment.

These provisions gave the chief minister the ability to impose new costs
and benefits on licensees.

Creating Ransack Rents

Strengthening his allocation rights was only half of Mustapha's agenda.
The other half was to create "ransack rents." At the beginning of his
term, two colonial-era institutions limited the quantity of forest land that
Mustapha could distribute with short-term licenses. One was the system
of long-term concessions, which had placed 70 percent of the commercial forest under sustained-yield management; the other was the Land
Ordinance of 1962, which gave extensive property rights to forest-
dwelling groups.

Sabah's forest dwellers practiced a traditional form of swidden agriculture; at the end of 1968, their swiddens covered 571,000 hectares of
"forested" land, about 13 percent of the forest estate (Munang 1987).
Swidden farmers hindered commercial logging, since they claimed property rights to large parts of the forest. Moreover, swiddeners used fire to
clear and fertilize their land; sometimes these fires damaged loggable
areas, or spread into logged-over forests.

The Land Ordinance of 1962 set out relatively lenient procedures for
granting land titles to natives, recognizing communal rights, establishing
native reserves, and compensating natives for land taken by the state.
Mustapha's new forest enactment limited native rights in the forest

reserve to those granted specifically by the chief minister; these rights could also be rescinded by the minister at any time, and cancelled after three years if not exercised. Swidden farmers often had to let their swiddens lie fallow for more than three years, to allow the forests' nutrient-poor soil to regain its fertility after cultivation; under the new law, they would lose their right to this land.

The forest enactment also set penalties for unauthorized swidden farming on land set aside for logging that were remarkably harsh – seven years in prison and a fine – by far the harshest for any of the "crimes" listed in the forest enactment.[37] In the 1963–7 Sabah Alliance government, Donald Stephens and UPKO had championed the rights of the forest-dwelling Kadazans, Dusuns, and Muruts. But with UPKO disbanded and Stephens out of politics, Mustapha was free to eviscerate the property rights of Sabah's upland population.

The Forest Enactment 1968 gave Mustapha the authority to nullify the property rights of forest dwellers at will. But it had little effect on Sabah's concessionaires, who held property rights to over two-thirds of the state's commercial forests.

In 1969, 1.9 million hectares of forest land had been set aside for Sabah's twelve long-term concessionaires, who held twenty-one-year contracts that were designed to be renewed indefinitely. For their first twenty-one years, the concessionaires had access to about 375,000

---

37 The forest enactment also set standards of evidence that made it virtually impossible for swiddeners to defend themselves in court:

1. Any person who kindles, keeps or carries any fire, or leaves any fire burning, near a Forest Reserve in such a manner as to endanger such Reserve or any forest produce therein shall be guilty of an offence and liable to imprisonment for seven years and to a fine.
2. The fact that any fire has escaped into a Forest Reserve and damaged any forest produce therein shall be conclusive proof that the person who kindled such fire is guilty of an offence under subsection (1) of this section.
3. Where any fire escapes into a Forest Reserve from any alienated land and causes damage to any forest produce, the occupier of such alienated land shall be guilty of an offence under subsection (1) of this section unless he proves –
   a. that such fire was not kindled by himself, his servants or agents or any member of his family; *and*
   b. that on becoming aware of such fire on his land, he took all reasonable measures to prevent such fire spreading to such Reserve.

   The penalties for these acts – seven years in prison and a fine – were made harsher still by a 1984 amendment to the forest enactment. The forest enactment also set severe penalties for unauthorized swidden farming on land set aside for agricultural conversion: three years imprisonment and a $50,000.00 fine.

hectares of forest; the remaining 1.53 million hectares were held in reserve, for them to log as their contracts were renewed. After eighty years of logging these primary forests, their rotation would begin again on land that was logged eighty years earlier. Since the concessions had been awarded by the colonial government, their holders were not indebted to USNO.

Mustapha's top advisor, Syed Kechik, drew up a strategy to gain control of these 1.53 million hectares of reserved forest land.[38] Syed Kechik realized that the concessionaires – two-thirds of whom were Sabahan Chinese – would fight the expropriation of the land that was promised to them. But after UPKO was dissolved in 1967, USNO's remaining coalition party, the SCA, had lost almost all its leverage: even without the SCA's votes, Mustapha held a two-thirds majority in the assembly. Moreover, to blunt any popular objections to the move, Mustapha transferred about 60 percent of the expropriated land – about 855,000 hectares – to the Sabah Foundation (*Yayasan Sabah*), a state-owned enterprise that promised to make cash payments to all citizens, and to fund public projects.[39]

The concessionaires were caught off guard by Syed Kechik's tactics; they were also intimidated by Mustapha's unchallenged political author-ity.[40] To soothe their concerns, Mustapha allowed them to log their remaining plots more quickly; in 1969, their harvests jumped 47 percent. All of a sudden, the concessionaires were no longer near the beginning of perpetual eighty-year felling cycles; instead they were in the middle or near the end of terminal twenty-one-year licenses. By late 1969, Mustapha had fully dismantled the institutions designed by the British to protect the sustainability of the forests.

---

38 Much of the credit – or blame – for Mustapha's strategies may belong to his shrewd longtime advisor, Syed Kechik. Syed Kechik was a lawyer from Kedah, West Malaysia, and a longtime USNO insider who held a variety of important posts in the Sabah government between 1965 and 1976. Kadazan leader Peter Mojuntin once referred to him as the " 'Rasputin' behind Tun Mustapha's throne" (Sta. Maria 1978: 226). He was also the recipient of at least three timber licenses covering 71,200 hectares of forest (Campbell 1986).

39 The remainder – almost 700,000 hectares – went back into the pool of forest reserves that the chief minister could distribute through annual and special licenses.

40 At the time he broke up the concession system, Mustapha's authority was aug-mented by emergency powers, which were granted to him following the May 13, 1969 riots in West Malaysia. Mustapha took the opportunity to jail the only remaining opposition assemblyman, Yap Pak Leong, who was held for thirty-one months without charge.

At the same time, Mustapha had created a new institution – the Sabah Foundation – that initially looked like a promising replacement for the concession system. The foundation had been established in 1966 as a modest government initiative to fund education with public grants; after receiving control of one-third of Sabah's commercial forests, it became the largest organization – except for the government itself – in the entire Malaysian Federation.

Mustapha's influence over the Sabah Foundation was at least as great as his authority over the forest department. The Sabah Foundation removed 855,000 hectares of prime commercial forest from the purview of both the forest department and the assembly.[41] Mustapha appointed his top aide, Syed Kechik, as the foundation's director; he also named himself chairman of the Sabah Foundation Board. Mustapha and his successors as chief minister would each use the Sabah Foundation for both ambitious social projects and political patronage.[42]

Windfall Use Under Mustapha 1967–75

By 1970, Chief Minister Mustapha had gained the ability to spend the timber windfall at a rate that reflected his political needs. The pressures of regular competitive elections kept Mustapha's hold on the chief ministership insecure, and he allocated timber licenses, and authorized logging, at rates that were exceptionally high – despite the admonitions of both domestic and foreign forestry experts.

Mustapha's abandonment of the policy of sustainable harvesting drew criticism from both the Forest Department and foreign consultants. A 1971 Forest Department research paper documented that the forests were being overcut, and proposed tighter logging restrictions and a shortened cutting rotation (Munang 1979). In 1972, a confidential report commissioned by the government and prepared by a Canadian consulting firm, warned that a majority of the Commercial Forest

---

41 The forest department had no authority to conduct any resource management activities on Sabah Foundation land. After the assembly passed legislation that enabled the foundation to operate logging concessions in December 1967, it had little further influence over the foundation's activities.

42 Mustapha was also able to lower the costs of his actions by diminishing government transparency. After 1969, the forest department no longer disclosed the names, locations, or concession sizes of the major licensees.

Reserve was no longer being operated on a sustained-yield basis, and criticized

> the inadequate authority and power of the (Forest) Department to carry through its role of forest administration and management independent of political or other external forces. (Hedlin Menzies and Associates 1972: 155)

A second confidential report, prepared by another consultant, noted that

> the timber production authorized at the present time in Sabah, and the short-term tenure of concessions and licenses will result in high levels of cut, followed by sharply declining levels of production. (Moss 1972: 5)

The report also urged the government to appoint a separate minister of natural resources, and then to curtail the minister's discretionary powers.

When Mustapha took office in 1967, the harvest was at 5.7 million cubic meters, about 20 percent above sustainable levels. By 1976, when USNO was voted out of office, it had reached 12.6 million cubic meters, some 260 percent of the sustainable rate.

Sabah's rising logging rate partly reflected the rising number of annual and special licenses. From 1967 to 1976, the number of annual licenses rose from 184 to 654, while the number of special licenses went from 16 to 35[43] (see Table 5.2). On the eve of decolonization, the holders of annual and special licenses produced 29 percent of Sabah's timber, and were due to be phased out. By 1976 these short-term licensees were cutting 75 percent of the state's timber, and had come to dominate the industry.[44]

Mustapha gave annual and special licenses to top USNO officials; to USNO supporters and allies; to former opponents, to bring them into the USNO fold; and to USNO directly and indirectly. He also awarded licenses to himself (Ross-Larson 1976; Hunter 1976).[45] Mustapha

---

43 When measured from the beginning of Mustapha's rule in April 1967, the rise in the number of short-term licenses was undoubtedly more dramatic – though precise figures were never made public. Between April and December 1967, the Mustapha government issued fifty-eight new annual and special licenses (Roff 1974).

44 Mustapha's Forest Rules and Forest Enactment also cut the maximum duration of special licenses from ten to five years.

45 Over the course of his eight years in office, Mustapha distributed licenses covering 1.86 million hectares of forest; according to his successor as chief minister, Harris Salleh, "the bulk of this went to persons who were relatives or close friends of [Mustapha's]" (Campbell 1986: 52).

Table 5.2. *Sabah Logging Permits By Type, 1955–91*

	Concessions[a]	Special Licenses	Annual Licenses
1955	4	—	59
1962	11	7	60
1967	12	16	184
1968	12	16	179
1969	12	16	156
1970	12	19	215
1971	12	28	192
1972	13	33	175
1974	13	35	570
1975	13	49	440
1976	13	35	654
1977	13	80	672
1978	13	72	766
1979	13	81	808
1980	12	92	603
1981	13	105	717
1982	13	103	622
1987	13	62	217
1991	13	76	620

[a] The number of concessions rose from twelve to thirteen in 1972, since the forest land turned over to the Sabah Foundation was considered a concession. Although these thirteen concessions continued to exist legally in the 1980s and 1990s, many of them were no longer producing timber.
Sources: Government of Sabah (various); Hedlin Menzies and Associates (1972); Lee (1976); Hani (1991); Food and Agriculture Organization (1992).

wielded timber licenses so adroitly that public opposition to his rule virtually disappeared and he took to living in London and Australia for most of the year.[46]

RENT SEIZING AND FOREST MISUSE, 1976–95

Between 1976 and 1995, three governments held office in Sabah: from 1976 to 1985, Harris Salleh's Berjaya government; from 1985 to 1994,

46 Mustapha also used logging permits to support the missionary efforts of the United Sabah Islamic Association – whose secretary-general was Syed Kechik – and to reward prominent citizens for converting to Islam (Ross-Larson 1976).

Joseph Pairin Kitingin's PBS government; and beginning in 1994, a six-party coalition led by UMNO-Sabah, which rotated the position of chief minister. Each of these governments denounced its predecessor for engaging in "timber politics" and promised a program of reform. Yet each chief minister held the same allocation rights as his predecessors – retaining the natural resources portfolio instead of appointing an independent minister, and closely controlling the Sabah Foundation. Each used timber licenses for political and personal gain. The gap between the authorized logging rate, and the sustainable rate, continued to widen.

The Berjaya party's central campaign theme in 1976 was the "rape" of the forests under Mustapha; its central promise was forestry reform.[47] Shortly after taking office, the Harris government announced that the condition of the forests was worse than it anticipated. A spokesman charged that logging rates were so high under Mustapha that, should they continue unchanged, all primary forests would be exhausted in ten years. Some 328,000 hectares of concessions issued by Mustapha were cancelled[48] (Rowley 1977).

Harris had promised to put aside the forest land taken from Mustapha's clients, in order to slow the rate of forest depletion. Instead, he reallocated the land to his own backers. Just over half (166,000 hectares) went to a series of pork barrel projects linked to his own Berjaya party: the Ex-Serviceman's Association, the Sanya Youth Cooperative, the Education Department Cooperative, and the Rural Development Corporation. The balance (162,000 hectares) was distributed to 1,500 Berjaya supporters and officials; the size of their reward was determined by a strict formula that ranked them by political importance (Davies and Lauriet 1980).[49]

Harris's policies led to a record number of annual and special licenses, and record harvests in 1977 and 1978. Logging rates leveled off

---

47 The Berjaya government was originally led by Donald Stephens who, following a conversion to Islam, became known as Tun Fuad Stephens. Harris Salleh became chief minister after Stephens was killed in a July 1976 plane crash.

48 This figure almost certainly understates the change in license ownership under Harris. Over 90 percent of all licenses were annual licenses, and many would have expired before he could cancel them. Among those not canceled were licenses held by Harris and other Berjaya leaders, who had obtained them earlier while serving in USNO (Guntur 1990).

49 Raffaele's sympathetic biography of Harris notes that at the time he left office in 1985, Harris's personal wealth totaled "several hundred million ringgit" – roughly $100 million. Most of this wealth came from timber concessions (Raffaele 1986: 176–7).

between 1979 and 1985, stabilizing at close to 300 percent of sustainable levels.

The PBS government that came to power in 1985, headed by Joseph Pairin Kitingin, followed a similar path. The Pairin government pledged its support for sustainable forestry, and in 1987 announced a freeze on the issuance of all new concessions. But the decree had little meaning: by the time of the announcement, Pairin had already given out licenses for all of Sabah's unlogged forest land (Pardo 1987). Moreover, despite the nominal freeze, the PBS government began to issue new licenses that authorized felling in logged-over forest land – a practice that can lead to severe forest damage. Although Pairin discontinued the government's longstanding practice of disclosing the number of licenses issued annually, nongovernmental reports show that from 1987 to 1991, the number of special licenses rose from 62 to 76, while the number of annual licenses went from 217 to 620 (Table 5.2). Like Mustapha and Harris, Pairin also served as his own minister of natural resources.[50]

The rapid decline in Sabah's forests gave Pairin a smaller pool of rents to distribute. Perhaps to compensate, Pairin began to use export permits for raw logs to reward political supporters.[51] After Pairin broke with Malaysian Prime Minister Mahathir in October 1990, the two struggled for the exclusive right to allocate log export permits, with each attempting to penalize firms that politically backed the other (*Asiaweek* 1993).[52]

The "National Front" coalition government that ousted PBS in 1994 followed a similar pattern, albeit with a larger role for the central government in Kuala Lumpur.[53] Shortly after the election, federal Minister of Primary Industries Lim Keng Yaik traveled to Sabah and announced

---

50 The PBS government did adopt modest forestry reforms. In 1992, the forest enactment was amended twice, to set aside more land for protection and to promote reforestation.

51 In this regard, Pairin adopted the same strategy as Marcos – once the entire forest estate had been given to licensees, they both used export permits to direct a dwindling pool of timber rents to their supporters.

52 The federal government had never before claimed a right to regulate Sabah's log exports.

53 In the 1994 Sabah state elections, UMNO ran candidates on its own slate for the first time. UMNO-Sabah officials became the core of the new National Front government, tying Sabah more closely to the federal government than any time in the previous thirty years.

an audit of all logging concessions awarded by the PBS government. "Once the government has assessed and checked the timber situation," he told reporters, "we will see the last of logging politics in Sabah" (Tan 1994).

But the front's first two chief ministers, Sakaran Dandai and Salleh Said Keruak, each retained the natural resources portfolio, and each used timber licenses to reward supporters. Idris Hydraulic, a firm closely tied to UMNO and the National Front, received a massive 176,388 hectare concession (Chen 1994). The father of Anwar Ibrahim – Malaysia's deputy prime minister, who had directed the effort to oust PBS – was given a 20,200 hectare concession, even though he lived in Western Malaysia, not Sabah (Hassan 1995).[54]

Unsustainable Logging, 1976–95

From 1976 to 1993, the authorized logging rate fluctuated between 8.2 and 13.3 million cubic meters a year. These unsustainable yields triggered a stream of protests from both the forest department and foreign advisors.

During the Harris government, the forest department issued a series of reports on Sabah's future log supply; all showed that under existing policies, there would be a sudden drop in timber production between the mid-1980s and the mid-1990s (Munang 1979; Segal 1983; Hadi 1985). Under the Pairin government, the forest department's forecasts became even bleaker. In 1988, Forest Conservator Miller Munang announced that all forest tracts outside the Sabah Foundation had either been logged or soon would be, and that the government was currently authorizing logging at over four times the sustainable rate (Munang 1988). By 1991, the department estimated that the sustainable yield of the forests – now suffering from widespread degradation and relogging – was just to 1.2 million cubic meters, about one-seventh of that year's logging rate and just over one-tenth of the 1992 rate (Figure 5.1).

A series of FAO studies in the late 1980s confirmed the department's dire projections, and stated the problem more bluntly. One analysis described "the wanton destruction of the environment and degradation of the forest resource as a consequence of over-cutting"

---

54 After the concession was reported in the press, Anwar asked that it be canceled.

(Pardo 1987: 14). A second noted that "the present rate of exploitation is almost four times the accepted norms" (Bhargava and Chai 1988: 14). A third FAO report warned of "an apparent drift to disaster," and declared

there may be differences of opinion about when it will happen and how severe it will be, but a drastic cutback in timber exploitation in Sabah is inevitable. (Gane 1987: 32–3)

A 1991 World Bank study was graver still, arguing that the Sabah Forest Department's sustained-yield estimate of 1.2 million cubic meters was overly optimistic (World Bank 1991).

Some of these analyses alluded to the role of politics in Sabah's forest problems. Pardo noted that the forest department's generally sound objectives lacked political support, and remarked, "Those outside of the forestry sector who make the political decisions and choices either are not aware of the forest policy or do not take it seriously" (Pardo 1987: 19–20). The FAO's summary report stated that

Evaluation results indicate that the major factors which impede rational and orderly harvesting are: the manner in which harvesting licenses are issued; and the lack of planning and control of logging operations. . . . A high proportion of the Special Licenses and Form I [Annual] Licenses are awarded to individuals who have neither the knowledge nor the capital to work their areas effectively. (Food and Agriculture Organization 1992: 18–19)

The World Bank also exonerated the forest department, stating that

as the forestry agencies [of both Sabah and Sarawak] do not have *de facto* control of the forests, and are unlikely to gain it as long as excessive profits fuel an alliance among logging firms, concessionaires, and politicians, expansion or upgrading of these agencies alone would not materially improve this situation. (World Bank 1991: 23)

Despite these admonitions, the Pairin government kept timber production high through 1993, in part by authorizing the early relogging of logged-over forests.[55] While harvesting rates dropped in 1994 and 1995, it is difficult to know if this reflected new restraint by the government, or the advancing degradation of the forests.

---

55 In Sabah's primary forests, mechanized logging typically bares between 40 to 66 percent of the soil. While the forests will eventually recover if fully protected, early relogging further damages the soil, impedes natural regeneration, and reduces the long-term commercial value of the forests (Bhargava and Chai 1988).

The Decline of the Sabah Foundation

When Mustapha dismantled the concession system in 1969, he declared that the Sabah Foundation would henceforth protect the sustainability of Sabah's forests. But under the concession system, forest sustainability was guarded by a matrix of interlocking institutions, including the 1954 Forest Ordinance and Forest Rules, legal contracts with the concessionaires, and the bureaucratic authority of the forest department. Under the Sabah Foundation, the sustainability of the forests was protected by little more than the decisions of the chief minister. The foundation's mandate for sustainable logging was gradually abandoned.

The Sabah Foundation originally held a mandate to log its forests at a roughly sustainable pace, cutting 0.9 percent (7,770 hectares) every year, and setting aside 10 percent of its land as unsuitable for logging.[56] Around 1974, however, the Mustapha government ordered the foundation to temporarily boost its annual coupe by 50 percent – to 11,650 hectares – for each of the next twenty years. Mustapha soon revised these figures again, and authorized a doubling of the original coupe (15,540 hectares) over the next ten years.

Under Mustapha's successors, the size of the annual coupe grew even further. From 1978 to 1981, Chief Minister Harris raised the coupe to 2.3 percent a year (18,000 hectares). After 1981, the government stopped disclosing the size of the annual coupe. But in the late 1980s, when the Sabah Foundation fell into arrears on its royalty payments to the state, the Pairin government overrode the objections of the forest department and approved another, unspecified boost in the foundation's annual coupe.

By the early 1990s, virtually all of the state's primary forest reserves outside the Sabah Foundation had been logged out. Now the PBS and National Front governments began to dismantle the Sabah Foundation itself, and sell off its remaining parcels of unlogged commercial forests.

Through a complex series of contracts and privatizations, the National Front transferred much of the foundation's remaining primary forests to its political backers. In the most important deal, Joseph Ambrose Lee, a major National Front donor, received 160,000 hectares

56 This logging mandate was less conservative, by half, than the one it replaced. When this same forest land was held by the 12 concessionaires, 20 percent – not 10 percent – was set aside as unsuitable for commercial logging. This change was made before the state's first full forest survey in 1975.

of Sabah Foundation forest at a price far below market value. Also profiting from the deal was Lee's partner, Mohamed Shafie Apdal, a former political secretary to National Front Chief Minister Sakaran and state chairman of UMNO's youth wing[57] (Pura and Duthie 1994; Nantha 1995).

THE DECLINE OF THE FOREST DEPARTMENT'S REGULATORY INFLUENCE

Under the Forest Rules and Ordinance of 1954, the forest department was charged with protecting the forests from damaging harvesting practices. In the 1950s and 1960s, the department carried out prefelling inventories of licensed areas, tree marking, postfelling sample inventories, postfelling silvicultural treatments to promote regeneration, postfelling surveys to assess penalties for any regulatory violations, and follow-up inventories to monitor regeneration.

Yet gradually the forest department lost the ability to carry out these measures, for two reasons. First, it failed to get enough government resources to keep up with the logging boom in the 1960s and early 1970s (Lee 1982).[58] The second and more important reason was that a series of chief ministers removed most of Sabah's forest land from the department's jurisdiction; doing so allowed loggers to employ inexpensive felling practices that were egregiously harmful to the forests. Between 1967 and 1989, 77 percent of Sabah's loggable forests were taken out of the department's purview.

Part of this problem can be traced to a decision made in 1962, before the departure of the British. A survey of the state suggested that almost half of Sabah's loggable forests (2.1 million hectares) had soils that made them suitable for permanent agriculture. Reclassified as "State Land Forests," they were removed from the forest department's jurisdiction. Since the State Land Forests were to be cleared for agriculture, officials reasoned, there was no need for loggers to use costly techniques to

57 The deal was consummated by a "reverse takeover," in which North Borneo Timber – a firm owned by Lee and Apdal – paid for the concession by issuing shares to Innoprise Corporation, the Sabah Foundation's investment arm. Mohamed Shafie Apdal was also the executive director of Innoprise.

Lee also received a valuable set of gold and marble concessions, and a license to operate a Sabah Foundation concession in Papua New Guinea, which was reportedly worth $20–25 million in annual profits.

58 In 1977, for example, the department was forced to drop all efforts to provide silvicultural treatments to logged-over areas.

protect the remaining trees or promote regeneration; hence anyone who gained a license to harvest timber in the State Land Forests was exempt from all silvicultural restrictions.

The 1962 policy on this "conversion forest" land was consistent with well-established forestry principles at the time. But after 1967, Sabah's chief ministers abused this policy, and began granting annual and special licenses in the State Land Forests, regardless of the demand for agricultural land.

The forest department recognized that logging the State Land Forests at a high rate could have grievous economic and environmental repercussions. In 1972, the assistant conservator, Malu Udarbe, publicly warned that much of the timber boom was based on

the apparently unrestrained clearing of forested State Lands for agricultural expansion. As these forests near exhaustion there will be an expected drastic decline in log exports and a corresponding fall in timber revenue. (Udarbe 1972: 289)

If the excess State Land Forests had been returned to the purview of the forest department – forcing these loggers to abide by the department's silvicultural restrictions – some of it might have better survived the logging process and eventually regenerate. This did not occur. Instead, Sabah's chief ministers maintained the fiction that the land would soon be needed for agriculture and could therefore be logged with impunity. By the end of the 1980s, all 2.1 million hectares of State Land Forest had been logged, although just 600,000 hectares had been used for some form of agriculture. The remaining 1.5 million hectares had been clear cut and abandoned, and were judged by the FAO to need extensive, and costly, rehabilitation (Food and Agriculture Organization 1992).

The forest department's ability to enforce harvesting regulations was also eroded by the proliferation of annual licenses in the Commercial Forest Reserve – that part of the forest originally set aside for the holders of long-term concessions. Under colonial rule, annual licenses were issued exclusively for the logging of conversion forests (later designated "State Land Forest"). But after 1967, Sabah's chief ministers issued annual licenses for both the State Land Forests and the Commercial Forest Reserve. By 1988, one-third of the trees in the forest reserve – and over two-thirds of the trees in the entire state – had been cut by annual licensees (see Table 5.3). The small size of these licensed areas and the brevity of the permits made them almost impossible for the forest department to regulate.

Table 5.3. *Licensed Forest Area, Sabah 1988 (hectares)*

	Forest Reserve	State Land Forest[a]	Total Logged	Licensed but Unlogged
Concession[b]	1,208,221	106,806	658,057	656,057
Special License	500,646	384,458	382,347	502,757
Annual License	829,026	1,278,160	2,107,186	0
TOTAL	2,537,893	1,769,424	3,147,590	1,159,727

[a] According to Food and Agriculture Organization (1992), 2.1 million hectares of state land forest had been logged; the figures shown here may exclude areas that were converted to agricultural use.
[b] Three-quarters of this "concession" land belonged to the Sabah Foundation.
Source: Chai and Awang (1989).

Finally, in 1970, the department lost its authority over the land transferred to the Sabah Foundation, which eventually totaled 972,800 hectares. Of the state's 4.3 million hectares of loggable forests, 3.3 million – about 77 percent – were wrongly removed from the forest department's jurisdiction.[59]

The forest department's inability to properly regulate the timber industry was criticized by both the state's foresters and its foreign advisors. A 1987 study found that in most of the Commercial Forest Reserve, "Other than size limit there is no realistic control on the intensity of logging, logging sequence, method of extraction, transport route, etc." (Pardo 1987: 24). Bhargava and Chai noted that "Apart from girth limit and area to be harvested, there is no other form of control"; they also suggested that "the approach which exists even today has given a good-bye to all norms of management," a statement later echoed by Forest Conservator Miller Munang (Bhargava and Chai 1988: 18; Munang 1988: 11). The World Bank issued similar findings in 1991, noting

In the absence of Forest Department supervision, market demand and the desire of contractors to minimize costs presumably dictate actual practice.

59 This figure includes the 972,000 hectares granted to the Sabah Foundation; the 829,000 hectares of commercial forest reserve logged by annual licensees; and the 1.5 to 1.769 million hectares of State Land Forest that were logged, but apparently not converted to agricultural use. This constitutes between 77 percent and 83 percent of the 4.3 million hectares that were inventoried by Chai and Awang (1989).

Table 5.4. *Changes in Sabah's Forest Cover, 1975–92*

Forest Types	1975 Area (ha)	%[a]	1992 Area (ha)	(%)	1975–92 Change (%)
Mangrove	365,500	4.96	317,857	4.31	−13.0
Transitional, Beach, and Swamp	203,256	2.76	193,500	2.63	−4.8
Undisturbed Low and Upland Dipterocarp	2,800,236	37.99	412,975	5.60	−85.3
Montane	771,874	10.47	715,500	9.71	−7.3
TOTAL UNDISTURBED	4,140,866	56.18	1,639,882	22.25	−60.4
Disturbed, Immature, and Regenerating	1,399,024	18.98	2,769,573	37.57	+98.0
TOTAL FOREST LAND	5,539,890	75.16	4,409,455	59.82	−20.4

[a] Refers to percentage of Sabah's land area covered by forest type.
Source: Adapted from Awang (1994).

That is, everything of sufficient commercial value is cut, the residual is badly damaged, and nothing is done thereafter to assist regeneration. (World Bank 1991: 27)[60]

Most international observers did not blame this regulatory laxity on the forest department's incompetence, but on the intervention of politicians. A 1972 consultant's report noted that "the Forest Department's full role has been stifled through the abrogation of its essential powers to control alienation and harvesting, largely in the interests of political expediency" (Hedlin Menzies and Associates 1972: 257). Sixteen years later, an FAO analysis suggested little had changed. "The Forest Department is fully aware of what needs to be done," it found, but "social and political elements highly influence management, and consequently these conditions have been sacrificed at the altar of wood production and revenue maximization" (Bhargava and Chai 1988: 16, 19).

CONCLUSION

Of the four states in this study, Sabah had the strongest forestry institutions, at least until 1963. By the 1970s, these institutions had been evis-

60 The statement refers to both Sabah and Sarawak.

cerated, and by the 1990s, Sabah's primary forests were largely gone. Sabah's first accurate forest survey, completed in 1975, found that mature, undisturbed forests covered 56.2 percent of the state. By 1992, they covered just 22.3 percent. Over 85 percent of Sabah's most valuable forests – the undisturbed lowland and upland dipterocarp forests – were lost during this seventeen-year interval (Table 5.4).

Overrapid and underregulated logging has produced formidable environmental problems in Sabah, notably widespread soil degradation; soil erosion in turn has led to downstream flooding, the disruption of hydropower and pulp and paper plants, blocked transportation for barges and fishermen, fouled drinking water, and the siltation and destruction of all but a few of the coral reefs in Brunei Bay. Logging has also endangered many plant and animal species, particularly in the lowland rainforests where the biodiversity was once greatest (Murtedza and Ti 1993).

The most worrisome consequences, however, may still be ahead. Unlike the Philippines and Indonesia, Sabah has few economic assets besides its forests. Taxes and royalties from the timber industry have provided the government with as much as two-thirds of its revenues. Moreover, Sabah's difficult terrain, remote location, and sparse population make it a poor base for industrialization or intensive agriculture. While deforestation in the Philippines may be costly, it need not destroy the economy if other national assets are developed. But Sabah has few viable substitutes for a forest-based economy – and hence, a worrisome economic and environmental future.

6

Sarawak, Malaysia

An Almost Uncontrollable Instinct

There is in man an almost uncontrollable instinct to destroy forests ... with the rapid expansion of these industries a strong possibility of such a danger can be clearly foreseen.

Sarawak Forest Conservator F. G. Browne (1954: 33)

Sarawak is Malaysia's largest state, and has almost twice Sabah's forested area. Some 17 percent of Sarawak's forests lie along the coasts, and are classified as peat swamp and mangrove forests. The balance lies in the lowlands and uplands of the hilly interior.

The peat swamp forests hold valuable stands of ramin trees, which have been harvested commercially since the late 1940s. But the soils of the hill forests are relatively poor, compared with the rich volcanic soils of the Philippines, Sabah, and East Kalimantan (in Indonesia). Sarawak's hill forests yield less exportable timber per hectare than the other three regions, and was the last to undergo a major logging boom.

On joining the Malaysian Federation in 1963, Sarawak – like Sabah – retained autonomy over its forests. Yet when the timber industries of the Philippines, Sabah, and Indonesia boomed in the 1950s, 1960s, and early 1970s, Sarawak's timber industry remained small, since its less valuable forests could not yet be profitably logged.

But in the late 1970s, both Philippine and Indonesian log exports began to fall, producing a demand for Sarawak logs to feed the plymills of Japan, South Korea, and Taiwan. From 1975 to 1985, Sarawak's share of the international hardwood log market rose from 3.4 percent to 38 percent. In 1984, Sarawak became the world's leading exporter of hardwood logs, a position it held through the late 1990s. It also authorized logging at three to four times the sustainable rate, despite a storm of protests from both home and abroad.

Like the other case studies, this chapter looks at how the arrival of a timber windfall influenced the state's forestry institutions. The major difference between Sabah and Sarawak was timing. Thanks to its richer soils and forests, loggers in Sabah began to earn rents in the 1950s; in Sarawak's hill forests, rents only became widely available after 1975. The delayed timing had three important consequences. First, because Sarawak's timber industry was small under British rule, the colonial government never established the strong forestry institutions in Sarawak that it did in Sabah – most importantly, a system of long-term sustainable concessions. As a result, Sarawak's rent-seizing politicians had less to dismantle than their Sabah counterparts.

Second, in the 1960s and early 1970s, politicians in Sarawak believed they would soon undergo the same kind of timber boom that neighboring Sabah was enjoying; they hence began to struggle over allocation rights before the boom instead of after it. Finally, the Sarawak timber boom reached its peak in the late 1980s and early 1990s, coinciding with an international movement to conserve tropical rainforests. It hence received far more international attention than the earlier booms in the Philippines, Sabah, and Indonesia; and its government faced much heavier external pressure for reform. These pressures had little effect.

POLITICS IN SARAWAK

The section of northwest Borneo that is now Sarawak was first brought under a common form of government by Sir James Brooke and his heirs between 1841 and 1941. After a period of Japanese occupation, Sarawak came under direct British rule between 1946 and 1963.

The Brookes governed most of Sarawak's ethnic groups indirectly, through each community's social hierarchy. The Chinese communities had well-established patron-client hierarchies within each regional and dialect group, which reached down to the newest Chinese immigrants and up to the local *Kapitan China*, who served as an envoy to the Brooke administration. Similarly, the Brookes worked with the traditional leaders of the Malays, the Melanus, and some of the smaller non-Muslim groups, including the Kenyah and Kayan. Sarawak's largest native groups, the Iban and the Bidayuh, were among the most egalitarian of Borneo's dayak societies, and fit awkwardly with the Brooke system of government. To mend this problem, the Brookes organized a system of appointed village headmen and regional and subregional chiefs who administered government policies in exchange for state benefits; these benefits, in turn, helped them maintain their status.

After 1946, Sarawak was run by a British governor and a bureaucracy whose senior positions were filled largely by expatriates. After the adoption of a new constitution in 1956, Sarawakians were allowed to elect members of the colony's advisory body, the *Council Negri*. But the governor was free to ignore measures approved by the council, and enact legislation that the council opposed, when he believed that doing so was "expedient in the interests of public order, good faith or good government" (Clause 39).

Since 1963, Sarawak's formal political institutions have been almost identical to Sabah's. They include a parliamentary government with a unicameral legislature whose members are elected by pluralities from single-member districts; a state constitution, which can be amended by a two-thirds vote of the legislature; and an exceptional degree of independence from the Malaysian federal government, including autonomy over the governance of the forests.

Much of Sarawak's political history has also paralleled Sabah's: Sarawak's political parties have generally been divided along ethnic lines; after joining the Malaysian federation, Sarawak was governed by a transitional regime, until the first direct elections were held (in Sarawak's case, in 1970); and ever since these first elections, Sarawak's chief ministers have established coalitions that assure them a two-thirds majority in the legislature, and hence a combination of executive, legislative, and constitutional powers.

Upon joining the Malaysian federation in 1963, Sarawak's ethnic composition was similar to Sabah's: 24 percent of the population was classified as "Muslim native," including both Malays and Melanus; 43 percent were "non-Muslim native," mostly Iban and Bidayuh; and 33 percent were ethnic Chinese. Each of these three groups provided the foundation for two political parties: Barjasa and PANAS had predominantly Malay and Melanu constituencies; SNAP and Pesaka largely represented non-Muslim native groups; and SCA and SUPP were principally Chinese parties.[1] Some of these parties – particularly PANAS, SNAP, and

---

1 Party names are abbreviated as follows: Sarawak National Party (SNAP), Sarawak United People's Party (SUPP), Sarawak Chinese Association (SCA), Barisan Rakyat Jati Sarawak (Barjasa), Parti Negara Sarawak (PANAS), Parti Pesaka Anak Sarawak (Pesaka), Partai Pesaka Bumiputera Bersatu (PBB), Parti Bangsa Dayak Sarawak (PBDS). Several of these parties – particularly SUPP, SNAP, and the short-lived Machinda – tried to build interethnic allegiances, but had limited success.

Pesaka – incorporated "traditional" patronage hierarchies into their party structures.

From 1963 to 1970, Sarawak was ruled by a series of transitional governments, until the first direct elections could be held (Table 6.1). The first transitional government included five of Sarawak's six major parties; the only excluded party was the left-leaning SUPP, which was viewed as a potential agent of communist subversion. Sarawak's transitional governments, however, were politically weak and chronically unstable, with each coalition party jockeying for control over the levers of state patronage – including government contracts, appointments to government boards, overseas travel opportunities, minor rural infrastructure projects, and timber concessions (Leigh 1974). With heavy pressure from Kuala Lumpur to maintain a stable coalition and no clear mandate from the electorate, the transitional chief ministers (Stephen Ningkan and Tawi Sli) had only limited influence over the cabinet and assembly.

Sarawak's first direction elections in 1970 proved to be a watershed. Like his Sabah counterpart, Sarawak's new chief minister, Abdul Rahman Ya'akub, now held a firm hand over the cabinet. After assembling a coalition government with a two-thirds majority in the state parliament, he also gained legislative and constitutional powers. Rahman Ya'akub used these powers, and his close ties to the federal government, to establish direct, discretionary, and exclusive control over state patronage, includ-

Table 6.1. *The Governments of Sarawak, 1963–97*

Year	Chief Minister	Coalition Parties
1963–6	Stephen Ningkan	SNAP, Pesaka, Barjasa, PANAS, SCA
1966	Tawi Sli	Pesaka, Barjasa, PANAS, SCA
1966	Stephen Ningkan	SNAP, SUPP
1966–70	Tawi Sli	Pesaka, Bumiputera[a], SCA
1970–81	Abdul Rahman Ya'akub	PBB[b], SUPP, SCA[c], SNAP[d]
1981–97	Abdul Taib Mahmud	PBB, SUPP, SNAP, PBDS[e]

[a] In November 1966, Barjasa and PANAS merged to form Parti Bumiputera.
[b] In January 1973, Pesaka merged with Parti Bumiputera to form Partai Pesaka Bumiputera Bersatu (PBB).
[c] The Sarawak Chinese Association (SCA) dissolved following the 1974 state elections, after being excluded from the government coalition.
[d] SNAP joined the government coalition in November 1976.
[e] PBDS was a member of the government coalition between 1983 and 1987, and rejoined it shortly before the 1996 elections.

ing timber concessions. Rahman Ya'akub and his successor, Abdul Taib Mahmud, used this patronage to retain uninterrupted control of the government for the next three decades.

From 1970 to 1981, Rahman Ya'akub used his formidable powers to bring order to Sarawak's fractious ethnic politics. In January 1973, he merged his own Malay-Melanu Parti Bumiputera with the native-based Pesaka to form Partai Pesaka Bumiputera Bersatu (PBB); in November 1976, after jailing the leader of the opposition SNAP – a second non-Muslim native party – he brought SNAP into the government and formed an all-party coalition. In the 1979 election, the coalition won forty-five of the assembly's forty-eight seats.

In 1981, Rahman Ya'akub turned the post of chief minister over to his nephew, Abdul Taib Mahmud, and took the largely ceremonial position of *Yang di-Pertua Negri* (head of state). Yet Rahman Ya'akub retained considerable influence over the distribution of state patronage. The division of authority between Rahman Ya'akub and Taib eventually produced a bitter dispute between uncle and nephew. In the 1987 election, Rahman Ya'akub formed a new political party (Permas) and ran against Taib; Rahman Ya'akub's position was strengthened by his alliance with a party devoted to the rights of non-Muslim natives, Parti Bangsa Dayak Sarawak (PBDS), which had previously backed Taib.

In the 1987 vote, Taib's coalition won twenty-eight of the assembly's forty-eight seats. Eight opposition members then defected to the government, giving Taib a comfortable 36–12 margin. In the 1991 election, Taib and his coalition partners won forty-nine of the assembly's fifty-six seats, putting the Permas-PBDS challenge behind it.[2]

As in Sabah, Sarawak's parties have spent large sums to purchase the support of both voters and legislators. In Sarawak's two close elections, campaign spending spiraled up to astonishing levels. In 1970, candidates spent an estimated $3.2 million to influence just 250,000 votes; at almost $13 per vote, election spending per capita was 30 percent higher than in the 1967 Sabah election (Milne and Ratnam 1974). In 1987, the rival

---

2 For the 1991 vote, eight new seats were created in the assembly, and the electoral districts were redrawn; the net effect was to weaken the non-Muslim native vote. Although the opposition PBDS increased its share of the vote from 17.6 percent in 1987 to 21.5 percent in 1991, it lost eight of its fifteen seats. In 1994 PBDS rejoined the government coalition. Rahman Ya'akub's opposition party, Permas, lost all of its seats in 1991 and later disbanded. For a full account of these events, see Chin (1996).

parties spent between $25 million and $80 million on a campaign that lasted just nine days, a cost of between $40 and $130 per vote (Jomo 1989).

THE FORESTS UNDER COLONIAL RULE, 1948–63

When James Brooke arrived in Borneo in 1839, he thought he had found a "trader's paradise," filled with valuable "antimony, timber, Malacca cane, bird's nest, pipe-clay, sago, vegetable oils, perhaps gold and diamonds" (cited in Colchester 1989). But for over a century, Sarawak's vast timber reserves proved to be poorly suited for large-scale exploitation.

Under Brooke rule, efforts to exploit the hill forests made little progress. The most ambitious venture, launched by the Borneo Company Ltd. in 1938, fell apart when one of two Siamese elephants brought in to carry logs from the forests slipped down a ravine and was strangled by vines[3] (Smythies 1963). On the eve of World War II, timber accounted for less than 1 percent of Sarawak's total exports.

After 1946, the British colonial government began to promote commercial logging in both Sarawak's hill forests, and in its coastal peat swamp and mangrove forests; it also developed a new forest policy, and a new set of forestry institutions. In 1953, the colonial government adopted a new forest ordinance, with the same goals as the forest ordinance adopted by the Sabah government in 1954:

a. To reserve permanently for the benefit of the present and future inhabitants of the country land sufficient:
  i. for the maintenance of the climate and physical condition of the country, the safe-guarding of water supplies and the prevention of damage to rivers and agricultural land by flooding and erosion;
  ii. for the supply in perpetuity at reasonable rates of all forms of forest produce required by the people for agricultural, domestic and industrial purposes.
b. To manage the Forest Estate with the object of obtaining the highest revenue compatible with sustained yield, in so far as this is consistent with the two primary objects set out above.

---

3 After the war, the same company brought in twenty-three new elephants – some from a circus – and tried again to log the hill forests. After failing a second time, they sold off the herd.

When Forest Conservator F. G. Browne presented the new ordinance to Sarawak's Council Negri, he noted that in the 1930s

Only the most primitive logging methods were used, and exploitation of the forests rarely extended far from the banks of floating streams. Except for the destruction of forests by shifting cultivation, there was no need to worry very much about the rate at which timber was being cut, and the law was a relatively simple one. (Browne 1954: 32)

He then pointed out that the annual timber harvest had grown steadily since the war, and would require a more comprehensive set of government institutions. Browne prophetically warned the council,

There is in man an almost uncontrollable instinct to destroy forests; and until a country begins to be very short of timber few people pay any attention to the necessity for its sustained production. There is no immediate, general danger that the Colony will run short of wood or other forest products, but with the rapid expansion of these industries a strong possibility of such a danger can be clearly foreseen. (Browne 1954: 33)

Sarawak's new forest institutions had three components that were similar to the forest institutions of Sabah. The first was the political autonomy conferred on the forest conservator, who held broad powers to allocate licenses and manage the forests. The conservator's autonomy also gave a measure of autonomy to the forest department, which he headed. Like their counterparts in Sabah and the Philippines, Sarawak's foresters believed that commercial logging and forest conservation were complementary goals. The colonial government urged department officials to give public lectures, and use the news media, to educate the public about the importance of forest conservation.

The second was an extensive set of logging regulations, devised to protect the regenerative and ecological capacities of the forests. In sections of the hill forests that were set aside for the permanent use of loggers, loggers were required to survey and demarcate the boundaries of their annual coupes; prepare topographical workmaps; carefully plan and construct roads; and fell only selected types of trees. Six months after felling, the forest department was obliged to inspect the logged-over forests for evidence of improper harvesting practices, and fine concession managers accordingly.

The third component was a large export duty on unprocessed ramin (*Gonystylus bancanus*), which was logged in the peat swamp forests, and was Sarawak's most valuable timber species at the time. The export duty was meant to promote the wood-processing industry; it was also high enough to dampen most rent-seeking pressures. To encourage logging in the less-profitable hill forests, duties on other species remained low.

But Sarawak also lacked two of Sabah's most important forest institutions. One was a system of secure, long-term timber concessions that could serve as the foundation for sustainable forest management. In the late 1940s, the Sarawak government approved between fifteen and twenty large concessions in the hill forests. But almost all proved to be unprofitable, thanks to a combination of high logging costs and low timber yields.[4] In neighboring Sabah, by 1963 almost 70 percent of the commercial forests were under contract for sustained-yield logging by concession holders. Until these contracts were altered by Chief Minister Mustapha in 1969, they bound both the concession holders and the Sabah government to a simple form of sustained-yield forest management. The Sarawak government had no similar contracts.

Sarawak also lacked even a minimal system for protecting the customary land rights of forest dwellers, and for preventing the spread of commercial logging onto land that was needed for swidden farming. Sabah's 1962 Land Ordinance made it relatively easy for upland peoples to have their customary land rights recognized by the state; but Sarawak's colonial government was still drafting a similar set of laws when colonial rule came to an end in September 1963. The transitional government considered a group of land bills in 1965, which would grant forest dwellers ownership of any land on which they exercised their customary rights. But the land bills touched off a bitter fight that split the Ningkan government; the government fell and the land bills were never adopted.

Sarawak's forest institutions were hence less comprehensive than Sabah's. To a greater degree than in Sabah, the sustainability of the forests rested on the personal authority of the forest conservator. The 1953 Forest Ordinance stated that the ecological functions of the forests must be protected, and that the timber harvest should not exceed sustainable levels. Yet with no system of long-term concessions in place, no rules that allowed upland natives to protect their traditional land, and

---

4 One of the few logging firms that survived was owned by James Wong, who later became the head of SNAP, and in the 1980s and 1990s, Sarawak's Minister for Tourism and the Environment.

much of the forests still unsurveyed and unclassified, the forest conservator had considerable discretion over how to interpret these mandates.

Two incidents in the early 1960s illustrate the importance of the forest conservator's powers in keeping logging to sustained-yield levels. The first concerned Sarawak's coastal swamp forests. In the 1950s and 1960s, the high price of ramin made logging in the peat swamp and mangrove forests quite profitable. Commercial logging in the peat swamp forests had begun in 1948, when Australian soldiers who had served in Sarawak during the war returned to export ramin to Europe. Ramin exports rose throughout the 1950s and early 1960s (Figure 6.1).

To keep logging in the peat swamp forests from exceeding sustainable levels, the government had to determine how quickly logged-over areas could regenerate: a faster regeneration rate would permit a high sustainable yield, while slower regrowth would mean a lower sustainable yield. The forest department began growth trials for ramin in the late 1940s; by 1960, foresters had gathered enough data to realize they had overestimated the growth rate of ramin, and inadvertently authorized peat swamp logging at a pace that could not be sustained. The forest conservator immediately reduced the cutting rate, changed the thirty-year felling cycle to sixty years, and ceased to issue new sawmilling licenses (Porritt 1997).

The second incident concerned the hill forests. Although hill forest logging was negligible in the 1950s, the rapid growth of the international hardwood market, and the development of mechanized logging equipment suitable for the tropics, raised hopes that a boom was imminent. A 1961 survey of timber quality in the Rejang River basin – considered the most promising area – proved disappointing. But after curtailing logging in the swamp forests, the forest conservator came under pressure to issue more permits for logging in the hill forests. In December 1961, a member of the Council Negri, John Meda, asked the government to issue timber licenses to non-Muslim natives, who resented the domination of the logging and sawmilling industries by Sarawak's ethnic Chinese. In 1962, there was a sharp rise in requests for logging permits from foreign timbermen, including ethnic Chinese lumbermen from Sabah who feared they would soon lose their annual licenses, and Filipinos and South Koreans in search of new log supplies. At the end of the year, the British Colonial Office reported that the "rapid development of the logging industry in the hill forests appears to be imminent" (Colonial Office 1963: 114).

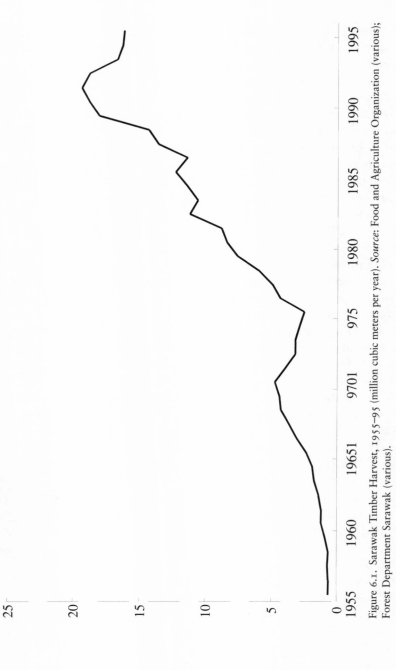

Figure 6.1. Sarawak Timber Harvest, 1955–95 (million cubic meters per year). *Source:* Food and Agriculture Organization (various); Forest Department Sarawak (various).

The forest conservator responded with restraint. He turned down council member Meda's request for licenses, restating the department's policy of granting licenses only to applicants with the requisite capital, knowledge, and experience to work the forests efficiently (Porritt 1997). He temporarily froze the issuance of all new licenses, and in 1963 the colonial government decided to approve licenses only for locally based firms.

The conservator's ability to curtail overharvesting in the peat swamp forests, and to turn down requests for licenses from both politicians and foreign timbermen, suggest he enjoyed a considerable degree of political autonomy. It also shows how important this autonomy was to the protection of the forests.

When colonial rule ended in September 1963, timber had become one of Sarawak's largest exports, second only to rubber. Sarawak's forest institutions included an exceptional level of autonomy for the forest conservator; a comprehensive set of felling regulations; and an export duty on ramin that was large enough to offset rent-seeking pressures. But unlike Sabah, Sarawak's hill forests were unprotected by long-term, legal contracts that bound concessionaires and the government to sustained-yield harvesting practices; and the customary land rights of Sarawak's forest dwellers had little legal protection.

RENT SEIZING UNDER TRANSITIONAL RULE, 1963–70

Between 1963 and 1970, Sarawak was ruled by a series of weak transitional governments, while the state's new political parties prepared for the upcoming elections. Each of the parties recognized how high the stakes would be in these elections. The victorious party (or coalition) would gain considerable majoritarian powers and a monopoly on state patronage. The losers could be forced to dissolve, just as Sabah's UPKO had dissolved after barely losing the 1967 election. Until these elections were held, the control of even small pockets of patronage might be crucial.

During the period of transitional rule, two of the three institutions that guarded the sustainability of the forests began to fall apart. One was the influence of the forest conservator. Under the 1953 Forest Ordinance, the conservator had the power to classify land, and hence decide whether it would be protected for ecological purposes, reserved for native customary use, or leased for commercial logging; he also had the authority to issue and cancel all logging permits. In 1964, the transitional government transferred most of these powers to the minister of forests.[5] Until 1964, the quality of forest management depended heavily on the judgement of the conservator, a professional forester; after 1964 it depended almost as heavily on the decisions of the minister of forests.

The minister's power to issue licenses and classify land would mean little if taxes and royalties were high enough to capture the resource rents available to commercial loggers; under the colonial government, these taxes and royalties were relatively high, particularly for ramin – the most important export species. But while ramin prices changed little in the 1960s, the export price of Sarawak's hill timber rose steadily, while taxes and royalties remained fixed (see Table 6.2). Permits for logging the hill forests began to produce supranormal benefits; so did the power to distribute them.

There were countervailing factors, however, that helped limit rent seizing during the transitional period. Until the early 1970s, a small but persistent communist insurgency in the hill forests discouraged would-be loggers; those who went ahead with logging were often forced to pay off the insurgents, keeping profits low. Moreover, during the final three years of the transitional regime (1967–70), the rival coalition parties reached a stalemate in their battle over allocation rights.[6]

Between 1963 and 1966, the minister of natural resources (who controlled the forests portfolio) was Teo Kui Seng, a member of the SCA. The 1964 amendments to the forest ordinance gave Teo many of the powers once held by the forest conservator; soon after its passage, logging rates shot up. In 1964, timber production rose by 8 percent; in 1965, by 26 percent; in 1966, by an additional 29 percent.

In September 1966, the Ningkan government was displaced by a new coalition headed by Pesaka's Tawi Sli. Abdul Taib Mahmud – a young Melanu lawyer from the Barjasa party – had been the driving force behind Ningkan's removal. Taib took over a new ministry of development and forestry; he also became the new cabinet's deputy chief minister. Holding these two posts, for a brief time Taib became the cabinet's

5 See Sarawak Law No. 68 of 1964.
6 Because the Sarawak government has never issued data on the number of licenses issued, it is impossible to know how much of the increased production was caused by an increase in the number of licensees, and how much was caused by other factors – such as rising profits, road building, and the spread of improved logging equipment – that encouraged existing licensees to harvest their plots more intensively.

Table 6.2. *Prices and Royalties for Sarawak Timber by Type, 1961 and 1968*

Type of Timber	1961: Unit Price ($US)	1968: Unit Price	Change (%)	1961 Royalty (% of Price)	1968 Royalty (% of Price)	Change in Export Volume, 1961–8 (%)
Ramin	23	23	0	6	6	+57
Jongkong	10	12	+20	11	9	+220
Meranti	9	17	+89	13	6	+1,360
Kapur	11	16	+45	10	7	+3,440
Other Non-Coniferous	9	14	+56	13	8	+573

Source: Adapted from Amanin (1971).

most influential member, overshadowing even the chief minister, Tawi Sli (Leigh 1974).

By 1967, however, Pesaka had become worried about the growing influence of Taib and the Parti Bumiputera.[7] To curtail his power, the Pesaka-led cabinet voted to rescind Taib's right to allocate logging permits, and to make them subject to the full cabinet's approval. In November 1967 Pesaka forced Taib to resign, and transferred the forestry portfolio to Tajang Laing, a member of their own party.

But just as Pesaka had been able to restrain Taib and his Parti Bumiputera, Taib and Parti Bumiputera were able to restrain Pesaka. Taib made his departure conditional on a freeze on the allocation of timber licenses – a freeze that was supposed to last until an FAO study of the forests was carried out.[8] Since the FAO would not be able to complete the study before the upcoming elections, Taib could tie the cabinet's hands on timber patronage, just as his cabinet rivals had tied his own. To make sure the freeze would not be reversed, he made his resignation conditional on two signed agreements: one between Sarawak and the federal government, and a second between the federal government and the FAO.

---

7 In November 1966 – shortly after the Tawi Sli government was formed – the two Malay-based parties, Barjasa and PANAS, merged to form Parti Bumiputera. Taib was named secretary general of the new party.

8 The freeze only applied to the hill forests; all loggable areas in the peat swamp forests had already been licensed out (Kavanagh, Rahim, and Hails 1989).

Taib's attempt to impose a licensing freeze on his rivals was only partly successful. Almost immediately after taking office, Tajang Laing granted a large concession in the Niah region to his own party, Pesaka. Pesaka named a leading Chinese entrepreneur, Wee Hood Teck, as one of the concession's main contractors; in return, Wee helped fund Pesaka in the upcoming election campaign.

Yet Pesaka's ability to issue new timber licenses was soon thwarted by the federal government, which informally backed the Parti Bumiputera against Pesaka. The federal government threatened to challenge the Niah timber license under the federal anticorruption law. Then in May 1969, following riots in West Malaysia, the federal government turned control over every state government, including the Sarawak state government, to a State Operations Committee (SOC). In each of Malaysia's other states, the chief Minister was named head of his own state's SOC; but in Sarawak, Kuala Lumpur appointed a civil servant, who quickly reimposed the freeze on timber licensing.

In an interview published in the November 16, 1969 *Sarawak Tribune*, the chairman of Sarawak's SOC, Tun Razak, hinted at the importance of the licensing issue in his appointment:

the [Sarawak] SOC should not be headed by the [Sarawak] Chief Minister because the powers that are given to this Committee are so tremendous.... It has been obvious right from the inception of SOC that one of its first actions was to look into the ways and means of ensuring that the State's main natural assets – forestry – is given out in a fair and justified manner.... This act of SOC controlling the issue of logging licenses had undoubtedly incurred the displeasure of certain groups.

During the seven-year transitional period, two of the institutions that had previously curtailed rent seizing – the influence of the forest conservator, and the state's capture of the timber rents – deteriorated; as a result, the major political parties began to struggle for control of the forest ministry, and the licensing authority it held. From 1964 to 1967, when first SCA and then Parti Bumiputera held the forests portfolio, timber production rose by an average of 25 percent a year; from 1967 to 1970, when the coalition parties reached a stalemate, it rose by an average of 9 percent each year. From 1963 to 1970, log production climbed from 1.73 to 4.74 million cubic meters. Were it not for the cabinet stalemate, they might have risen further still.

Since each of Sarawak's five major parties had at one time or another held some influence over the distribution of licenses, and since the outcome of the 1970 election was uncertain, each party was able to gain

Table 6.3. *Major Party Funders, Sarawak, 1963–9*

Party	Major Funders	Business Interests
SNAP	James Wong	Timber
	Wee Hood Teck	Various, including Timber
	Wee Boon Ping	Various, including Timber
SCA	Ling Beng Siew	Timber
Pesaka	Ling Beng Siew	Timber
	Temenggong Jugah	Timber
	Wee Hood Teck	Various, including Timber
SUPP	Wee Hood Teck	Various, including Timber
	Wong Tuong Kwang	Timber
Bumiputera	Ling Beng Siew	Timber
	Tun Mustapha Harun	Timber

Sources: Leigh (1974); Milne and Ratnam (1974); Ross-Larson (1976); Searle (1983); Sanib (1985).

some financial backing from the timber industry. Two of the biggest loggers – Wee Hood Teck and Ling Beng Siew – hedged their bets by donating to three parties each.

Some of the parties – including SNAP, SCA, Pesaka, and possibly SUPP – relied principally on loggers for their financing (see Table 6.3).[9] As one Chinese businessman observed,

It is best not to join a party but to be friends with everyone. If you join a party you lose business from those who belong to other parties. It is best to support a party only when it is (in) the government. (quoted in Milne and Ratnam 1974: 468)

RENT SEIZING UNDER CHIEF MINISTER RAHMAN YA'AKUB, 1970–81

The 1970 elections brought an end to seven years of unstable coalition governments, and ushered in a new phase of politics in Sarawak. At the head of the new government was Parti Bumiputera, which represented Sarawak's muslim natives; the party would remain in power through the

9 Several figures who gained concessions under colonial rule also used their timber profits to finance their own careers in politics – including Ling Beng Siew, James Wong, Temenggong Jugah, and Temenggong Oyong (Milne and Ratnam 1974).

end of the century.[10] The Parti Bumiputera won just twelve of the assembly's forty-eight seats, and had received less than 15 percent of the popular vote. With Kuala Lumpur's backing, however, Parti Bumiputera emerged at the head of a new coalition government. Abdul Rahman Ya'akub, Taib's uncle and mentor, became the new chief minister.

With the transitional period over, Rahman Ya'akub began to wield the dormant powers accorded to the chief minister by the state constitution. As chief minister, he could appoint and dismiss cabinet ministers, and enjoy strong executive powers. By inviting three other parties to join his coalition (Pesaka, SUPP, and SCA), he gained control of a two-thirds majority in the assembly, and hence both legislative and constitutional powers.

Yet from 1970 to 1975, most of the state's timber windfall dried up. The freeze on new concessions was still in effect, while the FAO carried out its study; the communist insurgency was active in many upland areas; and the international market for dipterocarp logs was hurt by both a global recession, and a glut of Philippine, Sabahan, and Indonesian wood. From 1970 to 1975, Sarawak's hill timber exports dropped from 1,517,000 to 184,000 cubic meters (Figure 6.1). Logging continued to be profitable in the peat swamp forests, but all loggable areas had been licensed out since 1967.

Still, Rahman Ya'akub was a gifted strategist who recognized the long-term value of gaining more complete authority over the forests; he may have also realized that timber prices would eventually rise and produce a large windfall.

When Rahman Ya'akub named his cabinet in 1970, he retained the forestry portfolio, giving himself direct allocation rights; his control of the cabinet and assembly also made these rights exclusive. Over the next decade, he took two measures that made his allocation rights more discretionary, and two further measures to boost the windfall's size, by curtailing the land rights of forest dwellers.

Gaining New Discretion

In the early 1970s, Rahman Ya'akub began to transfer some of the forest department's powers to a pair of new organizations that were more politically pliable and less transparent than the department. In 1971,

---

10 In January 1973, Parti Bumiputera became Partai Pesaka Bumiputera Bersatu (PBB) after merging with Pesaka.

Rahman Ya'akub established the Sarawak Foundation, a state-owned enterprise modeled on the Sabah Foundation. He promptly awarded it an 81,000 hectare concession, and gave it control of the Timber Cess Fund, which was raised from a tax on the logging industry. He also named himself as the foundation's chair.

Two years later, Rahman Ya'akub established the Sarawak Timber Industry Development Council (STIDC); he again named himself chair. The STIDC's nominal purpose was to promote value-added industries in the timber sector. Yet the STIDC also encroached on the forest department's authority over logging permits, giving the chief minister a second, more direct channel of influence over licensees. By 1980, an FAO report noted that "there exists a feeling among some of the staff of the Forest Department that progressively the Department will become little more than an agent for STIDC" (Food and Agriculture Organization 1980: 12). The STIDC was also given four large and several smaller logging concessions of its own, even though its mandate was to regulate, not participate, in logging operations. The FAO criticized this arrangement, arguing that by operating its own timber concessions, STIDC was prevented from "assuming its function of regulating, controlling and advising private industry" (Food and Agriculture Organization 1980: 26).[11]

In 1979, Rahman Ya'akub removed the few remaining legal constraints on his discretion over timber licensing. Under the 1964 amendments to the forest ordinance, the forest minister (now Rahman Ya'akub) had the power to issue and rescind logging permits, but applicants held the right to appeal his decisions to the forest conservator. A 1979 amendment to the forest ordinance made the minister's decisions final. It also removed a clause that had protected concessionaires against the "arbi-

---

11 Rahman Ya'akub also used the fight against Sarawak's communist insurgency to intimidate commercial loggers who supported other political parties. In September 1973, Rahman Ya'akub launched "Operation Judas," and arrested twenty-nine prominent ethnic Chinese businessmen and professionals whom he claimed were giving financial and material support to the Sarawak Communist Organization (SCO). Operation Judas was part of Rahman Ya'akub's larger effort to break the back of the SCO; but it also had a second motive. Among those arrested were Ling Beng Siew, Ding Jack Sung, and Wong Tong Kwang, all of them prominent timber merchants. Ling, Wong, and several of the other detainees had been active in Sarawak's Chinese political parties, SUPP and SCA. A year later, Rahman Ya'akub accused James Wong of disloyalty and arrested him as well; Wong was another major timber merchant and the leader of the opposition SNAP. The arrests gave the timber merchants – and other prominent Chinese leaders – an unsubtle hint that they were expected to support Rahman Ya'akub (Chin 1996).

trary" denial of renewal applications. To quash any residual ambiguity, Rahman Ya'akub pushed a second amendment through the assembly six months later, denying applicants any right to appeal his decisions.

Rahman Ya'akub's 1979 initiatives may have reflected the ballooning timber windfall: Between 1975 and 1979, the export price of Malaysian logs tripled, as exports from the Philippines and Indonesia trailed off (Figure 6.2). They may have also been spurred by a drop in political costs of rent seizing behavior: In the 1979 state election, Rahman Ya'akub's all-party coalition won forty-five of the assembly's forty-eight seats, leaving almost no one in the parliament to accuse him of abusing his power.

Ransack Rents

Between 1974 and 1980, Rahman Ya'akub also took two measures to increase the size of the windfall by curtailing the rights of forest dwellers. In each case, he acted when the influence of Sarawak's non-Muslim natives had been temporarily weakened.

In 1970, the forest department estimated that 2,250,410 hectares of forest – about 24 percent of the total forested area – were under swidden cultivation. Although both the colonial government and the transitional government had failed to recognize customary land rights, the ubiquity of the swiddens, and the political influence of the upland electorate, were substantial obstacles to the spread of hill forest logging.

In 1974, Rahman Ya'akub jailed the head of SNAP, a party that represented Sarawak's forest-dwelling natives.[12] Rahman Ya'akub then pushed an amendment to the land code through the assembly, giving the government new powers to extinguish native land claims.

Rahman Ya'akub took no further actions on the volatile issue of native land rights until after the 1979 vote. But two months after his landslide 1979 victory, the assembly passed a second amendment to the land code, and an amendment to the forest ordinance, that gave the government broadened powers to arrest, evict, and penalize anyone found to be farming, collecting firewood, trespassing, or conducting other listed activities on land set aside for logging. Previously, the director of forests could evict and penalize violators only with the approval of a judge; the new amendment removed the court's jurisdiction.

---

12 The jailed SNAP leader was James Wong Kim Ming – an ethnic Chinese timber-man who had allied himself politically with the non-Muslim natives.

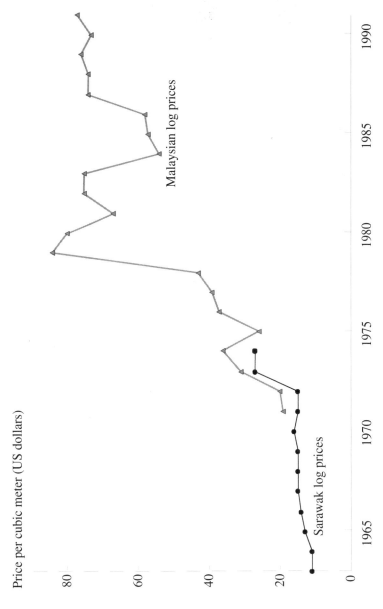

Price per cubic meter (US dollars)

Malaysian log prices

Sarawak log prices

80

60

40

20

0

1965   1970   1975   1980   1985   1990

Figure 6.2. Sarawak and Malaysian Log Export Prices, 1963–91 (US$ per cubic meter). *Source*: Food and Agriculture Organization (various).

Now forest dwellers could exercise their customary land rights only on areas set aside as "Communal Forests." Just 30,300 hectares – 1.3 percent of the area under swidden cultivation and less than one-third of 1 percent of Sarawak's total forest area – were protected as communal forests. Throughout the 1970s, this miniscule area remained unchanged. In 1980, Rahman Ya'akub reduced it by 82 percent to just 5,400 hectares.

Windfall Use Under Rahman Ya'akub, 1970–81

By the late 1970s, Rahman Ya'akub had used his ability to issue and rescind timber licenses to put together an all-party coalition. All assemblymen who joined the ruling coalition, and a wide range of ruling party officials, reportedly received shares in timber concessions, or in timber-processing firms. Active opposition to Rahman Ya'akub practically disappeared, as the advantages of joining the government coalition became overwhelming. To build this patronage network and support his other activities, Rahman Ya'akub authorized logging at unsustainable rates.[13]

In 1972, the FAO issued its long-awaited report on the Sarawak forests and forest industries; it included a comprehensive forest survey, and a long-term plan for the timber industry. One of the report's central recommendations was a limit on the annual allowable cut, for the peat swamp and hill forests collectively, of 4.39 million cubic meters of wood each year (Food and Agriculture Organization 1972: 15).

While demand was slack in the mid-1970s, there was little chance that loggers would breach this limit. But after prices bottomed out in 1975 the annual timber harvest grew quickly. In 1978, production reached six million cubic meters, more than 30 percent above the recommended limit. A confidential follow-up report by the FAO warned

---

13 As in the other cases, timber licenses in Sarawak were made valuable through undertaxation; license holders were hence able to accrue much of the timber windfall. Gillis (1988b) found that before 1980, revenues from Sarawak's forest sector, as a fraction of the sector's total export value, were "extraordinarily low" – much lower than in Indonesia or Sabah. Even after royalty hikes in 1980, he noted that forest taxes still totalled just 18 percent of export values, compared to 28 percent for Indonesia and 37 percent for Sabah. Gillis was unable to estimate actual rent capture.

A more detailed study by Vincent (1990) estimated that between 1966 and 1985, the Sarawak government captured just 18 percent of potential timber rents. A 1991 World Bank study, which covered 1966 to 1989, estimated rent capture at 35 percent (World Bank 1991).

the government that the logging rate had become unsustainably high (Wadsworth 1980).

The concerns of the FAO were cautiously echoed by a 1979 forest department report. Using generous assumptions, the department estimated the sustainable yield at 5.94 million cubic meters; if an additional increment of forest land was released for agricultural conversion, this total could be temporarily boosted to about 6.8 million cubic meters (Chai 1979).[14] In 1981, the government approved a cut of 8.8 million cubic meters, more than twice the FAO's recommended limits, and 29 percent above the forest department's more charitable recommendation.[15]

RENT SEIZING UNDER CHIEF MINISTER TAIB, 1981–95

By the time he left office in 1981, Chief Minister Rahman Ya'akub had gained full allocation rights to Sarawak's timber windfall; he did not, however, transfer all of these rights to his hand picked successor, Abdul Taib Mahmud. The 1981–95 period hence has two important features. The first was the struggle between Rahman Ya'akub and Taib for control of the allocation rights; the second was Taib's diminished security in

14 The forest department report assumed that logging Hill Mixed Dipterocarp Forests (MDF), in the permanent forest estate, would yield an average of 53.3 cubic meters of commercial timber per hectare; had they adopted a more realistic yield of 45 cubic meters per hectare, the maximum sustainable yield would drop to 5.27 million cubic meters without the addition of conversion forests, and 6.12 million cubic meters if conversion forests were included.

I calculate the increment from conversion forests by taking the average demand for new agriculture land in Sarawak – about sixteen thousand hectares each year in the 1970s, 1980s, and 1990s – and multiplying it by 53.3 cubic meters per hectare, a yield that is more plausible in Sarawak's conversion forests, where no felling restrictions apply.

15 The Sarawak government does not disclose the number of licenses it issues; it is the only state government in Malaysia that withholds this data. It also fails to issue complete information on the area of land that is licensed for logging. While it does publish information on the number of hectares under "Working Plans" (areas in the Permanent Forests under license) and "Felling Plans" (areas in the State Land Forests under license), it also authorizes logging on an additional, undisclosed number of hectares (see Forest Department Sarawak 1970: 59). According to one forest department report, in 1980 1.22 million hectares that had been licensed for exploitation – about a quarter of the total – came under neither Working nor Felling plans (Forest Department Sarawak 1981).

For this reason, the most accurate indicator of logging activity is the harvesting rate. In interviews and public documents, the forest department suggests that the authorized logging rate, and the actual logging rate, are identical; the figures in this chapter assume this to be correct.

office between 1986 and 1991. The drop in Taib's security may have led him to authorize a sudden jump in the logging rate, so that he could spend his patronage resources more quickly.

The Split Between Rahman Ya'akub and Taib

In 1981, Rahman Ya'akub decided to turn the post of chief minister over to his nephew Taib, and take a five-year term as Sarawak's ceremonial head of state. Rahman Ya'akub, however, was reluctant to give up his control of patronage. Although Taib became chief minister, Rahman Ya'akub retained influence over the state's principal levers of patronage, including land development permits, government supply contracts, and most importantly, timber licenses. As part of this arrangement, Taib appointed Haji Noor Tahir, a close Rahman Ya'akub ally, as the new minister of forestry.[16]

For his first few years as chief minister, the arrangement worked smoothly; but by 1985, Taib and Rahman Ya'akub were locked in a bitter dispute over allocation rights. The falling out between uncle and nephew was even more unlikely than it might appear: Rahman Ya'akub had raised Taib since he was a boy, and had been his political mentor for two decades.[17] Taib now abolished the forestry ministry and placed its functions under the ministry of resource planning – a portfolio he held himself. Yet he allowed most or all of Rahman Ya'akub's clients to keep their timber license shares; perhaps he hoped to win them over to his side.

In 1987, Rahman Ya'akub formed a new party to challenge Taib at the polls. He also struck an alliance with PBDS, a new party devoted to the rights of non-Muslim natives, which had grown disillusioned with Taib. In March 1987, 27 of Sarawak's forty-eight assemblymen suddenly announced their support for Rahman Ya'akub, and called on Taib to resign. Among the defectors were four of Taib's cabinet ministers and three assistant ministers. In retaliation, Chief Minister Taib revoked some thirty timber licenses held by the defectors and other

16 The division of patronage authority between Rahman Ya'akub and Taib may explain why the logging rate jumped from 8.8 million cubic meters in 1981 to 11.2 million cubic meters in 1982. It was the largest jump in logging rates to date, and reversed a three-year trend toward smaller increases in timber harvesting.

17 The dispute may have been exacerbated in 1984 by a 28 percent drop in timber prices, which hurt both Rahman Ya'akub's old client network and Taib's newer one.

Rahman Ya'akub clients.[18] The licenses covered 1.21 million hectares of forest; estimates of their value ranged from $3.6 billion to $9 billion. Rahman Ya'akub responded by releasing a list of concessions held by Taib's clients and family, covering 1.6 million hectares. The concessions on the two lists covered over 40 percent of the area licensed for logging (Leigh 1991).

The 1987 election was the first closely contested campaign in Sarawak since 1970, and the first since the timber boom began. Competing licensees, and aspiring licensees, treated the election as a rent-seeking contest, investing in their candidates sums that reflected the expected value of gaining (or losing) their concessions.[19] By contrast, Sarawak's major timber firms – who contracted with licensees to carry out the actual logging operations, and had to retain their standing with both factions – made substantial contributions to both sides. According to one assemblyman, the contractors "go with the government of the day but put bets on both horses" (Pura 1990). Just nine days were allowed for the campaign; estimates of election spending range from $25 million to $80 million – between $40 and $130 per vote (Leigh 1991). Backed by the federal government in Kuala Lumpur, Taib's coalition prevailed, capturing twenty-eight of the assembly's forty-eight seats.

After the 1987 election, Taib persuaded eight opposition members to defect to the government coalition. But Rahman Ya'akub's new party, Permas (Parti Persatuan Rakyat Malaysia Sarawak) and the remaining PBDS members formed a vigorous opposition and continued to challenge Taib's authority. For the 1991 election, the two opposition parties mounted a new campaign against Taib. Only after Taib and his allies won a resounding victory – capturing forty-nine of the assembly's fifty-six seats – was the challenge to Taib's rule over.

Timber Production and Protests, 1981–95

After a large rise from 1981 to 1982, timber production remained flat between 1982 and 1986; it rose sharply once again from 1986 to 1991,

---

18 The precise number of concessions revoked was never made clear; many of the names on the list of revoked licenses were kept confidential. Taib stated that the revocations were necessary "to prevent Sarawak from being overwhelmed by the 'politics of timber'" (Leigh 1991: 192).

19 Other constraints on campaign spending – such as client liquidity, and the absorptive capacity of the political parties during the nine-day campaign – undoubtedly placed lower limits on these sums.

despite protests from foreign governments, international organizations, Sarawak's forest dwellers, and Taib's own allies in the federal government (Figure 6.1). This latter jump was probably caused by a drop in Taib's political security.

Between 1982 and 1986, the Sarawak government authorized timber harvests of between 10.6 and 12.3 million cubic meters a year. The government had no obvious reason to boost these rates any further. Harvesting levels were already two to three times the sustainable rate, and had been once again criticized by the FAO in a confidential 1982 report to the government.[20] Moreover, the Sarawak government was awash in timber revenues: between 1980 and 1986, revenues from timber grew from 71 to 216 million ringgit, while total state revenues rose from 402 to 1,013 million ringgit. In 1985, the government's ten-year economic plan projected no future increases in timber production.

Yet from 1986 to 1991, log production rose from 11.4 to 19.4 million cubic meters, a level between four and five times the sustainable rate.[21] The rise in logging rates was even more striking when the pressures on Taib are taken into account. International attention was first drawn to Sarawak's forest policies in 1987, when members of the nomadic Penan and other forest-dwelling groups began to blockade logging roads in the upland forests. Most native groups did not oppose all commercial logging, but rather the encroachment of loggers onto land where they held traditional – albeit legally unrecognized – customary rights.[22] Environmental NGOs in Malaysia and abroad helped draw attention to the blockades, and to Sarawak's unsustainable logging policies.[23]

20 The FAO report advised the government to take "urgent action" to reduce the harvesting rate, or "otherwise the policy of sustained yield management and of the development of forest industries will be jeopardized" (Food and Agriculture Organization 1982: 57–8).

21 The rise came despite Taib's 1987 cancellation of thirty licenses covering 1.21 million hectares of forest, approximately 17 percent of the area licensed for logging; presumably these licenses were quickly reallocated.
    After they were revoked, Taib announced that the concessions would be reallocated through the STIDC, which Taib chaired. Normally they would have been reallocated by the forest department, which was slightly more transparent and slightly harder for Taib to manipulate.

22 Loggers also violated native cemeteries and damaged native water supplies, fish stocks, game, fruit trees, and the many other trees and plants whose products they used (World Rainforest Movement and Sahabat Alam Malaysia 1990).

23 The government's reaction to the native blockades, and the environmental NGOs, was callous. In November 1987, the Taib government amended the forest ordinance to criminalize the disruption of commercial logging and authorize heavy

In 1988 and 1989, politicians in Western Europe and North America – prompted by international NGOs – began to take notice. In July 1988, the European Parliament unanimously passed a resolution calling on all European Community states to ban hardwood imports from Sarawak "until it can be established that the logging does not cause unnecessary environmental damage and does not threaten the way of life of the indigenous peoples" (Colchester 1989: 9–10). Local and national governments in Germany, the Netherlands, and Austria took measures to restrict the use of tropical hardwoods. In 1989, the U.S. House of Representatives Foreign Affairs Committee sent a staff mission to Sarawak, which issued a report that criticized the state's logging policies and treatment of upland natives.

The Malaysian federal government responded publicly to the threat of timber boycotts with counterthreats.[24] Internally, however, it criticized Sarawak's forest policies, and in early 1989 began to pressure Taib to reduce the harvesting rate, to enforce its neglected silvicultural regulations, and to better accommodate the concerns of the Penan. It also urged Taib to invite a potentially sympathetic mediator – the International Tropical Timber Organization (ITTO), a U.N.-sponsored body that promoted the hardwood timber trade – to examine Sarawak's forestry practices. Taib reluctantly agreed to the ITTO visit.

The ITTO's 1990 report found that Sarawak's maximum sustainable yield was 4.1 million cubic meters – less than a quarter of the current rate, and below the 1972 FAO recommendation of 4.39 million cubic meters. The ITTO noted that the "scale of concession allocation (is) greatly in excess of any prudent estimate of the sustainable productive capacity of the Permanent Forest Estate" (Mission Established Pursuant to Resolution I(IV); hereafter Mission 1990: 68).

Yet the ITTO report acknowledged that "a precipitate reduction in the rate of harvest to this level" was politically impossible, and drew up an alternative plan. If the government expanded the permanent forest estate by 1.5 million hectares, and began an program of silvicultural

---

fines and imprisonment; by the end of 1990, more than two hundred natives had been arrested under the new law (*Sarawak Tribune* 1987; Rowley 1990). Both Malaysian and foreign environmental activists were banned from the state.

24 Primary Industries Minister Dr. Lim Keng Yaik warned in 1992, "If the Austrian Government insists on eco-labeling tropical timber-based products, Malaysia will retaliate.... For example, we can eco-label their chocolate products, which are produced at polluted factories" (Ghazali 1992).

treatments to hasten regrowth in logged-over areas, the maximum sustainable yield could be boosted to 9.2 million cubic meters, according to the report (Mission 1990: 34–6).

Many observers found the ITTO report too lenient. A 1991 World Bank draft report urged the government to immediately reduce its logging rate to 6.75 million cubic meters a year (World Bank 1991: iv–v). A study by Castilleja for the World Wildlife Federation (WWF) put Sarawak's maximum sustainable yield at 3.3 million cubic meters (Castilleja 1990). Even a 1994 ITTO follow-up study placed the maximum sustainable yield – under the ITTO's earlier, generous assumptions – at seven million cubic meters.

Although Taib vowed to implement the ITTO's recommendations, his government made only minor policy adjustments. For two and a half years after the ITTO report was issued publicly (March 1990 to September 1992), the government continued to raise harvesting rates. Over the following two years (1993 and 1994), log production was cut by 16 percent, to 16.3 million cubic meters; harvesting remained at this level in 1995.

Although Taib was a close political ally of Malaysian Prime Minister Mahathir, he resisted federal pressures to improve his state's forest policies. In 1992 and 1993, Primary Industries Minister Lim suggested publicly that states should distribute timber concessions through auctions, and limit bidding to actual timber firms. Both times Taib stated that these proposals did not apply to Sarawak (Tan 1992; *Business Times* 1993). Lim later complained to a journalist, "in [Sarawak's] Permanent Forest Estate, they give the concessions to the professionals in sustainable logging. But to be candid, they give the concessions in the State Land Forests to their friends" (Pearce 1994: 32).

The jump in the state's annual allowable cut coincided with Taib's greatest political challenge, which stretched from 1987 to the 1991 vote. Taib apparently responded by spending his patronage resources more quickly than ever before – despite heavy pressure from many sources, including his ally, Prime Minister Mahathir. Exactly twelve months after the 1991 vote, the forest department ordered all licensees to reduce their output. Between 1993 and 1995, the authorized logging rate stabilized between 16.7 and 16.2 million cubic meters a year, three to four times the maximum sustainable yield.

Although Sarawak's forest department maintains an exceptional degree of secrecy, over the course of the 1980s new details emerged about the patronage practices of the state's chief ministers. Both Rahman

Ya'akub and Taib used timber concessions for at least three purposes: first, to assemble supermajority, interethnic coalitions in the state assembly and at the local level; second, to raise campaign funds from ethnic Chinese timber contractors; and, finally, for personal and family enrichment.

Politicians in Sarawak typically received shares in license-holding firms, or in timber processing firms, rather than licenses themselves; many have paid only nominal sums – as little as one Malaysian ringgit – to receive these shares. In the 1990s, the chief minister's typical "gift" to a member of the assembly was worth 5 to 10 million ringgit (2 to 4 million U.S. dollars). Besides members of the assembly, Rahman Ya'akub and Taib gave concession shares to other important state and local officials; to Sarawak's representatives in the federal parliament; and to members of their own families[25] (Institute of Social Analysis [INSAN] 1989; Pura 1990; Leigh 1991).

25 Although the forest department issued hundreds of licenses (the actual number is secret), almost all licensees used one of seven major firms as contractors; collectively, these seven firms held an estimated 70 percent of all logging contracts, and were widely believed to provide politicians with most of their campaign funds (Pura 1990; World Bank 1991).

Contractors typically paid licensees both a lump sum for the contract rights (reportedly $400 per hectare in 1991), plus an annual fee based on the quantity of timber extracted (Institute of Social Analysis 1989; World Bank 1991: 22). A study of contracting arrangements in the Baram area found that licensees collected close to 20 percent of the gross logging profits between 1980 and 1987. Most of the balance went to contractors, with a small profit made by the subcontractors who actually did the logging (Lian 1989).

The major contracting firms are principally owned by Fuzhou Chinese entrepreneurs from the city of Sibu. Although the Fuzhous account for just 10 percent of Sarawak's population, by the 1990s they included some of Asia's most influential timbermen – including Tiong Hiew King (Rimbunan Hijau Group), Lau Hui Kang (KTS Group), Hii Yu Peng (Delta Group), Ling Beng Siew (Ling Beng Siew Sdn Bhd and Hock Hua Bank), and Wong Tuong Kwang (WTK Group).

After World War II, the Fuzhous took advantage of a boom in rubber and pepper prices to finance new timber and sawmilling operations – displacing the Hokkien Chinese who previously owned most sawmills. In the 1990s, they used their profits from logging in Sarawak – and from successful public offerings on the Kuala Lumpur Stock Exchange – to invest in timber operations in Indonesia, Cambodia, Burma, Solomon Islands, Papua New Guinea, New Zealand, Guyana, and China.

Some of Indonesia's wealthiest industrialists in the 1980s and 1990s were also Fuzhous, including Liem Soie Liong (aka Sudono Salim, Salim Group), Tan Tjoe Hin (aka Hendra Rahardja, Harapan Group), and Bong Son An (aka Burhan Uray, of the timber-based Djajanti Group) (Leigh 1988; Chew 1990; Pura 1994).

The Decline of Regulatory Enforcement

Like their counterparts in Sabah, the Rahman Ya'akub and Taib governments undermined one of Sarawak's remaining forestry institutions – the forest department's silvicultural regulations – by placing much of the forest estate outside the department's jurisdiction. They also failed to give the department the resources, and political backing, it would need to enforce these regulations.

The Sarawak Forest Department's Selective Felling System calls for an extensive sequence of operations to minimize the ecological damage caused by commercial logging, and protect the regenerative capacities of the forests. These regulations, however, only apply to land classified as "Permanent Forest Estate" (PFE), which is nominally reserved for sustained timber production. They do not apply to land classified as "State Land Forests" (SLF), which is to be cleared and converted to oil palm, rubber, cocoa, or pepper plantations in Sarawak's vast interior (Table 6.4).[26]

Yet the government authorized logging in the SLF at rates that far exceeded the state's need for plantation land. Between 1974 and 1991, Sarawak's noncoastal plantations grew by an average of 16,000 hectares a year. In 1992, government planners estimated the state would need 10,000 to 15,000 hectares of land for new plantations annually, through the year 2003. Although the government does not reveal the area of SLF logged annually, figures from the late 1980s and early 1990s imply that between 100,000 and 160,000 hectares of SLF were logged each year (Forest Department Sarawak various). Perhaps 90 percent of the forests logged in the state land forest were not needed for agriculture.

Even in the Permanent Forest Estate, the forest department lacked the necessary resources to properly regulate commercial loggers. A study by Kavanagh, Rahim, and Hails (1989) found little enforcement of regulations on road building, operable terrain limits, tree selection, and harvesting techniques. The ITTO noted that "management planning for the Hill Dipterocarp forests is good but falls down in execution," due to chronic understaffing and underfunding; it urged the government to assemble a "staff supported by the material resources needed to do the

26 The Sarawak government acknowledged that most of the SLF land should be reclassified as PFE land. It explained its failure to do so by suggesting that the process is slow and arduous. In 1960 the colonial government anticipated that the reclassification process would be completed by 1965 (Smythies 1963).

Table 6.4. *Sarawak Forest Estate, 1970 and 1991 (million ha.)*

Forest Classification	1970	1991	Change
Permanent Forests[a]	3.094	4.450	+1.356
State Land Forests	6.308	3.712	−2.596
Communal Forests	0.030	0.005	−0.025
Totally Protected Areas[b]	—	0.275	+0.275
TOTAL	9.432	8.455	−0.977

[a] Forests set aside for permanent timber production, including forest reserves and protected forests.

[b] Includes both national parks and wildlife sanctuaries.

Note: There are many discrepancies between the figures of the Sarawak state government and the Malaysian federal government; I assume here that the state figures are more accurate.

Source: Forest Department Sarawak (various).

job and by firm political backing" (Mission 1990: 61, 66). According to the World Bank, "Staff are often well-trained, competent, and professional in orientation, but professional objectives are too often overridden by political concerns" (World Bank 1991: 102).

Although government records provide little information on enforcement, they suggest that it has not kept up with the pace of logging. Between 1970 and 1991, Sarawak's timber harvest rose by a factor of five, yet the number of forest offenses recorded by the department dropped from 336 to 201.[27] In 1991, not a single forest offense was recorded in the Miri section, even though it contained over 30 percent of the state's licensed forest area.

CONCLUSION

The Sarawak case offers a third demonstration of how a windfall's arrival – or in this case, anticipation – can harm a state's commodity institutions by creating incentives for rent seizing. The ultimate impact on the forests themselves has been difficult to assess, since the forest department has produced few reliable figures on deforestation and forest

27 These offenses are not broken down by type, and may include not just improper logging practices but swidden farming or hunting in restricted areas and a wide range of other proscribed activities.

degradation.[28] Two decades of studies, however, suggest that logging in Sarawak's hill forests has almost certainly led to extensive damage. The use of heavy equipment for the construction of roads and skid trails, for example, has led to widespread soil erosion and the clogging of stream beds with silt, sand, and gravel. The consequences for Sarawak's forest dwellers have been, and will continue to be, far-reaching.

The case also illustrates how variations in the political security of an officeholder – in this case, Chief Minister Taib – may cause variations in the rate at which he spends his patronage resources, and hence authorizes logging. In the Philippines, Marcos's heightened security after 1972 gave him an incentive to slow deforestation; in Sarawak, Taib's insecurity between 1986 and 1991 gave him an incentive to accelerate the pace of logging, despite protests in Sarawak, Kuala Lumpur, and abroad.

28 The Sarawak government has, however, consistently criticized the impact of swidden farmers on the forests, albeit with unreliable figures. Some important critiques of the government view include Hong (1987); Colchester (1989); and Aiken and Leigh (1992).

7

Indonesia

Putting the Forests to "Better Use"

Indonesia's abundant forest resources are still untapped. It is high time that (the forests) *be put into better use. . . . Gentlemen, old cracks in the business will need no further detail on this subject matter.*

Sudjarwo, Indonesian Director General of Forestry, 1968
(Philippine Lumberman 1968a)

In the late 1960s, Philippine log exports began to decline; at the same time, Indonesia's timber exports began to soar. By 1973 Indonesia had replaced the Philippines as the world's leading hardwood exporter.[1] Timber also became Indonesia's largest source of foreign exchange, after oil.

The case of Indonesia differs from the others in three important ways. First, its forestry institutions were far weaker. In the Philippines, Sabah, and Sarawak, rent seizing damaged the institutions that fostered sustained-yield forestry. The Indonesian government had no such institutions in the 1960s and early 1970s; there was little to dismantle. But the Indonesian forests had been protected, in part, by *nonstate* institutions – the institutions of *adat*, or customary law. Of the four cases in this study, Indonesia and Sabah had made the greatest strides – before their timber booms – toward recognizing the customary land rights of forest dwellers. Shortly after the timber boom began, the Indonesian government rescinded those rights, to boost the size of the windfall.

---

1 All discussion in this chapter of Indonesia's forests refer to the forests of the Outer Islands – that is, all islands except for Java and Bali. Java and Bali are heavily populated and have few remaining natural forests; due to their rich volcanic soils, they permit the cultivation of teak. See Barber (1989), Boomgaard (1992), and Peluso (1992b) on the political history of Java's teak plantations.

Second, Indonesia's boom was *not* triggered by rising international timber prices; rather, it was caused by the government's efforts in 1966 and 1967 to lower the costs of cutting and exporting timber. In the other three cases, the timber boom was caused by an exogenous price shock. But in Indonesia the timber boom was deliberately created by the Suharto government. For this reason, this chapter takes pains to distinguish between the policies adopted in 1966 and 1967, which helped cause the boom, and the policies adopted in 1970 and after, which were influenced by the boom.

Finally, in the other cases, politicians used their influence over timber rents to support networks of patronage, or for personal enrichment. This occurred in Indonesia, too, until the late 1970s. Yet after 1980 Indonesia's President Suharto was increasingly secure, and could rely on the state's abundant oil revenues and booming economy to fund his political needs. As a result, the government's most influential cabinet ministers began their own efforts to capture allocation rights to the windfall, so they could subsidize their favored industrialization projects. Indonesia's timber rents were not only used for patronage and corruption; they were also used for ill-conceived efforts to build up the country's plywood and aircraft industries.

POLITICS UNDER INDONESIA'S "NEW ORDER"
GOVERNMENT, 1966–98

The Republic of Indonesia gained independence from the Netherlands in 1949. From 1949 to 1957, the country was governed by a series of weak parliamentary governments; from 1957 to 1965, it was ruled autocratically by President Sukarno; and from 1966 to May 1998, it was ruled autocratically by Suharto, a former major general in the Indonesian army.

Under Suharto's "New Order" government, power within the Indonesian state grew highly centralized; key positions in the bureaucracy were staffed with military officers; channels for popular representation were restricted by state-sponsored groups organized along corporatist lines; freedom of the press was curtailed, and views considered hostile to the regime were criminalized; and the electoral system was heavily biased toward Golkar (*Golongan Karya*), the government's own political party.

Many scholars have emphasized the importance of patronage in New Order Politics. Jackson argued that "Patron-client bonds are frequently the vital connecting link in coalitions spreading across *aliran* (religious), ethnic group, and family demarcations (Jackson 1978: 14)." For both Crouch (1979) and Robison (1986), politics was not simply organized on patrimonial lines: the pursuit of patronage was often the substance of politics. Mackie suggested that the term "neopatrimonial"

> characterizes Suharto's government in the 1980s better than any other term, underlining the unprecedented concentration of power that Suharto has been able to amass, both economic and political, within the control of his tight circle of ministers. Against that, other countervailing centres of economic power or political influence outside the state . . . are still puny and relatively impotent. (Mackie 1990: 88)[2]

Political leaders in the Indonesian archipelago have long used patronage to augment their authority. Indonesia's first president, Sukarno, utilized patronage during the 1959–65 "Guided Democracy," a period of autocratic rule (King 1982). Yet the organization and political salience of patronage changed in important ways under Suharto. During the critical years between 1966 and 1980, when Suharto consolidated his authority over Indonesia's politically fragmented armed forces, he developed institutionalized forms of patronage that were unusually effective.

Suharto and the Military

Suharto had a weak political base when he first took power following the abortive coup of September 30, 1965. At the time, Suharto was a major general in charge of Kostrad (*Komando Cadangan Strategis Angkatan Darat*), the Army Strategic Reserve Command. The coup plotters targeted seven military officers senior to Suharto; six were killed. As the senior most general not pursued by the coup plotters, Suharto quickly took charge of the army's response to the crisis. Yet because of his relatively modest rank, he had only a weak political base – even within the military – when he assumed de facto presidential authority in March 1966. Suharto had never been a part of the army's inner circle. He was

2 A "neopatrimonial" ruler is usually defined as one who maintains authority through patronage, rather than ideology, impersonal law, traditional forms of legitimation or hereditary succession (Snyder 1992). Important modifications to the emphasis on New Order patronage have been offered by Emmerson (1983), Liddle (1985), and MacIntyre (1990).

neither well known nor highly regarded outside of Kostrad and the army's Diponegoro Division, which he had headed.

Moreover, at the time of the coup, the Indonesian armed forces were politically and administratively fractured. Some military units were aligned with the Indonesian Communist Party (PKI); others were stridently anticommunist. To establish himself as a national political leader, Suharto had to first consolidate his authority over the four branches of the military, and curtail the danger of intra-service violence. As Vatikiotis suggests,

> This perhaps is the central issue of any historical study of Suharto. How was a man whom no one in the military establishment particularly liked or respected, able to get so far? (1993: 17)

Suharto's ability to gain control over the huge, fractious, and politically splintered armed forces in the 1960s and 1970s was critical to the survival of his government. His tactics included an early purge of pro-Sukarno and extreme anti-Sukarno elements; a major reorganization of the four services, placing the army, navy, air force, and national police under a unified command; and the establishment of a web of intelligence operations to monitor dissent within the ranks. Equally important was Suharto's use of patronage to reward supporters, to buy off potential opponents, and to create personal loyalties that superceded administrative and ideological boundaries.

The Institutions of New Order Patronage

To say that Suharto used state assets to buy political support would understate his formidable political skills. Rather than use patronage in an ad hoc manner, or rely on dyadic personal ties with his many clients, Suharto crafted a set of patronage institutions that created a stable set of incentives for generations of military officers, who had few if any personal links with him. To appreciate the utility of these institutions, it is helpful to explain three of the problems, common to systems of political patronage, that they were able to overcome.

First, the use of major state assets for patronage commonly has economic drawbacks: It typically entails discrimination against more efficient foreign and domestic entrepreneurs, and the imposition of growth-impeding trade restrictions. Conversely, political clients may lack the investment capital and the business experience to competently manage the assets they receive.

Second, the use of state assets for patronage can have political draw-backs. When a leader uses *private* wealth for patronage, it may be seen as legitimate and even beneficent; when he uses *public* wealth for patronage, it can be viewed as a form of corruption – a diversion of public assets for private gain.

Third, regardless of who owns the patronage, clients may try to cheat – to take the benefits offered by the patron, but without providing any quid pro quo.

Suharto's patronage institutions helped him surmount each of these problems. First, Suharto encouraged his military clients to exploit their patronage through joint ventures with better-capitalized, more experienced business partners – usually foreign or ethnic Chinese firms.[3] Typically, individual military officers or military units would provide their foreign or Chinese partners with personal protection, along with access to the government licenses, tax breaks, contracts, and credit they received. The military officials, in turn, would gain a share of the resulting profits and skilled management for their enterprises. Suharto himself established close alliances with Chinese entrepreneurs in the 1950s, when he was the chief supply and financial officer for the army's Diponegoro Division in Central Java. After becoming president, Suharto helped turn these alliances into a widespread, informal institution.

The military-backed joint venture was a distinctly New Order institution. Before 1965, President Sukarno shunned foreign investment, and military officers only dealt with Chinese entrepreneurs through *pribumi* (non-Chinese Indonesian) brokers. The rise of joint ventures in the New Order allowed both military officers and their Chinese partners to cut out the *pribumi* middlemen (Robison 1978). This both reduced the transaction costs of military-Chinese alliances, and helped align the

---

3 The ethnic Chinese community in Indonesia has a long and complex history, dating back to at least the fifteenth century. Today most ethnic Chinese are Indonesian citizens and have taken Javanese or Muslim names, but according to one source, in 1985 half a million were still classified as resident aliens (*Warga Negara Asing*) (Shin 1989).

In the 1990s there were perhaps four million ethnic Chinese in Indonesia, about 2 percent of the population. Yet due in part to the success of their alliances with the military, they had come to dominate the economy. A 1989 survey found that 163 of the 200 largest business groups in Indonesia were owned by Chinese interests. Another study, from 1990, noted that thirty-four of the top fifty business groups were controlled by Chinese families (Capricorn Indonesia Consult 1990). Schwarz (1994) estimated that businesses owned and run by Chinese families were responsible for 70 percent of all private economic activity in Indonesia.

commercial incentives of both parties: the profits were typically shared according to a formula that dampened incentives for opportunistic behavior.

Joint ventures mitigated many of the economic drawbacks of using state assets for political patronage. On one hand, joint ventures allowed the military to profitably exploit its assets; on the other, they gave Indonesia's most experienced, and best capitalized entrepreneurs – the ethnic Chinese – indirect access to government assistance. Perhaps most important, commercial alliances with the military gave investors relatively secure property rights – a critical function after the expropriation of Dutch businesses under Sukarno, and the state-sanctioned massacres of 1965–6.

To mitigate political drawbacks of using state assets for patronage, Suharto turned a colonial-era institution – the *yayasan* (charitable foundation) – into a conduit for patronage. In the early 1990s, Suharto controlled an estimated eighteen *yayasan*, with perhaps \$2–3 billion in assets. Suharto's *yayasan* were funded by corporate donations, by mandatory contributions from government employees, and by businesses built on government licenses, including timber licenses. Though ostensibly set up for charitable purposes – such as building mosques and helping destitute children – these *yayasan* were also used for political purposes, such as rewarding political supporters and funding Golkar (Shin 1989: 248; Robison 1993).

Since they were private organizations, Suharto's *yayasan* were free from any audits or accountability. Because they were held by Suharto personally – not the office of the president – they fostered personal loyalty. And as charitable organizations, they were free from taxation.[4]

Finally, Suharto fostered long-term loyalty among high-level military officers by compensating them generously upon their retirement. These "patronage pensions" commonly took the form of preferential access to credit or government licenses; the opportunity to serve as the domestic partner for a foreign investor; or lucrative sinecures in Suharto's vast web of firms and *yayasan*. Like the *yayasan*, Suharto developed patronage

---

4 The critical flaw in these institutions was their reliance on the stature and longevity of a single man, Suharto. This was painfully revealed in 1997 and 1998, when uncertainty about Suharto's health and political future led many investors to panic and withdraw their money from Indonesia. The resulting plunge in the currency produced an economic shock that helped force Suharto from office.

pensions in the late 1950s, while serving in the Army's Diponegoro Division (Robison 1977).[5]

Suharto's patronage pensions created three incentives to keep his military clients loyal. First, in any patronage system, clients are most liable to defect once they have been compensated; those who are still "owed" compensation should refrain from defecting, lest they forfeit their payoff. Because Suharto typically "paid" his officers after they retired, they had an incentive to remain loyal during active duty. Second, the incentive of officers to support Suharto grew stronger over the course of their careers, since the size of their future compensation grew with the length of their service, and the time of their retirement drew closer.[6] Finally, since their patronage pensions came from Suharto personally, and not the Indonesian state, officers realized they would only be rewarded if Suharto was in power when they retired. For senior officers, Suharto's removal could entail the loss of a lifetime's worth of political compensation.

Buoyed by Suharto's patronage, the commercial holdings of the armed services grew quickly after 1965.[7] Almost all of the leading businessmen who enjoyed government patronage under Sukarno lost their empires; most of their assets were transferred to the military. In the Suharto era, the military's commercial assets were widely believed to provide between

5 Although *yayasan* existed under Dutch colonial rule, Suharto and one of his long-time aides, Sudjono Humardhani, helped pioneer their use as a political tool. In 1957, when Suharto was the military commander of the Diponegoro Division in Central Java, Sudjono established two *yayasan* (and several corresponding companies) in the name of Suharto and the Diponegoro command. The original funds came from the military's seizure of Dutch assets, which were then supplemented by

   collections of donations such as those from kopra, salt, customs, sugar, telephone, electricity, lotteries, the Association of Indonesian Batik Co-operatives, cement, motor transport, radio, kapok, cloves, fertilizer auctions and others. (Malley 1990)

   They also apparently raised funds from smuggling. Under the threat of corruption charges, Suharto lost his command and almost left the army. The tools that nearly put Suharto in jail would later help him govern the nation.
6 Those with the longest careers also tend to be highest in rank, which made the strategy most effective in the upper reaches of the military.
7 Even before 1965, the Indonesian military had extensive commercial holdings. Some began in the late 1940s and 1950s, when military units were forced to raise their own funds – first to fight the Dutch, then to fund their postindependence operations. Others date to 1957–8, when the government expropriated Dutch-owned firms and placed their assets under military supervision. These commercial operations, which sometimes included smuggling, were typically begun out of necessity; but they often became vehicles for the personal enrichment of officers (Robison 1978; Crouch 1978).

50 and 80 percent of its total operating budget. During the 1970s, the principal sources of these off-budget funds were the oil parastatal (*Pertamina*), a parastatal that monopolized the trade in essential commodities (*Bulog*), and the timber industry (Jenkins 1980).

FORESTRY INSTITUTIONS AND POLICIES, 1966–9

When the Suharto government came to power in 1966, three-quarters of the Indonesian archipelago was covered with forests. Past efforts to promote commercial logging in the Outer Islands had amounted to little. Yet by 1973, Indonesia had become the world's leading supplier of tropical timber. After oil, raw logs were the nation's largest source of foreign exchange.

Indonesia's timber boom differed from the timber booms in the Philippines, Sabah, and Sarawak in two important ways. First, unlike the other three governments, the Indonesian government had virtually no concern for – and no formal institutions to support – sustained-yield forestry. Second, Indonesia's boom was *not* triggered by the shock of rising log prices; instead, it was initially caused by the government's deliberate efforts to lower the costs of logging. By carefully examining this period, we can distinguish between the policies in 1966–7 that *led* to the Indonesian timber boom, and the policies beginning in 1970 that were *influenced* by it.

Forestry Institutions Before the Timber Boom

Until 1967, a long series of attempts to promote commercial logging in Indonesia's Outer Islands had failed. Timber exports from East and South Kalimantan boomed for a few years shortly after 1900, and again during the 1930s with the arrival of the first Japanese investors. But before 1967, the few operations that succeeded were periodically crippled by insecure property rights, fluctuations in world timber prices, and the lower costs and higher returns of logging in the Philippines and Sabah. Even foreign investors in the early 1960s, who had both the requisite capital and a guaranteed market, did poorly move footnote.[8] As late as 1966, Indonesian timber exports were worth just $4 million.

---

8 In 1963, the Sukarno government agreed to a "production sharing" contract between Perhutani – a newly formed Indonesian parastatal that was given exploitation rights to sections of Kalimantan – and a Japanese consortium known as the

The weakness of the timber industry was mirrored by the weakness and decentralization of the government's forestry institutions. Since 1957, jurisdiction over the Outer Island forests had been awkwardly divided between Indonesia's central and provincial governments, with most in the hands of the latter. Government Regulation 64 (1957) had given provincial officials broad authority to manage the forests within their boundaries; it also gave them the right to distribute timber concessions of up to 10,000 hectares in size. Provincial forestry bureaucracies were accountable to the provincial governor, not the forestry department in Jakarta. The central government could only control timber exports (which were negligible) and exploit the handful of forest areas that had been ceded to Perhutani, the forestry parastatal.

The Basic Agrarian Law of 1960 further marginalized the forestry department by recognizing *adat* (traditional) property rights as long as they did not conflict with the "national interest." Forest dwellers used *adat* laws to determine the ownership and use of specific trees and their products, hunting and fishing rights, the use of land for shifting cultivation, and the "rights of disposal" (*hak ulayat*) over communal property.

Until 1967, these two laws created a relatively hospitable setting for forest dwellers, and for the small-scale loggers who supplied local markets; conversely, they created an inhospitable setting for large-scale commercial logging.

The two laws left the Indonesian forestry department with little authority over the forests of the Outer Islands. Although the department had been set up in the mid-nineteenth century, it was almost exclusively concerned with forest management on Java. One Dutch observer in the 1920s wrote that the forests of Kalimantan – the archipelago's most valuable dipterocarp forests – were controlled by a "many-headed creature," composed of "the population, chiefs of native jurisdictions, local European and native civil servants, self-governments, heads of the regional administration, etc."; the central forestry department was nowhere to be found (Beversluis 1929, cited in Potter 1988). Java's forests covered some three million hectares; the forests of the Outer Islands, in the mid-1960s, covered 143 million hectares.

Kalimantan Forest Development Cooperation Company, Ltd. Most of the startup costs were funded by a 2.66 billion yen loan from the Japanese Overseas Economic Cooperation Fund. Yet production fell far short of the original target, and eventually left Perhutani with a $10 million debt (Manning 1971; Japan Tropical Forest Action Network 1992). Several smaller production sharing agreements between Perhutani and Japanese firms were also signed.

The Sources of the Timber Boom

In 1966, the new Suharto government faced an economic crisis. The Indonesian economy had collapsed during the final years of the Sukarno regime: inflation had reached triple digits; factories were operating at less than a quarter of their capacity; and government revenues and expenditures were steadily dropping. Indonesia's declining exports were especially worrisome. From 1961 to 1966, the real value of all exports fell by 13 percent, due to hyperinflation, the nationalization of Dutch-owned firms, and the policy of "confrontation" with Malaysia and Singapore – the latter a major processing center for Indonesian goods. As a consequence, Indonesia had little foreign currency to finance imports or pay its foreign debts.

To pull the country out of its economic crisis, the Suharto government needed to reschedule its debt and gain additional foreign aid. Indonesia's major lenders and donors – the International Monetary Fund (IMF), World Bank, and a consortium of Western states – agreed to help but insisted that the government craft a plan that would also attract private foreign investment.[9] Many foreign investors were attracted to Indonesia's extractive sectors, including oil, mining, and timber.

In 1967 the New Order government took four measures to promote timber exports and attract foreign investors. The first was the adoption of a new foreign investment law that offered foreign investors generous tax holidays, the free repatriation of profits, and a guarantee of compensation if their Indonesian subsidiaries were ever nationalized. Sixteen months later, the government adopted a second investment law that gave domestic firms the same benefits. Forestry was named a "priority sector," enabling firms to deposit only 25 percent of their intended investment in state banks as collateral, instead of the usual 50 percent.

Second, the government aggressively recruited foreign investors for the timber sector. In November 1967, Indonesia sent twenty high-level officials to Geneva to woo the chief executives of some seventy foreign concerns. The director general of forestry, Sudjarwo, and two of his assistants were included in the delegation (Winters 1995).

After the meeting, Sudjarwo embarked on a twelve-country trip around the world to "invite interested parties in friendly countries" to

---

9 It would be misleading, however, to suggest that these policies were simply imposed on the Indonesian government: Suharto's top economic advisors favored a similar strategy. See Bresnan (1993), Winters (1995).

invest in the Indonesian timber industry. Logging firms in the Philippines – Indonesia's main competitor – were a special target. In his address to the Philippine Chamber of Wood Industries and the Philippine Lumber Producers Association, Sudjarwo spoke bluntly about Indonesia's plans for the forests:

Present conditions dictate that for a rapid stabilization of the economy, improvement of foreign currency earnings and provision of productive employment must be given the highest priority . . . Indonesia's abundant forest resources are still untapped. It is high time that it will be put into better use to give its appropriate share in the stabilization of the Indonesian economy. . . . Gentlemen, old cracks in the business will need no further detail on this subject matter. (*Philippine Lumberman* 1968a)

The third step was to set forest royalties and taxes low enough to give logging firms in Indonesia a cost advantage over their competitors in the Philippines and Sabah. Extraction costs in Indonesia's vast, unexploited forests were initially higher than in the Philippines and Sabah; to compensate, the government kept forest charges to a minimum. The Suharto government established a modest tax on timber exports, and levied only negligible royalties and license fees.[10] New investors were made exempt from corporate and dividend taxes for five to six years; in practice, these tax holidays commonly lasted for ten to fifteen years.[11] The tax breaks gave logging firms in Indonesia a 10 percent cost advantage over their Philippine competitors.[12]

Finally, in May 1967 the government adopted a Basic Forestry Law (BFL) that centralized much of the state's authority over the forests, and swept away many of the legal and jurisdictional obstacles to large-scale commercial logging.

The 1967 BFL placed all of Indonesia's forest land – 75 percent of the country – under the purview of the directorate general of forestry in Jakarta. Overnight, the forestry department's jurisdiction grew from three million to 146 million hectares. Before their timber booms, the forest departments of the Philippines, Sabah, and Sarawak had decades

---

10 Timber exports were subject to a 10 percent ad valorem tax; royalties were set at $1–3 per cubic meter for the most common species; and license fees were just $.50 per hectare for a twenty-year concession.

11 Gillis (1988) found that "most timber companies – foreign and domestic – paid no income taxes at all from 1967 through 1983." He estimated that the tax revenues foregone due to the tax holiday and its abuse, along with related types of tax evasion in the timber industry, totaled $2 billion from 1967 to 1983.

12 This figure is based on data from *Philippine Lumberman* (1968d, 1968e); Coats (1971); Manning (1971); Koehler (1972); and Grossman and Siegel (1977).

of experience in governing logging operations, on sustained-yield principles, in dipterocarp forests; they also had an important measure of political autonomy. The Indonesian forestry department had neither the experience, nor the autonomy, of its three counterparts. Moreover, during the first years of the timber boom, its overwhelming priority was to promote the industry's rapid growth, not to protect the forests. It would not get around to issuing silvicultural regulations until 1972, five years into the timber boom.

The BFL gave the central government the authority to grant exploitation rights (*Hak Pengusahaan Hutan*) to private firms directly, without going through either the provincial governments or Perhutani, the forestry parastatal. Regional and local officials still held the ability to issue smaller concessions, but most of their authority was usurped by the central government. Indonesia's forest dwellers also had their influence curtailed: the BFL subordinated *adat* rights to the forestry department's authority, stating that

The enjoyment of *adat* rights, whether individual or communal, to exploit forest resources directly or indirectly . . . may not be allowed to disturb the attainment of the purposes of this law. (BFL, article 17)

The 1967 policy changes brought a flood of foreign investment into Indonesia's timber sector. Between 1967 and 1972, forestry was Indonesia's third most attractive sector for foreign investors, after manufacturing and mining; by 1978, foreign firms had sunk $376 million into logging and wood-processing ventures (see Table 7.1).

Other accounts have emphasized the role of Japanese firms in the Indonesia timber sector.[13] Yet the largest investors were Philippine and Malaysian logging firms who had begun to run low on timber supplies in their own states, or who hoped to expand their base of supplies.[14] The second-largest group of investors was composed of Japanese and Korean firms who sought to gain more control over the cost, quality, and

13 cf. Nectoux and Kuroda (1990); Dauvergne (1997).
14 There is evidence that Philippine firms – who for a time were prevented from investing in the Indonesian timber industry by the Philippine Central Bank, which feared capital flight – financed their investments with funds they held in third countries, including Hong Kong. In 1968, the *Philippine Lumberman* (a trade journal) noted sarcastically, "For a country in dire need of capital and trying hard to attract foreign investments, the Philippines appears to have a good store of entrepreneurs with facilities to invest in other countries, such as Indonesia" (*Philippine Lumberman* 1968d).

Table 7.1. *Realized Foreign Investment in the*
Indonesian Forest Sector, 1978

Nationality	Investment ($US mil)	No. Firms	Concession Area (mil. ha.)
Philippines	72.6	11	1.380
Hong Kong	53.0	15	1.387
Malaysia	49.1	19	2.419
United States	48.7	4	1.081
Japan	46.2	12	1.263
South Korea	33.3	7	0.890
Singapore	10.3	5	0.420
Others	62.7	4	0.606
TOTAL	375.9	77	9.336

Source: Gillis (1987).

pace of their timber supplies. Some of Japan's largest trading houses – including Mitsubishi, Sumitomo, and Mitsui – gained their own concessions; others, like C. Itoh, gave credit to local firms, to be repaid with future log supplies. By the end of 1973, 58 percent of all approved investments in the forest sector came from overseas (Manning 1971; Robison 1986).

The New Order government's policy changes, and the flood of foreign investment, led to a remarkable leap in timber exports. In 1966, Indonesia exported $4 million worth of timber, about 0.59 percent of the total value of all exports. In 1967 timber exports began to soar: Over the next six years, the volume of log exports rose by an average of 108 percent annually (see Figure 7.1). By 1973, timber exports were worth $3.2 billion, and constituted 18 percent of all exports. After oil, timber had become Indonesia's most important source of foreign exchange. Equally striking was the rise in Indonesia's share of the world market for hardwood logs. In 1966, Indonesia had a 1.5 percent share; by 1973 it held a 36 percent share and had become the developing world's leading log exporter.

The Indonesian timber boom was caused in part by the New Order government's efforts to lower extraction costs, and in part by the rising overseas demand for wood. Between 1967 and 1973 the volume of timber traded in international markets almost doubled. Yet the world's leading hardwood exporter, the Philippines, passed

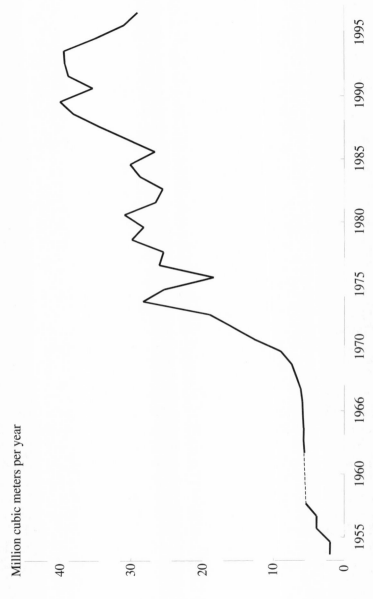

Million cubic meters per year

Figure 7.1. Indonesian Timber Harvest, 1953–96 (million cubic meters per year). *Source:* Food and Agriculture Organization (various).

its historical production peak in 1968 and was unable to meet these demands.

Still, Indonesia's timber boom was mostly caused by domestic, not international factors. If the rising demand for timber was an important factor, we would see Indonesian exports rising in response to rising timber prices. But from 1966 to 1969, exports rose from 334,000 to 3,728,000 cubic meters – a factor of eleven – despite a 20 percent *drop* in the export price of Indonesian wood (Figure 7.2). This suggests that the most important initial force behind the logging boom was the reduction in logging costs, caused by the change in government policies.

THE IMPACT OF THE TIMBER BOOM

Although the Indonesian government had been eager to promote log exports, the timber boom was far larger than the government anticipated. In the early 1970s, the Suharto government reacted to the surge in timber production with a new set of forest policies. The 1967 policies were designed to promote log exports and attract foreign investment. After 1970, however, New Order officials began to engage in rent seizing: nullifying the allocation rights of provincial officials, in order to make their own rights more exclusive; dismantling the customary rights of forest dwellers, to boost the size of the windfall; and distributing timber rents to Suharto's clients in the military.

In the Philippines, Sabah, and Sarawak, rent seizing led to the dismantling of state institutions that had previously kept logging to sustainable levels. Yet the Indonesian government had no such institutions in the 1960s and early 1970s; there was little to destroy. But there were *nonstate* institutions that protected the forests: the institutions of *adat*, or customary law. The 1967 BFL had partly usurped *adat* to promote commercial logging; new regulations in 1970 and 1971 went even further. Of the four cases in this study, Indonesia and Sabah had gone the furthest – before their timber booms – to recognize the customary land rights of forest dwellers. Now Indonesia, like Sabah, would rescind those rights in order to boost the scale of the windfall.

Gaining Exclusive Allocation Rights

By 1969, the New Order government presided over a remarkably successful timber industry. Logging firms were reporting annual profits of

Price per cubic meter (US dollars)

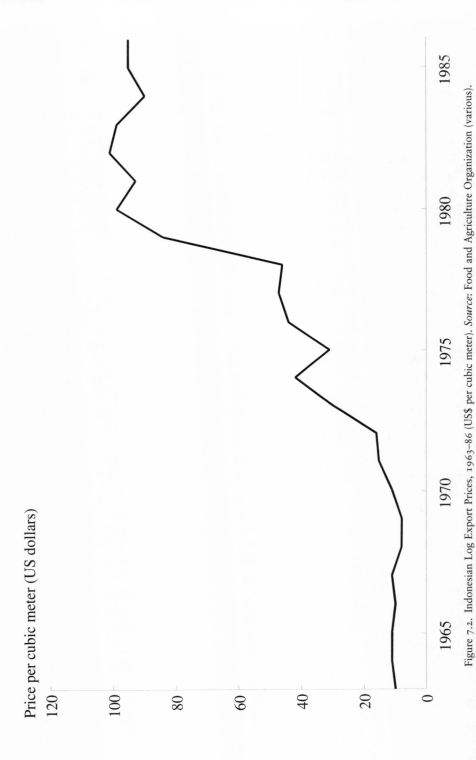

Figure 7.2. Indonesian Log Export Prices, 1963–86 (US$ per cubic meter). *Source*: Food and Agriculture Organization (various).

between 30 and 50 percent, and were almost certainly earning substantial rents.[15] With timber selling for $8 per cubic meter, foreign and domestic firms were besieging the forestry department with concession applications; over the next four years, the price of Indonesian timber rose by 500 percent to $40 a cubic meter. The unexpected rise in timber prices created unexpected profits. In 1973–4, the volume of timber exports exceeded the government's target by 400 percent; the value of these exports surpassed their target by 700 percent (Palmer 1978). The "endogenous" shock of 1967–9, created by government policies, gave way to an "exogenous" shock between 1970 and 1973, created by the jump in timber prices.

Suharto already held direct allocation rights in the forest sector, thanks to his July 1966 reappointment of Sudjarwo as director general of forestry. Sudjarwo had been the head of the forestry department since 1964; he was the highest-ranking official from the Sukarno regime that Suharto retained. Sudjarwo, however, did not owe his political survival to his professional training. Fortuitously, Sudjarwo had family ties to Suharto's wife and links to Suharto himself through Javanese mystical practices. Sudjarwo was given unusually broad powers over foreign firms, even by the standards of the New Order government. In most sectors of the economy, foreign investment was regulated by the National Investment Coordinating Board (BKPM); but the board was given no jurisdiction over natural resource sectors, including the timber sector. Sudjarwo soon proved to be an important political asset for Suharto, who appointed him to top fund-raising positions in some of his key *yayasan* (Magenda 1991).

Yet Sudjarwo's influence – and, by extension, Suharto's – over the timber industry was nonexclusive. Under the original terms of the BFL, the forestry department could only give out timber concessions larger than 10,000 hectares. Provincial governors retained the authority to grant timber concessions of up to 10,000 hectares; district heads *(Bupati)* could grant concessions of up to 5,000 hectares; and sub-district heads *(Camat)* could grant concessions of up to 100 hectares in size.

The division of authority allowed provincial and local officials to gain a fraction of the forest windfall. Perhaps inadvertently, it also allowed

---

15 On the supranormal profits available to concessionaires in the early 1970s, see Coats (1971); Manning (1971); Koehler (1972); Grossman and Siegel (1977); Ruzicka (1979); and Gray and Hadi (1990).

local smallholders to profit from the timber boom, by creating concessions that were small enough to exploit with minimal capital, and that
could be acquired by local residents with no influence in Jakarta. By
1970, over two million hectares of these small forest concessions had
been given out by regional authorities.

Even though the New Order government had targeted foreign
investors, between 1967 and 1970 the timber boom was dominated by
the holders of these small concessions, who responded to the government's incentives with the same alacrity as the large foreign firms. Most
of these smallholders employed a traditional, nonmechanized logging
technique called *banjir kap* ("cutting during the flood"). The *banjir kap*
method was far less damaging to the forests than mechanized logging.
Mechanized logging required the building of roads through the forests,
and the use of heavy equipment; it typically led to widespread soil degradation and damage to uncut trees. *Banjir kap* operators cut logs by
hand and floated them out of the forest on swollen rivers during the
monsoon season, using no roads, trucks, or bulldozers. Between 1967
and 1970, *banjir kap* loggers accounted for 62 percent of Indonesia's
timber production.

In 1970, Sudjarwo issued Government Regulation No. 20/1970,
which set a new minimum concession size of 50,000 hectares and thereby
removed the ability of provincial officials to grant timber concessions.
The government's rationale was that only large concessions could attract
foreign investors, who were needed to finance wood-processing facilities.
But the timber agreements signed by foreign firms had only weak provisions calling for investments in wood-processing plants, and these provisions were largely unenforced.

Government Regulation No. 20/1970 also stipulated that all
logging be mechanized, putting *banjir kap* operators out of business. The
forestry department had complained that *banjir kap* operators were
difficult to regulate, and failed to reforest logged-over areas. But the
argument rang false: The department showed little concern for regulating much larger concessions, which violated the reforestation regulations
with impunity.

Nor was there any obvious economic reason to outlaw the practice
of *banjir kap*: These small operators were providing the economy
with the jobs and foreign exchange it needed; the industry's profits
were flowing to Indonesians, not foreigners; and local people found
banjir kap logging more lucrative than working for large concession-

aires.[16] At the same time, since they needed little capital investment, *banjir kap* loggers could sell their timber at a lower price than large concession holders, making Indonesian wood more competitive internationally. All of this should have pleased the government. But for the Suharto government foreign firms had at least one advantage over *banjir kap* loggers: they could be used to transfer rents to the Indonesian military.[17]

Creating Ransack Rents

The BFL had already diluted *adat* rights to help make timber extraction profitable. In 1971, the government adopted GR No. 21/1971, which weakened *adat* rights further by stipulating that commercial loggers would have precedence over *adat* rights when the two were in conflict, and by giving logging firms themselves authority to regulate *adat* rights on their own concessions. Article Six states:

1. The rights of the *adat* community and its members to harvest forest products . . . shall be organized in such a manner that they do not disturb forest production.
2. Implementation of the above provision is [delegated to the Company] which is to accomplish it through consensus with the *adat* community, with supervision from the Forest Service.
3. In the interests of public safety, *adat* rights to harvest forest products in a particular area shall be frozen while forest production activities are under way.

The implications of this regulation were vast. By the late-1970s, timber concessions covered more than one-quarter of the country. In these areas, the traditional rights of forest dwellers to use the land for swidden cultivation, and to gather plants, animals, and other forest products, were curtailed or extinguished. Conversely, rescinding *adat* rights

---

16 According to Peluso (1983: 179), "Virtually every able-bodied man living in the most remote parts of East Kalimantan took part in banjir kap. Farmers joined schoolteachers, government officials and shopkeepers in cutting logs or in organizing work groups. . . . Millions and millionaires could be made practically overnight; everyone along the trade networks prospered."
17 Japanese purchasers delivered the coup de grace to *banjir kap* operators when, in 1971, they refused to purchase any Indonesian logs produced by nonmechanized processes.

made timber concessions more valuable, and increased the pool of timber rents available to the government.[18]

Timber Patronage and the Military

Before 1971, most foreign investors held their timber concessions through wholly owned Indonesian subsidiaries. But over the course of the 1970s, Sudjarwo used a combination of informal and formal measures to force most foreign firms to take on domestic partners – partners he had the authority to nominate. By 1979, 66 of the industry's 77 foreign firms operated through joint ventures with Indonesian partners (Gillis 1987).

Sudjarwo's power to allocate timber licenses and design joint ventures gave him indirect control over most of Indonesia's timber windfall, thanks to the government's policy of radically undertaxing the timber industry. From 1967 to 1969, low taxes and royalties may have been justified by the government's efforts to attract foreign investors, and to help Indonesian timber capture a share of the international market. By 1970, however, the low level of rent capture was attracting public criticism, and by 1972 – with production booming and investors clamoring for new concessions – it was clear that profits had grown unjustifiably high in the forest sector. Yet from 1973 to 1986 the state's share of the logging rents fell from 25 percent to just 5 percent; most of the remainder went to licensees.[19]

By distributing licenses and designing joint ventures, Sudjarwo parceled out most of the timber windfall to Suharto's clients and patronage institutions, and to the Suharto family itself. By the mid-1970s, Sudjarwo had approved:

---

18 The literature on the *adat* rights of local peoples in Indonesia, and their infringement by logging firms, is extensive. Important works include Barber (1989); Zerner (1992); Peluso (1992a); Peluso (1993); Tsing (1992); and Barber, Johnson, and Hafild (1994).

19 The timber sector's low taxes and royalties were criticized as early as 1970 by the government's own Commission of Four (Mackie 1970). On the Indonesian government's low rent capture also see Ruzicka (1979); Gray and Hadi (1990); WALHI Economic Team (1991); and Haughton, Teter, and Stern (1992).

Taxes and royalties on the timber sector have, at one time or another, included a Forest Concession License Fee (*Iuran Hak Pengusahaan Hutan*), a Forest Products Royalty (*Iuran Hasil Hutan*), an Additional Royalty for river dredging and resettlement (*Iuran Hasil Hutan Tambahan*), a Reforestation Fee (*Dana Reboisasi*), a Land and Improvement Tax (*Pajak Bumi dan Bangunan*), a Scaling and Grading Fee, a corporate income tax, and various timber export taxes.

- concessions for each of the four major services (army, navy, air force, police), to help fund networks of Suharto loyalists and to finance off-budget projects;
- concessions for Kostrad (*Komando Cadangan Strategis Angkatan Darat*, the Army Strategic Reserve Command) and Opsus (*Operasi Khusus*, Special Operations), two branches of the military charged with some of Suharto's most important political tasks, including military intelligence;
- three concessions for Lt. General Ibnu Sutowo, the autocratic president and director of Pertamina, who helped finance both Golkar and many of Suharto's patronage operations;
- three concessions for a group of retired army officers, who called themselves the Konsultasi Pembangunan Group;
- two unusually large concessions for the Hanurata Group, which was wholly owned by two of Suharto's *yayasan*: Yayasan Harapan Kita, and Yayasan Bantuan Beasiswa Yatim Piatu;[20]
- and ten concessions for P. T. Tri Usaha Bhakti, the Defense Ministry's holding company. The funds held by Tri Usaha Bhakti were used to provide retiring officers with pensions, and to fund client networks running through the command structure. Many of Tri Usaha Bhatki's concessions were run in partnership with the business groups of regional military commands. (Robison 1977)[21]

To exploit their concessions, the military-backed firms relied on either subcontracting agreements (which were illegal but unofficially permitted) or joint ventures with foreign or Indonesian Chinese firms. Both arrangements produced easy profits for the military. According to a report by the American Embassy in Jakarta (1980), subcontractors typically paid the concession holder $10 to $30 per cubic meter of timber, while incurring both the costs and risks of the enterprise.

---

20 These concessions were run as joint ventures with the Salim Group and the Bob Hasan Group, each owned by one of Suharto's closest business associates (Liem Sioe Liong and Bob Hasan, respectively). The Hanurata Group later gained a 10 percent share of another timber firm, Santi Murni Plywood; a further 13 percent was distributed to Suharto's children, brother, and father-in-law.
21 In 1969, Suharto carried out a major reorganization of the military, truncating the autonomy of the army, navy, and air force, and greatly enhancing the power of the minister of defense – an office Suharto held himself – as well as the commander of the armed forces. To help finance and control the reorganized military, the defense ministry formed Tri Usaha Bhakti, a holding company whose shareholders were senior military officers.

Joint ventures were also lucrative. The military partner provided only the license and a nominal fraction of the capital; even this capital might be financed by the foreign partner through a "signing bonus" or an agreement to charge it against future revenues. The commercial partner supplied all or virtually all of the capital, managed the concession, and marketed the timber. In the four cases described by Robison (1978), firms linked to the military provided an average of 0.25 percent of the initial capital, yet received an average of 36 percent of the equity in the joint venture.

The International Timber Corporation of Indonesia (P. T. ITCI), a joint venture between Tri Usaha Bhakti and the U.S.-based Weyerhaeuser, illustrates these arrangements. Weyerhaeuser had initially applied for an Indonesian timber concession in 1969 through a wholly owned subsidiary, P. T. Weyerhaeuser Indonesia: it was granted a relatively undesirable 100,000 hectare site in East Kalimantan, which it never fully developed. But in 1971, Weyerhaeuser found it could gain access to a much larger, and more valuable 601,000 hectare concession by acting as the foreign partner for Tri Usaha Bhakti, which held the concession rights.

Tri Usaha Bhakti retained a 35 percent share in ITCI, their joint venture. Yet besides the concession itself (which it had received at no cost), Tri Usaha Bhakti had provided just .5 percent ($160,000) of ITCI's initial capitalization of $32 million.[22] Moreover, it played no role in exploiting the concession or marketing the timber. By 1978, ITCI's annual sales were worth $67 million, and after-tax profits were 45 to 50 percent of sales (Sacerdoti 1979). For Tri Usaha Bhakti, ITCI yielded an annual profit of $10 to $12 million, with virtually no investment.[23]

The Problem of Regulatory Enforcement

In the Philippines, Sabah, and Sarawak, timber booms hurt the forest department's ability to enforce preexisting silvicultural regulations. In Indonesia, the timber boom made the government's silvicultural and reforestation regulations virtually impossible to enforce from the time they were first issued.

22 Tri Usaha Bhakti also received a $3.5 million "signing bonus" from Weyerhaeuser – more than enough to finance the cost of its contribution to ITCI's initial capitalization.

23 The secrecy of Indonesian government records makes it impossible to know the full extent of the military's holdings; it also makes it difficult to know what proportion of the industry was in the hands of the military or other political clients. Anecdotal evidence suggests it may have been a majority, possibly a large majority.

In 1972, the department issued a comprehensive set of silvicultural regulations – the *Tebang Pilih Indonesia* (TPI), or Indonesian Selective Cutting System – that was designed to govern all aspects of the logging process, including basic forest planning, road construction, inventories, felling, and regeneration.[24] While silviculturally laudable, the TPI system was costly for concession-holders to implement. Ignoring the regulations, conversely, allowed concessionaires to boost their profits by logging recklessly, and by retaining the funds they would otherwise spend on reforestation and proper forest management. According to one Indonesian forester,

The guidelines are strict enough, but they are not properly enforced. If they were, the logging people say it would hardly be profitable to do any logging here. (Lauriat and Sacerdoti 1977: 64)

In the 1970s, concessions owned by the military enjoyed even greater impunity than other licensees. According to Crouch, bureaucrats in Jakarta were

in a weak position to recommend restrictions on projects with which powerful army officers were associated. . . . Even when restrictions were imposed, as in the case of joint ventures in forestry, contractual obligations limiting the felling of trees, requiring replanting, and the establishing of processing facilities were rarely observed, and there was little effective supervision of the quantity of exports on which royalties to the government were calculated. (Crouch 1978: 323–4)

The government's reforestation provisions were particularly ineffectual. Rather than replant, concessionaires were doing the opposite:

---

24 The TPI system stipulated that in most settings only trees with diameters greater than fifty centimeters at breast height could be felled, and it prohibited logging on steep slopes. It also specified that a certain number of "mother" trees must remain standing after each area was logged, to foster natural regeneration; that when the residual number of mother trees was too low, the concession-holder must replant the area with seedlings from its own nursery; and that concession-holders must protect logged-over stands from further logging for thirty-five years, remove undesired species and liana climbers, prevent gully erosion, and take other measures to protect the area. The TPI regulations were set out in Decision Letter No. 35/1972 of the director general of forestry.

Since in practice, the residual number of mother trees almost always fell short, the TPI regulations made the reforestation of virtually all logged-over areas mandatory. Lesley Potter (1991: 185) notes that in Kalimantan, "Hardly ever was the desired number of 25 trees per hectare found; usually only 2 or 3 trees in this size class would be located and these were vulnerable to destruction during logging activities."

quickly re-entering logged-over stands to remove any remaining trees, a practice that can produce long-term harm to the forests by excessively compacting the soil and damaging regenerating trees (Kuswata 1980).

One of the forestry department's own leading foresters noted that prior to 1980,

concession holders only complied with the (TPI) stipulation on diameter limit, while the other operational aspects (such as residual stand inventories, refining, nurseries, replanting/enrichment planting and forest tending) had not been carried out at all. Even though some concession holders had already implemented some silvicultural activities, for example in nursery and enrichment planting, most were for exhibition and cosmetic planting only. (Djamaludin 1991: 98)

When the forestry department did penalize logging violations, they often did so selectively and inflated their claims. In 1978, the department announced that a "crackdown" on logging violations had led to the cancellation of concessions covering 12.5 million hectares, and the withdrawal of 1.3 million hectares from the concessions of five other firms. But these claims were exaggerated: The department never disclosed any company names, and a 1988 study found that only 2.4 million hectares of concessions had *ever* been cancelled by the forestry department, much less in 1978 (Pusat Data Business Indonesia 1988: 163). Moreover, to the extent there was a crackdown, it seemed to be directed against foreign firms, to force them to grant more equity to their Indonesian partners.

Favored licensees were sometimes granted extralegal privileges by the forestry department. In one case, the Indonesian navy was allowed to log 10,000 hectares of high quality forest inside the South Sumatra Nature Reserve; in another case, 60 percent of the East Kutai Nature Reserve was temporarily excised, logged, and then restored to the reserve (Cribb 1988).

The department's neglect of regulatory enforcement continued well into the late 1980s. Before 1988, according to a study by the Indonesian forestry department, "practically no improvements were made in the actual performance of the concession holders, in their seriousness to fully implement TPI" (Djamaludin 1991: 98). The department's 1987 survey showed that some of the most important silvicultural tasks – including inventories of residual stands, and enrichment planting – had been carried out on less than 3 percent of the logged-over forests.

A 1989 FAO study confirmed this bleak picture, finding that

in about half of the provinces, the concessions exceed the forest areas classified and suitable for regular or limited production, and that conversion or unclassified forest has to make up for it. The area of concessions reported to be steeper than 45 percent (i.e., above the legal limit) is sometimes quite substantial and indicates that protection forest is also used. (Sutter 1989: 17)

The department's enforcement failures can partly be explained by the difficulty of monitoring firms that operated in the remotest parts of the archipelago. But political pressures also played a role. In 1980, Sudjarwo named an exceptionally conscientious forester, Djamaludin Suryohadikusumo, as Director General for Forest Utilization – a position in charge of enforcing the TPI system. Djamaludin made an unprecedented effort to enforce the department's regulations, and threatened to cancel the licenses of 131 timber firms who were out of compliance. Three weeks after appointing him, Sudjarwo demoted Djamaludin and sent him to South Kalimantan.

THE TIMBER INDUSTRY SHAKE-UP, 1979–95

In the late 1970s and early 1980s, the timber industry went through a series of tumultuous changes: the export of unprocessed logs – the industry's most lucrative product – was phased out; the state pushed hard to develop sawnwood and plywood industries; and most military firms left the industry and were replaced by ethnic Chinese firms. The shake-up reflected larger changes in the New Order state, some of which were caused by the 1978–9 oil shock.

In the 1960s and 1970s, the fiscally constrained Suharto government relied on nominally independent government agencies – principally the forestry department, Pertamina, and Bulog – to create and distribute rents to the regime's most important clients. But when the 1978–9 oil shock brought an unexpected windfall to the central government, Suharto used the opportunity to set up a new, more centralized procedure for dispensing patronage through government contracts.

Beginning in 1980, the oil windfall was placed in the hands of "Team 10" – a group of officials directed by Sudharmono, a longtime Suharto associate who was both the state secretary and (starting in 1983) the chairman of Golkar. According to Winters (1995: 141), Team 10 was

Suharto's vehicle for centralizing the patronage process, "drawing patronage power upward and into the center, and elevat(ing) to the level of formal national policy a pattern of tight micromanagement of opportunity and success throughout the archipelago that had not existed previously."

As Team 10 became the new locus of state patronage, the rents of the timber industry grew politically extraneous to Suharto, this opened the door to rent seeking by state actors at the penultimate level of government. Between 1981 and 1995, the state's most powerful bureaucracies – including the ministries of industry, finance, planning, and research and technology – fought with the forestry department over the industry's rents.[25] These ministries used timber rents to subsidize their own ambitious industrialization projects, rather than use them for patronage or corruption.

On April 22, 1981, the director-general of forestry – along with his counterparts in the ministries of trade and industry – issued a "Letter of Joint Decision" announcing strict limits on the export of unprocessed logs, and requiring firms to invest in plywood mills if they wished to obtain log export permits.[26] As a result, the export of raw logs – which produced the industry's largest and easiest profits – fell by 57 percent in 1981, and a further 49 percent in 1982. By 1985, raw log exports dropped to zero.[27]

The decision to force the logging industry into "downstream" wood-processing was a triumph for the ministries of industry, finance, and planning (BAPPENAS), who had long fought to overcome the resistance of the forestry department and the political clients it protected. The ban forced licensees to underwrite the sawnwood and plywood industries by selling their logs to wood-processing factories at a fraction of their export value. It was an egregiously inefficient way to build up Indonesia's manufacturing capacity. In 1982 alone, $293 million in rents – 37 percent of the industry's total potential rents – were used to subsidize the move into

---

25 The forestry department gained ministerial status in 1983. For clarity, I continue to refer to it as a "department" rather than a "ministry."

26 See "Letter of Joint Decision, Director General of Forestry, Director General of Miscellaneous Industry, Director General of Internal Trade, and Director General of External Trade," April 22, 1981, No. 78/KPTS/DJ/1981. This decree was the most important in a series of initiatives to move the timber industry downstream.

27 The oil shock also facilitated the log export ban by giving the state a comfortable surplus in foreign exchange reserves, which mitigated the drop in timber revenues that accompanied the move into plywood.

downstream processing; almost all came from the industry's share, not the government's (Gillis 1988a). Still, the ban had its intended effect: Plywood production rose from 1.01 million cubic meters in 1980 to 6.08 million cubic meters in 1986.

The ban had painful consequences for the logging industry in 1980–1. Over one hundred firms – about 20 percent of the industry – went bankrupt; many more failed over the next three years, while the survivors went heavily into debt.[28] Most foreign and military companies recognized that the era of easy profits had come to an end; rather than investing in wood processing factories and waiting for prices to recover, most sold off their holdings.

In the wake of the military's departure, the timber industry was taken over by a small number of Indonesian Chinese entrepreneurs. The Indonesian Chinese had been on the periphery of the timber industry since the beginning of the boom. Some, like Mohamad "Bob" Hasan (The Kian Seng), worked as partners or contractors for firms held by the military; others, like Burhan Uray (Bong Sun On) and Jos Sutomo (Kang King Toat), held their own concessions. But during the industry shakeup, these and other Indonesian Chinese entrepreneurs vastly expanded their holdings. They purchased concessions from foreign investors and military firms who were anxious to leave the industry; from smaller concession holders, who lacked the capital to invest in plywood mills; and from state banks who were left with bad loans from bankrupt concession holders. They financed their purchases with loans from state banks, foreign banks, and loans from Japanese trading houses.

By 1992, the timber industry had been reorganized into a small number of large business groups (see Table 7.2). The thirty-two largest groups collectively held 30.4 million hectares of concessions, which was half of the production forest and almost 16 percent Indonesia's total land mass.[29] At least twenty-seven of these thirty-two groups were owned by ethnic Chinese businessmen; most were largely or wholly owned by a single family.[30] Only the thirty-fifth largest group – Dwima, which held

---

28 The government cushioned the blow by telling state-owned banks to refrain from calling in their loans to the remaining timber firms – loans that totaled hundreds of millions of dollars – to protect them from bankruptcy.

29 These figures slightly understate the concentration of holdings in the timber industry, since several individuals owned multiple groups, which had separate legal identities.

30 Of the remaining five groups, one was a joint venture between Korean and pribumi firms (Korindo); one was controlled by the Suharto family (Hanurata); and three had unidentified owners. The concentration of Indonesian Chinese in

Table 7.2. *Major Indonesian Timber Concession Holders, 1994*

#	Company	HPH	Area (ha)	Major Owner	Type
1	Djayanti Jaya	27	3,302,000	Burhan Uray (Bong Sun On)	Chinese
2	Alas Kusuma	16	2,579,000	Tan Hok Lim	Chinese
3	Kayu Lapis	22	1,863,000	Andi Sutanto (Tan Siong An)	Chinese
4	Barito Pacific	36	1,766,000	Prajogo Pangestu (Phang Djun Phen)	Chinese
5	Kalimanis	7	1,322,000	Mohamad Hasan (The Kian Seng)	Chinese
6	Wapoga Mutiara	5	1,261,000	Kakan Sukandadinata, Piet Yap, Alexander Tsao Ming Lit	Chinese
7	Bumi Raya Utama	9	1,204,000	Adijanto (Tan Lim Han)	Chinese
8	Hutrindo	11	1,095,000	Alex Korompis (Kho Teng Kwee)	Chinese
9	Satya Djaya Raya	8	1,090,000	Susanto Lyman (Lie An Djian)	Chinese
10	Uniseraya	9	996,000	Muharno Ngadimin (Ng Tjiok Sun), Salim Widjaja (Liem Khway Lay)	Chinese
11	Iradat Puri	7	992,000	Mirawan H. S.	Chinese
12	Surya Dumai	7	987,000	Martias (Pung Kian Hwa)	Chinese
13	Korindo	7	973,000	N.A.	Korean, Pribumi
14	Sumalindo	7	797,000	Prajogo Pangestu (Phang Djun Phen), William Soeryadjaya (Tjia Kian Liong)	Chinese
15	Harapan Kita Utama	6	774,000	N.A.	N.A.
16	Jati Maluku Timber	4	748,000	Oei Ek Tjhong (Eka Tjipta Widjaja)	Chinese
17	Roda Mas	8	681,000	Tan Siong Kie	Chinese
18	Daya Sakti	7	677,000	Hadi Surya, Windya Rachman	Chinese
19	Kayu Mas	8	617,000	Njoto Widjojo (Njoo Kiem King Kie)	Chinese
20	Yusmin Trading	7	589,000	N.A.	N.A.
21	Sumber Mas	5	564,000	Yos Soetomo (Kang King Toat)	Chinese

Table 7.2. *(continued)*

#	Group	HPH	Area (ha)	Owner	Group
22	Benua Indah	4	563,000	Tan Jam Sia	Chinese
23	Dayak Besar Agung	4	554,000	H. M. Yusuf Hamka	Chinese
24	Gunung Raya Utama Timber	3	533,000	Simon Rahardja (Tjia Sin Tjing)	Chinese
25	Raja Garuda Mas	5	515,000	Sukanto Tanoto (Lim Sui Han)	Chinese
26	Sinar Mas	4	515,000	Oei Ek Tjhong (Eka Tjipta Widjaja)	Chinese
27	Porodisa	2	496,000	Jarry Sumendap	Chinese
28	Hanurata	2	488,000	Suharto family[a]	Suharto
29	Tanjung Raya	6	456,000	Pohan Burdiman (Pho Boen Tjit)	Chinese
30	Bina Lestari	5	446,000	Kho Soie Tiam	Chinese
31	Subago	4	443,000	N.A.	N.A.
32	Kodeco	3	435,000	Njoto Widjojo (Njoo Kiem King Kie)	Chinese
33	Brajatama	2	420,000	N.A.	N.A.
34	Segara Timber	6	418,000	N.A.	N.A.
35	Dwima	4	409,000	Slamet Sarojo, Soemadi, Soebagio Anam	military

[a] Held through Yayasan Harapan Kita and Yayasan Bantuan Beasiswa Yatim Piatu; all shares of these foundations were owned by members of the Suharto family. The Hanurata group concessions were run as joint ventures with the Salim Group and the Bob Hasan Group.

Sources: Robison (1986); Capricorn Indonesia Consult (1990, 1994); PT Data Consult Inc. (1993).

four concessions totaling 409,000 hectares – was closely linked with the military.[31]

By the 1990s, the remaining timber firms had fully recovered from the log export ban, and built a formidable – and highly profitable – industry

the timber industry was somewhat greater than in other major industrial sectors. Indonesian Chinese owned two-thirds of the country's largest firms, but over four-fifths of the major firms in the timber industry (Capricorn Indonesia Consult 1990; Schwartz 1994).

31 Some of the most influential Indonesian Chinese loggers had close ties to Suharto and his family. Bob Hasan (The Kian Seng) was the timber industry's most influential figure. Hasan had personal and business links to Suharto dating back to

based on the export of plywood and other value-added products. But the industry's profits touched off a second rent-seizing battle inside the state.

In 1980, the department began to impose on loggers a reforestation guarantee deposit (*Dana Jaminan Reboisasi dan Permudaan Hutan*) of $4 per cubic meter, to be refunded once the concessionaire had reforested logged-over areas. Few timber firms ever bothered to replant their concessions and reclaim their deposits; as a result, the deposit grew into an important source of revenue for the department. In 1989, the reforestation deposit was changed to a nonrefundable fee (renamed the *Dana Reboisasi*, or Reforestation Fund) and raised to $7 per cubic meter. It was raised again to $10 in 1990, and to an average of $16 per cubic meter in 1993 – by which time it had become the largest tax on the timber industry.[32]

The ballooning Reforestation Fund became an alluring target for both government and nongovernment rent seekers. In 1994, the fund was raided by then-Minister of Research and Technology Habibie, who secured a presidential decree to transfer $180 million (Rp. 400 billion) to a state-owned manufacturer under his purview, to help fund the con-

the 1950s, when he helped then-Colonel Suharto purchase supplies for the Diponegoro Division. By the 1990s, Hasan managed many of Suharto's business affairs and was engaged in joint ventures in timber with Suharto's second son, Bambang Trihatmodjo; in transportation with Hutomo Mandala Putra, Suharto's youngest son; and in timber, tea plantations, banking, and telecommunications with Suharto's eldest son, Sigit Hardjojudanto. Hasan also controlled APKINDO – the powerful plywood manufacturer's association, which controlled all plywood exports – and every other industry association of consequence (Shin 1989; Barr 1998).

In the 1990s, Prajogo Pangestu (Phang Djun Phen) was Indonesia's largest concession holder; he, too, found it useful to cultivate financial links with the Suharto family – including "joint ventures" in petrochemicals with Bambang Trihatmodjo, and joint ventures in sugar plantations and pulp and paper operations with Suharto's daughter, Siti Hardijanti Rukmana. There were also persistent reports – which Prajogo denied – that in 1990–91 he and businessman Liem Sioe Liong helped cover $420 million in foreign exchange losses suffered by a prominent Indonesian bank, Bank Duta. Seventy-two percent of the bank was owned by three foundations connected to Suharto (Schwarz and Friedland 1992; Pura, Duthie, and Borsuk 1994). Although Prajogo formally held some 2.55 million hectares of concessions (1.766 million through Barito Pacific, and another .797 million through Sumalindo), he was thought to have "access" to another three million hectares, possibly through subcontracting arrangements.

32 The rise in the reforestation deposit lifted the government's timber taxes and royalties from 3,520 Rupiah ($2.74) per cubic meter of wood in 1986 to 53,550 Rupiah ($25.50) in 1995. Rent capture rose commensurately, from 6 percent in 1986 to at least 30 to 40 percent in 1995.

struction of the N-250 aircraft; the money was treated as an "interest-free loan," with no specified terms or repayment schedule (*Jakarta Post* 1994). In February 1997, Mohamed "Bob" Hasan – one of the president's closest advisors and the head of APKINDO, the plywood producer's association – obtained $109 million (Rp. 250 billion) to finance his group's investments in pulp and paper (Barr 1998).

CONCLUSION

In 1967, the Suharto government began a vigorous campaign to promote commercial logging, in response to both pressure from foreign investors and governments, and the need to revive the economy. After several years of rapid growth, a fivefold rise in the export price of Indonesian timber gave President Suharto an incentive to make his allocation rights more exclusive, and to create ransack rents.

In some ways, rent seizing was less pronounced in Indonesia than in the Philippines, Sabah, and Sarawak. Neither Suharto nor Sudjarwo exercised the same level of discretion over licensing as their counterparts in the Philippines, Sabah, and Sarawak.[33] The Indonesian government provided concessionaires with long-term contracts, usually lasting for twenty years; politicians in the other states relied on short-term licenses, lasting between one and five years.[34] The Indonesian government banned raw log exports while the industry was booming, despite the pain it caused many timber firms. Among the other cases, only the Philippines banned log exports – and then only in 1986, after widespread deforestation, and the sudden departure of Marcos, had caused a sharp drop in the industry's influence.

Finally, for the first two decades of the timber boom the Indonesian government authorized logging at rates below what it thought was the maximum sustainable yield. A 1971 FAO study put the maximum sustainable yield at 48 million cubic meters a year; between 1967 and 1986, the legal log harvest never exceeded 30.9 million cubic meters (Sweatman 1971).

33 However, much is unknown about informal ways that Suharto may have influenced the licensing process; moreover, data released by the forestry department on license allocation are often incomplete and contradictory.
34 As Chapter 4 notes, the Philippine government switched from short- to long-term licenses after President Marcos declared martial law; Marcos then used monthly export quotas to maintain his leverage over licensees.

The government's restraint should be of little comfort. The FAO's estimates were unrealistically high, close to double later estimates; the government ignored, or was complicit with, countless violations of its own silvicultural regulations; and illegal logging pushed up the actual level of harvesting. Still, the Indonesian government's policies stand apart from the policies of the Philippine, Sabah, and Sarawak governments, which authorized logging at between four and ten times the sustained-yield rate.

The Indonesian government's restraint was most likely the result of economic concerns, not environmental ones. The 1974–5 global recession hurt Indonesian timber firms badly; the demand for hardwood timber disappeared, and firms were forced to let countless freshly cut logs rot in their holding ponds. To help support prices, the Indonesian government began to restrict the supply of timber. Around 1975, the forestry department began to impose limits on the number of trees that could be taken from each plot. Even though the area of forest under concession doubled between 1973 and 1980, the department was able to keep the total harvest roughly constant. As the government imposed a gradual ban on raw log exports between 1980 and 1985, log production once again dropped.

Some of the differences in the Indonesian case may have also been caused by Suharto's security in office, which gave him a low political discount rate – an incentive to use his political resources at a slower pace. Between the mid-1970s and the mid-1990s, Suharto was a secure autocrat, compared to officeholders in the Philippines, Sabah, and Sarawak who faced almost continuous challenges. Many of Suharto's political tactics – such as turning *yayasan* into patronage institutions, and providing patronage pensions for high-ranking officials – suggest that he employed long-term strategies for retaining his authoritarian powers. The use of Indonesia's forest resources at a relatively measured pace may have reflected this strategy.

Other scholars have emphasized the harmful role played by foreign actors, particularly Japan, in the Indonesian timber industry. But the impact of these actors on Indonesia's institutions and policies was limited. Foreign firms and governments helped persuade the new Suharto regime to promote commercial logging, and to foster foreign investment in the forest sector. Foreign firms also served as partners for political clients of the Suharto government.

Yet foreign investors never dominated the industry. From the early years of the boom, most of Indonesia's timber was logged by Indonesians. By the late 1970s, over five hundred firms had concessions; sixty-six were joint ventures between Indonesian and foreign firms, and just eleven were wholly owned by foreigners. Their policy influence, particularly after 1975, was modest at best. The poor quality of Indonesia's forest policies can be better explained by the weakness of the state's forestry institutions in the 1960s; by the government's overriding concern with boosting foreign exchange; and by both rent seeking and rent seizing.

8

Conclusion

Rent Seeking and Rent Seizing

This book began with three puzzles: Why did the governments of the Philippines, Malaysia, and Indonesia squander their forests? Why do most governments in the developing world squander commercially valuable forests? And why do developing states generally mishandle resource windfalls? The book's research design – which emphasizes validity over generality – gives me a good deal of leverage over the first question, but less over the second and third questions. Here I summarize the book's findings, and discuss the implications for both policy analysts and social scientists.

POLICY FAILURES IN THE PHILIPPINES, SABAH,
SARAWAK, AND INDONESIA

All four states in this study had exceptionally valuable forests. Three of them (the Philippines, Sabah, and Sarawak) initially had relatively strong forestry institutions, and nominal policies of sustained-yield harvesting. Yet all four governments wound up squandering their forests, by authorizing logging at unsustainable rates, by keeping royalties and taxes low, and by failing to enforce logging regulations.

There were undoubtedly many reasons for these policy failures. This book focuses on a single cause: the rents created by high timber prices. When timber prices rose high enough to generate rents, governments in three of the four states (the Philippines, Sabah, and Sarawak) stripped their forestry departments of much of their authority over the timber sector, and abandoned their policies of restricting logging to sustained-yield levels. In the fourth case (Indonesia), the government's forestry institutions were weak to begin with; still, the jump in timber prices after 1969 had a harmful effect on nonstate institutions that protected the forests, the institutions of customary law, or *adat*.

Why would timber booms have such a damaging effect on forest institutions and policies? Chapter 3 noted that observers offer two types of explanations for the policy failures caused by natural resource booms: cognitive explanations, which suggest that resource windfalls cause myopic disorders among policymakers; and societal explanations, which suggest that windfalls encourage nonstate actors – such as interest groups, political clients, and rent seekers – to demand a share of the windfall from the government.

The case studies suggest that neither irrational sloth nor irrational exuberance can explain why government policies so quickly deteriorated. Contemporaneous reports from both the government's own foresters, and from intergovernmental advisory bodies, show that policymakers in the Philippines, Sabah, and Sarawak were repeatedly warned that they were authorizing logging at unsustainable levels – in violation of their own nominal policies – and that doing so would have harmful economic, social, and environmental consequences. Of course, it is impossible to know how well informed individual policymakers were. Yet longitudinal comparisons within the Philippine, Sabah, and Sarawak cases suggest that limited information cannot explain their postboom policy failures, since their information was equally (or more) limited before their countries' timber boom, when policies were more prudent and sustainable. There is little evidence that policy failures were caused by cognitive shortcomings.

There is a great deal of evidence, however, the policy failures were partly caused by rent-seeking pressures from private actors. In all four cases, logging permits were distributed to major campaign donors, influential constituents, and the friends, relatives, and cronies of top politicians. When timber exports boomed in Sabah in the early 1960s, Chief Minister Donald Stephens found that the great majority of his visitors came to request timber licenses; his counterparts in the Philippines, Sarawak, and Indonesia no doubt felt similar pressures.

Chapter 3 suggests an additional reason why resource booms commonly lead to policy failures: rent seizing. It defines rent seizing as "efforts by state actors to gain the right to allocate economic rents"; it also specifies four hypotheses. The first is that when a state receives an economic windfall, public officials will attempt to gain the right to allocate it, in the form of economic rents, to others.

Do the case studies support this hypothesis? The answer is a quali-fied "yes."

In three of the four cases, there is a rough correlation between the time that rents arose in the timber sector, and the time that politicians sought the right to allocate timber concessions. In the Philippines, rents became available in the early-to-mid 1950s, and by 1956 President Magsaysay and members of congress were battling over allocation rights. The cases of Sabah and Sarawak are more complex, since in both states rents first became available under the British colonial government, which left local political leaders with no viable rent-seizing avenues. After the two states gained their own governments under the Malaysian flag in 1963, the struggle within the new cabinets over the allocation of forest concessions took center stage. Only in the Indonesian case is there no apparent causal link between the timber windfall and allocation rights, since President Suharto gained allocation rights in early 1967, before the timber boom occurred. By the time that timber concessions rose in value, they were already controlled by Suharto's close ally, Director General Sudjarwo.[1]

The second hypothesis is that politicians will try to maximize the value of their allocation rights, by making them more direct, exclusive, and discretionary. Although their ability to do so varied, politicians made these efforts in all four states. During his two elected terms as president, Marcos used a range of bureaucratic strategies to erode the forestry bureau's independence, and to gain more direct authority over license allocation; he also fought to exclude members of congress and members of his own cabinet from holding allocation rights. After declaring martial law in 1972, he took each of these measures further, and devised a clever system of export licenses that made his influence highly discretionary. Sabah's Tun Mustapha and Sarawak's Rahman Ya'akub took parallel measures to strengthen their allocation rights: both served as their own ministers of forestry; both transferred their forestry departments' powers to more secretive and flexible organizations (the Sabah Foundation, the Sarawak Foundation, and STIDC); and both amended the forestry laws to give themselves heightened discretion over the assignment and with-drawal of timber concessions. In Indonesia, when timber prices rose, President Suharto usurped the allocation powers of provincial governors and district heads. Although he delegated formal control over the

---

1 Note that the Indonesian case does not contradict the first hypothesis, since there may be other factors that cause politicians to seek allocation rights.

forestry sector to Director General Sudjarwo, Suharto's close personal ties with Sudjarwo, and Suharto's authoritarian powers, gave him relatively direct and discretionary control of the timber industry.

The third hypothesis is that these rent-seizing efforts lead to the weakening or dismantling of institutions that restrict resource exploitation. The governments of the Philippines, Sabah, and Sarawak were endowed with relatively strong forestry institutions prior to their timber booms: All had forestry departments that held a large measure of autonomy within the government, and that had historically sought to limit logging to sustained-yield levels. The rent-seizing campaigns of political actors dismantled these institutions or rendered them ineffectual. In both Indonesia and Sabah, the forests were protect by laws that recognized the customary land rights of forest dwellers. In both states, these laws were nullified in the wake of a timber boom.

The incentives for rent seizing and institutional dismantling are illustrated by Figure 8.1, which is a modified version of Figure 3.1. Supply

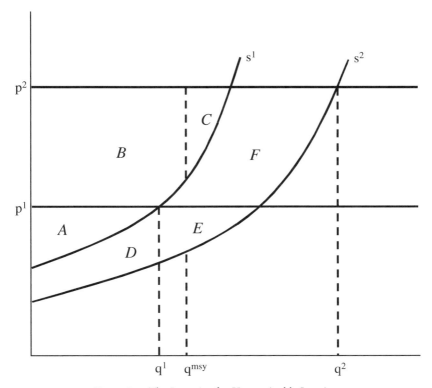

Figure 8.1. The Incentive for Unsustainable Logging.

curve S^1 represents the preferences of timber firms under "normal" conditions, when government institutions are properly regulating the industry. If prices are at the normal level P^1, firms will cut a quantity of timber q^1; in this illustration, this quantity is just below the maximum sustainable yield q^{MSY}. This approximates the situation in the Philippines before 1955, in Sabah before 1965, and in Sarawak before 1978. In each case, the price of timber then rose from P^1 to P^2, creating a new pool of rents B that acted as an incentive for rent-seizing behavior. In these three cases, politicians dismantled the forestry institutions that restricted their ability to allocate these rents.

Politicians also recognized that by enforcing regulations on sustained-yield harvesting, they were forgoing a further quantity of rents, represented by area C. By allowing firms to harvest above the maximum sustainable yield, they gained access to these rents as well.

Moreover, once they had stripped their forest departments of their political autonomy, state actors were able to reduce the logging costs of license holders by allowing them to ignore silvicultural and environmental regulations and by eviscerating the rights of forest dwellers. This enabled loggers to shift their supply curve from S^1 to S^2. As a result, firms could profitably log quantity q^2, creating a further cache of allocable rents – or "ransack rents" – represented by areas D, E, and F.

The fourth hypothesis concerns the rate at which politicians allocated the rents represented by areas A through F. It states that the rate at which a politician will allocate rents – approximated by the harvesting rate – will be influenced by the exclusivity of their allocation rights, and their security in office. This final hypothesis is difficult to illustrate (much less test), because the harvesting rate is influenced by many other factors, ranging from changes in technology to fluctuations in overseas timber markets. Still, there is evidence both within and across the cases to support this hypothesis. In the Philippines, Marcos took important measures to slow the harvesting rate after he declared martial law in 1972 and gained both more exclusive control over timber rents and greater security in office. Indonesia's Suharto held exclusive allocation rights and was an exceptionally secure autocrat through the mid-1990s. He also kept logging to the lowest rate of the four cases: In the 1970s and the first half of the 1980s, it was below what foresters believed was the sustained-yield rate, while in the 1990s it rose to between 1.5 and 2 times this rate.

The cases of Sabah and Sarawak are broadly consistent with hypothesis four, once we control for the creation of ransack rents. Both

Sabah's Tun Mustapha (between 1967 and 1970) and Sarawak's Rahman Ya'akub (between 1970 and 1979) dismantled restrictions on logging activity after taking office, shifting out the timber industry's supply curve and creating ransack rents; as a result, they also increased their states' harvesting rates. Once this process was complete, we can see the influence of exclusivity and political security on harvesting rates. Sabah's chief ministers have consistently held exclusive allocation rights; but since they have been perpetually insecure – and repeatedly defeated in elections – their allocation rates have been high, rising to ten times the sustainable level in the early 1990s. Sarawak's chief ministers have also held exclusive allocation rights, except between 1981 and 1985, when Taib was forced to share these rights with former Chief Minister Rahman Ya'akub. During the first year of this shared arrangement, harvesting rose 27 percent, from 8.8 million to 11.2 million cubic meters a year; over the next four years it leveled off. But between 1986 and 1991, Taib's security in office dropped sharply, as he faced two highly contested elections. During this spell the harvesting rate rose more than 70 percent, from 11.4 to 19.4 million cubic meters – between four and five times the sustainable level. Twelve months after the 1991 election, which Taib won decisively, the forest department ordered license holders to reduce their output.

While the data on timber rents, rent seeking, and institutional change are incomplete, the four case studies are broadly consistent with the hypotheses laid out in Chapter 3. Collectively, they illustrate how commodity booms can harm state institutions and policies, and lead to the overrapid dissipation of a windfall. They also show how rent seeking and rent seizing go hand-in-hand: When private actors have incentives to seek rents, public officials gain incentives to supply them – a process that may have disastrous consequences for the governance of natural resources.

WHY DO DEVELOPING STATES SQUANDER THEIR FORESTS?

The case studies suggest that rent seizing was an important source of policy failure in the Philippines, Malaysia, and Indonesia. Can this finding be applied to other developing states? It is impossible to know without examining other cases in detail. Still, three observations can move us closer to an answer.

First, the domain of relevant cases – that is, the states that are vulnerable to rent seizing in their forest sectors – consists of all developing states whose natural forests have enough commercial value to generate rents. In the late 1990s, developing states had an estimated 15.275 million square kilometers of forest; according to one study, rents were available in about 27 percent of these forests (Bryant, Nielsen, and Tangley 1997). These rent-generating forests were governed by at least a dozen states, including Brazil, Burma, Cambodia, Cameroon, Côte D'Ivoire, Congo-Brazzaville, Congo-Kinshasa, Equatorial Guinea, Gabon, Ghana, Laos, Papua New Guinea, and the Solomon Islands.

Second, the presence of forest rents – and, hence, the danger of rent seizing – in any given state depends in part on market conditions. The international demand for hardwood timber remained strong through the late 1990s, and was expected to remain strong well into the twenty-first century. At the same time, the major suppliers of the 1990s, Malaysia and Indonesia, were quickly depleting their forests. This suggests that international timber prices will continue to rise, and create rents in these and eventually other forested states.

Finally, there are indications that rent seizing has already been a problem in several states, notably Cambodia and Papua New Guinea. In Papua New Guinea the government established a new forest authority in the early 1990s to govern the fast-growing timber industry. The authority was designed to keep logging to sustainable levels and free from political interference; it was strongly backed by reformist bureaucrats, local nongovernmental organizations (NGOs), and the World Bank. Yet the authority was forced to battle both members of parliament and the prime minister, who repeatedly tried to strip away its autonomy and gain control of the licensing process.

Without examining a broader sample of cases, we cannot know if the poor forest policies of other states have been caused, in part, by rent seizing. But if rent seizing does affect other countries, twelve heavily forested states in Latin America, Africa, and the Southeast Asia-Pacific region appear to be most vulnerable in the coming years.

WHY DO STATES SQUANDER THEIR WINDFALLS?

According to classic models of economic development, commodity booms should boost economic growth in newly industrializing states. Yet Chapter 2 notes that developing states often grow more slowly after commodity booms. Their governments also tend to mismanage their windfalls. In some cases, policymakers may not know the correct policy response to a positive trade shock; in other cases, they may know the correct response but lack the administrative capacity to implement it. Chapter 2 notes, however, that often policymakers have both the requisite knowledge and administrative capacity, yet still handle their windfalls poorly. It is this last set of policy failures that present a major puzzle.

Because I only examine cases of timber-exporting states in Chapters 4 through 7, I cannot make strong inferences about states that export other types of natural resources. Let me instead offer three conjectures about the policy failures of commodity exporters.

First, commodity windfalls do not make public officials unduly short-sighted. Of course, policymakers are often myopic, and they often lack the information they need to respond properly to positive trade shocks. As Deaton (1999: 35) notes, commodity booms "provide serious challenges for the best-informed and most adept of social planners." My conjecture is simply that windfalls do not make state actors more short-sighted than they were before. This claim may seem obvious, yet a great many studies imply that windfalls cause myopic behavior.

Second, rent-seeking pressures from powerful individuals, classes, or interest groups create serious problems for policymakers. States with different regime types may distribute their windfalls to different constituencies; still, when states undergo resource booms distributive pressures are ubiquitous, and make the prudent use of windfalls difficult even for skillful political leaders.

Finally, windfalls may also cause rent seizing, which are efforts by state actors to capture the right to allocate rents to others. Rent seizing accompanies rent seeking: When private actors seek rents, public officials have an incentive to supply them. Rent seizing can be more pernicious and harder to mitigate than rent seeking, since state actors have rule-making and rule-enforcing powers, and hence the ability to dismantle institutions that would otherwise restrain them. Institutions can become endogenous to rent-seeking struggles, and collapse.

How well does the book's model of rent seizing fit the larger set of cases? There is no easy answer to this question, but other scholars have observed processes that look much like rent seizing in other settings. Bates (1981: 14) found that when agricultural marketing boards in Africa accumulated surpluses, the central governments "sought, and won, control over the revenues." Davis's (1983) study of ten African and Latin American coffee, cocoa, and tea exporters during the 1975–8 boom notes that governments repeatedly appropriated the surpluses held by stabilization funds. According to a World Bank study of eighteen agricultural exporters, stabilization funds were used by governments to facilitate "enormous transfers" of wealth from the rural sector to urban consumers, industry, and the state itself (Schiff and Valdes 1992). Similarly, studies by Auty (1990), Karl (1997), and Collier and Gunning (1999) have shown that oil and mineral-exporting states frequently have difficulty protecting their windfalls from political interference, and from appropriation for patronage, corruption, and pork barrel projects.

HOW CAN TROPICAL FORESTS BE BETTER PROTECTED?

The cases of the Philippines, Malaysia, and Indonesia hold both good news and bad news for those who wish to better protect the world's tropical forests from unsustainable logging. The good news is that poor information has *not* been an obstacle to improved rainforest management. Since at least the 1950s, foresters and public officials in Southeast Asia have understood the virtues of sustainable forest management; when allowed to do so, foresters have been able to implement at least rudimentary forms of sustained-yield management. Better information about forest ecology may improve public policies. But the disastrous forest policies of the states in this study were caused by political forces, not by a lack of information.

The bad news is that the international trade in tropical timber poses a serious threat to many of the remaining forests – a threat that has been poorly understood and may be difficult to mitigate. Some scholars have argued that the international timber trade may help protect tropical forests, by making it profitable for actors in developing states to sustainably manage their forests, instead of converting the land to nonforest uses. Others argue that the impact of the timber trade on tropical deforestation is small or negligible. A 1993 report prepared by the London Environmental Economics Centre, on behalf of the ITTO, concludes that

the international tropical timber trade is not a major source of tropical deforestation. Not only is the conversion of forests to other uses such as agriculture a more significant factor, but an increasing proportion of tropical timber harvested in producer countries is for domestic consumption ... only 6 percent of total tropical non-coniferous roundwood production enters the international trade. (London Environmental Economics Centre 1993: iii)

The ITTO study and others like it tend to underestimate the damage done by the timber trade. They correctly note that when developing states properly manage their forests, the international timber trade should do them no harm. But the international timber trade itself may damage the ability of states to manage their forests sustainably, by creating much larger rents than the domestic timber trade; these rents can set off both rent seeking and rent seizing. Timber exports can indirectly weaken forestry institutions and damage sustained-yield policies.

To better protect the forests, advocates should worry less about the ignorance of policymakers and more about the effects of international markets. The policy options are much the same for the forest sector as they are for other natural resource sectors.

WHAT SHOULD BE DONE?

There are at least four possible ways to mitigate the problem of rent seizing.

The most comprehensive approach would be to reduce the incidence of windfalls by stabilizing international commodity markets. Over the last several decades, international markets for natural resources have grown increasingly volatile (Reinhart and Wickham 1994). Yet for better or worse, international market stabilization has already been tried, and failed utterly. From the 1960s to the mid-1990s, international commodity agreements were forged to support the prices of sugar, cocoa, coffee, rubber, and tin; each of these agreements fell apart (Gilbert 1996). Negotiations to stabilize markets for some two dozen other commodities either produced no results, or ineffectual agreements. A study by Cashin, Liang, and McDermott (1999) suggests that the duration of price fluctuations in international commodity markets may make international stabilization funds impractical.

A second approach would encourage governments to better protect their windfalls by shrouding them in secrecy. Several states have already tried this. In the 1970s, the Indonesian government hid some of its oil revenues in clandestine accounts. The government of Cameroon placed its oil windfall in secret offshore funds that were controlled by the president's office. The Botswanan government listed its revenues from booming diamond exports in obscure items at the bottom of the state budget, to conceal their magnitude (Bevan, Collier, and Gunning 1993). The drawbacks of this approach are self-evident: While the opportunities for corruption are restricted to a smaller set of state actors, these actors will find corruption even easier than normal. Moreover, a strategy of secrecy can only be sustained as long as the incumbent government remains in office.

A third and more plausible option would be to keep the windfall out of the hands of the state. As Collier and Gunning (1999) suggest, private agents tend to manage windfalls better than their governments, provided they have uncontaminated information about the windfall's source and duration. States can transfer the job of capturing windfalls to the private sector by privatizing state-owned resource enterprises, and encouraging private trade groups to organize their own stabilization funds. There are two important constraints on this approach. First, even when a windfall goes directly to the private sector, a portion may still accrue to the state, since commodity booms tend to boost tax revenues. Second, privatization is likely to be a poor option when it comes to old-growth forests, particularly tropical forests where people live, farm, and hunt. Logging in the natural forests of the moist tropics creates numerous social and environmental externalities. Private actors have little incentive to internalize these costs, and in the absence of strong government regulation, can permanently damage the forests and the human communities that live in them. Still, for other natural resources, privatization may help forestall the problem of rent seizing.

The fourth approach would be to use third-party enforcement to help curtail rent seizing. When the state's normal enforcement mechanisms become endogenous to the rent-seeking process, third parties can help force the government to use its windfalls prudently. In the 1980s and 1990s, some international funders – including the World Bank, the IMF, and the Asian Development Bank – began to take on this role. After Marcos fell from power in the Philippines, members of the Aquino government covertly invited the World Bank and other donors to "impose" conditions on their loans to the government, to help bind the government to a plan of forestry reform (Ross 1996). In Papua New Guinea, the World Bank protected the government's forest authority from political interference by repeatedly threatening to withhold funds. During the 1997–8 Asian financial crisis, the bank forced the Indonesian government to reform its forestry practices. In Cambodia, the IMF has pressured the government to halt excessive logging and collect revenues from the timber industry.

This approach, too, has limitations. In general, attempts by international funders to impose policy conditions on reluctant governments have worked poorly (Mosley, Harrigan, and Toye 1991; Ross 1996).

Conditionality works best when the recipient state is small, and its government relies heavily on international donors; or when a larger government is in crisis and has little choice but to accept the donor's demands. In most other cases, governments find ways to evade or counteract the conditions they dislike.

NGOs also can act as third-party enforcers; in states that are larger and more democratic, they may be more effective than international donors. In the Philippines, a vibrant NGO movement has helped put far-reaching forestry reforms in place. To be effective, NGOs must find ways to offset the powerful incentives created by rents. One reason Philippine NGOs were effective was that by the late 1980s the remaining forest rents were small (Ross 1996). But when the rents are large – such as in Venezuela during the oil booms of the 1970s, or Sarawak during the timber booms of the 1980s and 1990s – NGOs can be overwhelmed.

IMPLICATIONS FOR THE STUDY OF POLITICAL ECONOMY, INSTITUTIONS, AND RENT SEEKING

This study has implications for two debates in the social sciences: one about international political economy, the second about institutions and rent seeking.

Scholars of international political economy have long studied the influence of international markets on developing states. From the early 1950s to the late 1970s, many argued that the international economic system placed developing states at a disadvantage. Third World states – particularly those that exported primary commodities – were said to be locked in a permanent state of underdevelopment, due to the declining terms of trade for primary commodities, the instability of international commodity markets, the influence of First World corporations and governments, and class alliances between First World and Third World elites.[2] These criticisms culminated in the 1970s in the push for a "New International Economic Order" that would overturn the international division of labor, and remove what were viewed as systematic biases against Third World development.

Since the early 1980s, these critiques have largely faded. Many economists and political scientists now suggest that international

2 See, for example, Singer (1950); Baran (1952); Gunder Frank (1966); Wallerstein (1974); Evans (1979); Cardoso and Faletto (1979).

markets have a beneficial effect on developing states, by encouraging them to adopt more prudent fiscal and monetary policies. Governments that maintain fiscal and monetary discipline and minimize corruption will be rewarded by foreign investors; those that do not will be penalized.

This study seeks to modify the conventional wisdom by pointing out one way that international markets can have a harmful effect on states, at least in natural resource sectors. In manufacturing sectors the standard logic may hold: governments are more likely to attract foreign investment when they maintain sound economic policies. But in resource sectors – particularly minerals, oil, and timber sectors – this incentive is much weaker, since rents will attract investors even when economic policies are poor and corruption is high. Investors in manufacturing sectors can, in the long run, earn only "normal" profits; they must hence pay close attention to the state's ability to maintain a stable economic environment, since instability and poor governance can erode their slim profit margins. But exhaustible natural resources create rents, allowing foreign investors to profit even when economic conditions are poor. Natural resources are also geographically specific: extractive firms must go where the resources are. In states that are politically and economically unstable, manufacturers will flee, but resource firms are more likely to stay – for example, in Angola, Burma, Congo-Kinshasa, Indonesia, Kazakhstan, Liberia, Nigeria, and Sierra Leone. International markets are less likely to reward the good institutions and policies, or penalize the bad institutions and policies, of states that export minerals, oil, and timber.

Moreover, international commodity markets can damage the institutions and policies of developing states, by creating incentives for both rent seeking and rent seizing. Rent seizing is exceptionally hard to remedy, because it harms the very institutions that states rely on to foil corruption. States with strong resource institutions, like the Philippines and Malaysia before their timber booms, may see these institutions dismantled. States without strong institutions, like Indonesia in the 1960s, may find it harder to build them. International markets may have a beneficent effect on states' manufacturing sectors, but they can have perverse effects on their resource sectors.

This book also has implications for the study of institutions and rent seeking. It describes a type of rent seeking that has been overlooked, and can lead to the deterioration of state institutions. It also shows how state institutions can become endogenous to the pursuit of rents. This may complicate the analysis of rent seeking in important ways. Most formal studies of rent seeking treat both institutions and rents as exogenous, and focus on the economic consequences of rent-seeking behavior in carefully specified settings. A handful of studies treat institutions as exogenous but rents as endogenous, noting that when state institutions are "weak," state actors may create rents that can be allocated to private actors (Appelbaum and Katz 1987; McChesney 1987).

This study shows one way that institutions can be treated as endogenous to the struggle over rents. It suggests that while weak state institutions may allow rent seeking, rent seeking can weaken state institutions – producing a downward spiral of eroding legal, administrative, and political restraints.

Treating state institutions as endogenous may make the analysis of rent seeking less tractable; but scholars should not grow entranced with their heuristic assumptions. Policy analysts routinely urge governments to strengthen their institutions to reduce rent seeking, corruption, and other ailments. Yet state institutions are sometimes harmed by the problems they are supposed to solve; they become endogenous to the conundrums of development.

Appendix

Chronologies of Events

CHRONOLOGY OF EVENTS IN THE PHILIPPINES

1946	Director of Forestry has sole authority to issue licenses; rejects government request to temporarily raise logging rates to aid postwar reconstruction.
1955	Magsaysay transfers licensing power to DANR appointees.
1955	Magsaysay cabinet excludes concessions below 6,000 ha from public bidding.
1956	Eleven members of congress revealed to own concessions.
1958	Garcia cabinet excludes concessions below 50,000 ha from public bidding.
1955–65	Members of congress and the cabinet share allocation rights.
1966	Marcos nominates Quejado, a nonforester, as director; widespread protests.
1968	Marcos gives Quejado power to bypass DANR Secretary Lopez, report to Marcos directly; Lopez threatens to quit; Quejado replaced by Santos.
1972	Marcos declares martial law.
1973	Marcos announces log exports will be banned in 1976; export quotas implemented; quotas issued monthly by presidential aides.
1976	Export ban postponed until 1982; monthly quotas continue.
1982	Export ban postponed indefinitely; monthly quotas continue.

Appendix

CHRONOLOGY OF EVENTS IN SABAH (I)

Year	Control of License Allocation	Sabah Foundation
1954	Concession system, harvesting regulations established; conservator has sole authority to issue licenses.	
1962	Forest Department loses jurisdiction over 2.1 mil ha forest land judged suitable for agriculture.	
1963	Conservator's authority over licenses transfered to forests minister.	
1963–7	Cabinet members struggle over forestry portfolio.	
1967	Mustapha folds Forests Ministry into chief minister's office.	
1969	Mustapha gains discretion over all licensing matters; breaks up concession system; Forest Department loses jurisdiction over land given to Sabah Foundation; forest dwellers lose land rights.	Gains 800,000 ha taken from concessions; charged with logging at sustained-yield pace: 0.9 percent annually.
1974		Logging authorized at 1.35 percent annually.
1975		Logging authorized at 1.8 percent annually.
1978		Logging authorized at 2.3 percent annually.
1980s		Further boost in annual logging rate; level unspecified.
1993–5		Remaining parcels of unlogged land sold off.

Appendix

CHRONOLOGY OF EVENTS IN SARAWAK

Year	Control of License Allocation	Forest Dweller Rights
1953	Conservator gains sole authority to issue licenses.	
1960	Conservator reduces harvesting to protect swamp forests.	
1962	Conservator freezes issuance of new licenses.	
1964	Conservator's authority transferred to forests minister; applicants may appeal to conservator.	
1965		Government rejects land bills that would recognize native customary rights.
1966–9	Cabinet members struggle over forestry portfolio.	
1969–70	Emergency government freezes license allocation.	
1971–3	Sarawak Foundation and STIDC begin to take over Forest Department functions.	
1974		Land Code amended to make it easier to extinguish native claims.
1979	Forest Ordinance amended to allow "arbitrary" decisions, and remove applicant's right of appeal.	Penalties raised for unauthorized activities in loggable forest.
1980		Communal forests reduced from 30,300 to 5,400 ha.
mid-1980s		Native protests and blockades.
1987		Government criminalizes blockades; cracks down onprotests.

CHRONOLOGY OF EVENTS IN INDONESIA

Year	Control of License Allocation	Forest Dweller Rights
1957	Regional officials allocate licenses, control almost all forest areas.	
1960		*Adat* rights recognized.
1964	Sukarno appoints Sudjarwo Minister of Forestry.	
1966	Suharto names Sudjarwo Director-General of Forestry.	
1967	Forestry Department can issue large licenses; regional officials still issue smaller licenses. Director General can nominate partners for foreign investors.	*Adat* rights curtailed to facilitate logging.
1970	Forestry Department gains control of all license allocation; *banjir kap* logging banned.	
1971		Loggers gain precedence over *adat* when they conflict.
1978–9	Oil shock	
1880–1	Government begins to phase out raw log exports; military and foreign firms leave, Chinese firms take over.	

References

Abramovitz, Janet N. (1991), *Investing in Biological Diversity: U.S. Research and Conservation Efforts in Developing Countries.* Washington, D.C.: World Resources Institute.

Ahern, George P. (1901), "Special Report of Captain George P. Ahern, Ninth U.S. Infantry, in charge of Forestry Bureau, Philippine Islands, covering the period from April 1900 to July 30, 1901." Washington, D.C.: Division of Insular Affairs, War Department.

Aiken, S. Robert and Colin H. Leigh (1992), *Vanishing Rain Forests: The Ecological Transition in Malaysia.* Oxford: Clarendon Press.

Amanin, Eugen (1971), "Notes on the Development of Forest Industries in Sarawak with Particular Reference to Industrial Incentive and National Profit," *Malayan Forester* 34, 6–19.

American Embassy Jakarta (1980), "The Timbering and Wood-Processing Industries of Indonesia," U.S. Department of State Airgram, April 11, 1980.

Ames, Barry (1987), *Political Survival: Politicians and Public Policy in Latin America.* Berkeley: University of California Press.

Angelsen, Arild and David Kaimowitz (1999), "Rethinking the Causes of Deforestation: Lessons from Economic Models," *The World Bank Research Observer* 14 (1, February), 73–98.

Appelbaum, Elie and Eliakim Katz (1987), "Seeking Rents by Setting Rents: The Political Economy of Rent Seeking," *The Economic Journal* 97 (September), 685–99.

Aquino, Belinda A. (1987), *Politics of Plunder: The Philippines Under Marcos.* Quezon City: Great Books Trading and University of the Philippines College of Public Administration.

Ascher, William (1998), "From Oil to Timber: The Political Economy of Off-Budget Financing in Indonesia," *Indonesia* 65 (April), 37–61.

(1999), *Why Governments Waste Natural Resources: Policy Failures in Developing Countries.* Baltimore, Md.: Johns Hopkins University Press.

Ascher, William and Robert Healy (1990), *Natural Resource Policymaking in Developing Countries.* Durham, N.C.: Duke University Press.

Asiaweek (1993), "Logger's Lament," *Asiaweek* (28 April), 48–50.

(1994a), "Sailing Against the Wind," *Asiaweek* (9 March), 22–6.

(1994b), "End of an Era," *Asiaweek* (30 March), 24–31.

Auty, Richard M. (1990), *Resource-Based Industrialization: Sowing the Oil in Eight Developing Countries*. Oxford: Claredon Press.

(1991), "Mismanaged Mineral Dependence: Zambia 1970–1990," *Resources Policy* (September), 170–83.

(1993), *Sustaining Development in the Mineral Economies: The Resource Curse Thesis*. London: Routledge.

Awang, Yahya (1994), "Forestry in Sabah: Brief," *Jabatan Perhutanan* Sabah.

Axelrod, Robert (1984), *The Evolution of Cooperation*. New York: Basic Books.

Baird, David R. (1987), "The Forestry Sector of Malaysia," Desk Study, Canadian International Development Agency, May 1987.

Baker, M. H. (1965), *Sabah: The First Ten Years as a Colony, 1946–1956. Singapore Studies on Malaysia*, Number One. Singapore: Malaysia Publishing House Ltd.

Baldwin, Robert E. (1966), *Economic Development and Export Growth: A Study of Northern Rhodesia, 1920–1960*. Berkeley: University of California Press.

Baran, Paul A. (1952), "On the Political Economy of Backwardness," *Manchester School of Economics and Social Studies* 20 (January), 66–84.

Barber, Charles Victor (1989), "The State, the Environment, and Development: The Genesis and Transformation of Social Forestry Policy in New Order Indonesia," unpublished Ph.D. Dissertation, University of California, Berkeley.

Barber, Charles Victor, Nels C. Johnson, and Emmy Hafild (1994), *Breaking the Logjam: Obstacles to Forest Policy Reform in Indonesia and the United States*. Washington, D.C.: World Resources Institute.

Barr, Christopher (1998), "Bob Hasan, the Rise of Apkindo, and the Shifting Dynamics of Control in Indonesia's Timber Sector," *Indonesia* 65 (April), 1–36.

Bates, Robert H. (1981), *Markets and States in Tropical Africa*. Berkeley: University of California Press.

Bautista, Germelino M. (1992), "The Forestry Revenue System in The Philippines: Its Concept and History," Natural Resources Management Program Policy Studies, Report 92-20, prepared by Louis Berger International, Inc., Manila, October 1992.

Beblawi, Hazem and Giacomo Luciani, eds. (1987), *The Rentier State. Nation, State, and Integration in the Arab World*, Giacomo Luciani, ed., Vol. 2, 4 vols. London: Croom Helm.

Bedard, Paul W. (1957), "Developments in Philippine Forestry: A Progress Report," U.S. International Cooperation Administration, March 23.

Bellin, Eva (1994), "The Politics of Profit in Tunisia: Utility of the Rentier Paradigm?" *World Development* 22, 427–36.

Bevan, David, Paul Collier, and Jan Willem Gunning (1993), "Trade Shocks in Developing Countries," *European Economic Review* 37, 557–65.

Beversluis, A. J. (1929), "'Het Wezen' van het Boschwezen in de Buitengewesten," *Tectona* XXII, 452–64.

References

Bhagwati, Jagdish N. (1982), "Directly Unproductive, Profit-seeking (DUP) Activities," *Journal of Political Economy* 90 (5), 988–1002.

Bhagwati, Jagdish and T. N. Srinivasan (1980), "Revenue Seeking: A Generalization of the Theory of Tariffs," *Journal of Political Economy* 88 (December), 1069–87.

Bhargava, S. K. and Domingo Chai Nai Ping (1988), "An Appraisal of Forest Management in Sabah," Development of Forest Sector Planning, FO: DP/MAL/85/004, Field Document 13, UN Food and Agriculture Organization, Rome.

Bilsborrow, Richard and Martha Geores (1994), "Population, land-use and the environment in developing countries: what can we learn from cross-national data?," in *The Causes of Tropical Deforestation: The economic and statistical analysis of factors giving rise to the loss of the tropical forests*, eds. Katrina Brown and David W. Pearce. Vancouver: UBC Press, 106–33.

Bleaney, Michael and David Greenaway (1993), "Long-Run Trends in the Relative Price of Primary Commodities and in the Terms of Trade of Developing Countries," *Oxford Economic Papers* 45, 349–63.

Blomqvist, Ake and Sharif Mohammad (1986), "Controls, Corruption, and Competitive Rent-Seeking in LDCs," *Journal of Development Economics* 21, 161–80.

Boado, Eufresina L. (1988), "Incentive policies and forest use in the Philippines," in *Public policies and the misuse of forest resources*, eds. Robert Repetto and Malcolm Gillis. Cambridge: Cambridge University Press, 165–204.

Bodin, Jean (1967 [1606]), *Six Books of a Commonwealth*. ed. and trans. M. J. Tooley. New York: Barnes and Noble.

Boomgaard, Peter (1992), "Forest Management and Exploitation in Colonial Java, 1677–1897," *Forest and Conservation History* 36, 4–14.

Boyce, James K. (1993), *The Philippines: The Political Economy of Growth and Impoverishment in the Marcos Era*. London: OECD Development Centre and Macmillan Press.

Bresnan, John (1993), *Managing Indonesia: The Modern Political Economy*. New York: Columbia University Press.

Broad, Robin (1995), "The Political Economy of Natural Resources: Case Studies of the Indonesian and Philippine Forest Sectors," *The Journal of Developing Areas* 29 (April), 317–40.

Broad, Robin and John Cavanagh (1993), *Plundering Paradise: The Struggle for the Environment in The Philippines*. Berkeley: University of California Press.

Browne, F. G. (1954), "Regional Notes: Sarawak," *Malayan Forester* 17, 32–5.

Bryant, Dirk, Daniel Nielsen, and Laura Tangley (1997), *The Last Forest Frontiers: Ecosystems and Economies on the Edge*. Washington, D.C.: World Resources Institute.

Buchanan, James (1980), "Rent Seeking and Profit Seeking," in *Toward a Theory of the Rent-Seeking Society*, eds. James Buchanan, Robert Tollison, and Gordon Tullock. College Station: Texas A & M University Press, 3–15.

Buchanan, James, Robert Tollison, and Gordon Tullock (1980), *Toward a Theory of the Rent-Seeking Society*. College Station: Texas A & M University Press.

References

Bureau of Forestry (1950), *Forestry Golden Book (supplement)*. Manila: Bureau of Forestry (Philippines).

Business Times (1993), "Timber Rights: S'wak Not Included," *Business Times* (6 February).

Callister, Debra J. (1992), *Illegal Tropical Timber Trade: Asia-Pacific*. Cambridge (England): TRAFFIC International.

Campbell, Bill, ed. (1986), *Sabah Under Harris*. Kuala Lumpur: Penerbit Warisan.

Capricorn Indonesia Consult (1990), *A Study on the Top 50 National Private Business Groups*. Jakarta: P.T. Capricorn Indonesia Consult Inc.

   (1994), *Company Profile of Woodbased Industry in Indonesia 1994*. Jakarta: P.T. Capricorn Indonesia Consult Inc.

Cardoso, Fernando Henrique and Enzo Faletto (1979), *Dependency and Development in Latin America*. Berkeley: University of California Press.

Cashin, Paul, Hong Liang, and C. John McDermott (1999), "How Persistent Are Shocks to World Commodity Prices?" IMF Working Paper 99/80.

Castilleja, Guillermo (1990), "Reducing the Annual Timber Harvest in Sarawak: How Much?" National Wildlife Federation, October 15, 1990.

Chai, Domingo Nai Ping and Yahya Awang (1989), "Current Forest Resource Scenario in Sabah," in *Opportunities and Incentives for Wood Processing in Sabah*, ed. Ti Teow Chuan, Proceedings of a seminar organized by Timber Association of Sabah held at Kota Kinabalu, 22–3 August, 1989, Kota Kinabalu: Timber Association of Sabah, 17–35.

Chai, Leo (1979), "Forest Resource Base, Policy and Legislation of Sarawak," *Malaysian Forester* 42 (4), 311–27.

Chaudhry, Kiren Aziz (1994), "Economic Liberalization and the Lineages of the Rentier State," *Comparative Politics* 27 (October), 1–25.

Chen, Agnes (1994), "Aokam-CASH Contest for Sabah's Forest Concessions Likely to End in a Draw," *Business Times* (16 August), 19.

Chew, Daniel (1990), *Chinese Pioneers on the Sarawak Frontier, 1841–1941*. Singapore: Oxford University Press.

Chin, James (1994), "The Sabah State Election of 1994," *Asian Survey* 34 (10, October), 906–15.

Chin, Ung-Ho (1996), *Chinese Politics in Sarawak: A Study of the Sarawak United People's Party*. Kuala Lumpur: Oxford University Press.

Clad, James and Marites D. Vitug (1988), "The Politics of Plunder," *Far Eastern Economic Review* (24 November), 48–50.

Coase, Ronald H. (1960), "The Problem of Social Cost," *Journal of Law and Economics* 3, 1–44.

Coats, Robert (1971), "Indonesian Timber," *Pacific Research* (May), 9–16.

Colander, David C., ed. (1984), *Neoclassical Political Economy: The Analysis of Rent-Seeking and DUP Activities*. Cambridge, Mass.: Ballinger Publishing Company.

Colchester, Marcus (1989), *Pirates, Squatters, and Poachers: The Political Ecology of Dispossession of the Native Peoples of Sarawak*. London: Survival International.

References

Collier, David (1993), "The Comparative Method," in *Political Science: The State of the Discipline*, 2nd ed., ed. Ada Finifter, Washington, D.C.: APSA, 105–19.

(1998), "Comparative Method in the 1990s," *APSA-CP* 9, 1–5.

Collier, Paul and Jan Willem Gunning, eds. (1999), *Trade Shocks in Developing Countries*. New York: Oxford University Press.

Colonial Office (1963), "Sarawak, Report for the Year 1962," Her Majesty's Stationery Office, London, 1963.

Corden, W. M. and P. J. Neary (1982), "Booming Sector and Deindustrialization in a Small Open Economy," *The Economic Journal* 92, 825–48.

Cribb, Robert (1988), "Conservation Policy and Politics in Indonesia," in *Changing Tropical Forests: Historical Perspectives on Today's Challenges in Asia, Australasia, and Oceania*, eds. John Dargavel, Kay Dixon, and Noel Semple, Canberra, Australia: Centre for Resource and Environmental Studies, Australia National University, 341–55.

Crouch, Harold (1978), *The Army and Politics in Indonesia*. Ithaca, N.Y.: Cornell University Press.

(1979), "Patrimonialism and Military Rule in Indonesia," *World Politics* 31 (4, July), 571–87.

Cuddington, John (1989), "Commodity Export Booms in Developing Countries," *The World Bank Research Observer* 4 (2, July), 143–65.

Cuddington, John T. (1992), "Long Run Trends in 26 Primary Commodity Prices: A Disaggregated Look at the Prebisch-Singer Hypothesis," *Journal of Development Economics* 39, 207–27.

Daily Mirror (1959), "Forest Ills Cure Eyed," *Daily Mirror* (1 December).

(1961), "Expert Bares Alarming Situation of PI Forests," *Daily Mirror* (23 March).

(1967), "Solons Act to Curtial Powers of Forest Chief," *Daily Mirror* (21 March).

(1969a), "Forestry Issues 969 Minor Products Licenses," *Daily Mirror* (16 October).

(1969b), "FM After Rich Logger-Solons," *Daily Mirror* (25 November).

Dauvergne, Peter (1997), *Shadows in the Forest: Japan and the Politics of Timber in Southeast Asia*. Cambridge, Mass.: MIT Press.

Davies, Derek and George Lauriat (1980), "Spicing Up Sabah's Recipe," *Far Eastern Economic Review* (18 July), 24–7.

Davis, Jeffrey M. (1983), "The Economic Effects of Windfall Gains in Export Earnings, 1975-1978," *World Development* 11, 119–39.

Deacon, Robert T. (1995), "Assessing the Relationship between Government Policy and Deforestation," *Journal of Environmental Economics and Management* 28, 1–18.

Deaton, Angus (1999), "Commodity Prices and Growth in Africa," *Journal of Economic Perspectives* 13 (3, Summer), 23–40.

DiLorenzo, Thomas J. (1988), "Property Rights, Information Costs, and the Economics of Rent-Seeking," *Journal of Institutional and Theoretical Economics* 144, 318–32.

Dion, Douglas (1998), "Evidence and Inference in the Comparative Case Study," *Comparative Politics* 30 (2, January), 127–45.

References

Djamaludin, Suryohadikusomo (1991), "The Implementation of Indonesian Selective Cutting and Replanting (TPTI) Silviculture System for Timber Improvement in the Logged-over Areas," in *Fourth Round-Table Conference on Dipterocarps*, ed. BIOTROP. Bogor, Indonesia: Southeast Asian Regional Centre for Tropical Biology, 95–110.

Dogan, Mattei (1994), "Limits to Quantification in Comparative Politics: The Gap between Substance and Method," in *Comparing Nations: Concepts, Strategies, Substance*, eds. Mattei Dogan and Ali Kazancigil. Cambridge, Mass.: Blackwell, 35–71.

Dougan, W. R. and J. M. Snyder (1993), "Are Rents Fully Dissipated?" *Public Choice* 58, 793–814.

Easterly, William (1991), "Economic Policy and Economic Growth," *Finance and Development* (September), 10–13.

Egerton, J. O. (1953), "Notes on Logging in The Philippines," *Malayan Forester* 16, 146–56.

Emmerson, Donald K. (1983), "Understanding the New Order: Bureaucratic Pluralism in Indonesia," *Asian Survey* XXIII (11, November), 1220–41.

Evans, Peter (1979), *Dependent Development: The Alliance of Multinational, State, and Local Capital in Brazil*. Princeton, N.J.: Princeton University Press.

Far Eastern Economic Review (1967), "Central Threats," *Far Eastern Economic Review* (29 June), 713–15.

Fernandez, Segundo P. (1960), "Codification of the Forest Laws of The Philippines," *The Philippine Lumberman* (December–January), 36–55.

Food and Agriculture Organization (1972), "A Development Strategy for the Hill Dipterocarp Forests of Sarawak," Forest Industries Development, Malaysia, FO: SF/MAL/68/516, Working Paper 12.

(1976), "Forest Resources in the Asia and Far East Region," Rome.

(1980), "The Coordination and Development of Forestry and Forest Industries in Sarawak," Forestry Development Project Sarawak, FO:MAL/76/008, Field Document No. 1, Kuching July 1980. Based on the work of P.M. South and Moore.

(1982), "Project Findings and Recommendations," Forestry Development, Sarawak, FO: DP/MAL/76/008, Terminal Report.

(1992), "Project Findings and Recommendations," Development of Forest Sector Planning, FO: DP/MAL/85/004, Terminal Report, UN Food and Agriculture Organization, Rome.

(Various), *Forest Products*. Rome: Food and Agriculture Organization of the United Nations.

Forest Department Sarawak

(1970), *Annual Report of the Forest Department Sarawak*. Kuching: Forest Department Sarawak.

(1981), "Progress on Forestry, 1976–1980," Report presented at the Asia-Pacific Forestry Commission, Eleventh Session, 6–10 April 1981, Suva, Fiji.

(Various), *Annual Report of the Forest Department Sarawak*. Kuching: Forest Department Sarawak.

Foresters' Conference (1947), "Proceedings of the First Postwar Foresters' Conference," *The Philippine Journal of Forestry* 5, 203–50.

Fyfe, A. J. (1964), "Forestry in Sabah," *Malayan Forester* 27, 82–95.

Gane, M. (1987), "Sector Analysis/Problem Identification," Development of Forest Sector Planning, FAO Field Document 9, FAO: UP/MAL/85/004, UN Food and Agriculture Organization, Rome.

Gelb, Alan and Jorge Marshall-Silva (1988), "Ecuador: Windfalls of a New Exporter," in *Oil Windfalls: Blessing or Curse?*, ed. A. Gelb and Associates. New York: Oxford University Press, 170–96.

Gelb, Alan and Associates (1988), *Oil Windfalls: Blessing or Curse?* New York: Oxford University Press.

Ghazali, Fadzil (1992), "KL May Eco-label Austrian Products," *Business Times* (6 October).

Gilbert, Christopher L. (1996), "International Commodity Agreements: An Obituary Notice," *World Development* 24, 1–19.

Gill, Tom (1959), "Diagnosis of Forestry Problems," *The Philippine Lumberman* (October–November), 5–10.

Gillis, Malcolm (1987), "Multinational Enterprises and Environmental and Resource Management Issues in the Indonesian Tropical Forest Sector," in *Multinational Corporations, Environment, and the Third World: Business Matters*, ed. Charles S. Pearson. Durham, N.C.: Duke University Press, 64–89.

——— (1988a), "Indonesia: Public Policies, Resource Management, and the Tropical Forest," in *Public policies and the misuse of forest resources*, eds. Robert Repetto and Malcolm Gillis. New York: Cambridge University Press, 43–114.

——— (1988b), "Malaysia: Public Policies and the Tropical Forest," in *Public Policies and the Misuse of Forest Resources*, eds. Robert Repetto and Malcolm Gillis. New York: Cambridge University Press, 115–64.

Golay, Frank H. (1961), *The Philippines: Public Policy and National Economic Development*. Ithaca, N.Y.: Cornell University Press.

Gomez, Edmund Terence and Jomo K. S. (1997), *Malaysia's Political Economy: Politics, Patronage, and Profits*. New York: Cambridge University Press.

Gooch, Winslow L. (1953), "Forest Industries of the Philippines," A Cooperative Project of The Bureau of Forestry, The Department of Agriculture and Natural Resources, The Philippine Council for United States Aid, and the United States Mutual Security Agency; Manila, May 1953.

Government of Sabah (various), "Annual Bulletin of Statistics, Sabah," Kota Kinabalu.

Grant, J. S. (1958), "The Aborigines of Sarawak," *Malayan Forester* 21, 245–50.

Gray, John A. and Soestrisno Hadi (1990), "Fiscal Policies and Pricing in Indonesian Forestry," U.N. Food and Agriculture Organization, UTF/INS/065/INS/: Forestry Studies, Field Document No. VI-3.

Gray, L. C. (1914), "Rent under the Assumptions of Exhaustibility," *The Quarterly Journal of Economics* 28, 466–89.

Greif, Avner, Paul Milgrom, and Barry Weingast (1994), "Coordination, Commitment, and Enforcement: The Case of the Merchant Guild," *Journal of Political Economy* 102 (4, August).

Grilli, Enzo R. and Maw Cheng Yang (1988), "Primary Commodity Prices, Manufactured Goods Prices, and the Terms of Trade of Developing Countries:

What the Long Run Shows," *The World Bank Economic Review* 2 (1), 1–47.

Grossman, Rachel and Lenny Siegel (1977), "Weyerhaeuser in Indonesia," *Pacific Research* IX (November–December), 1–12.

Grut, Mikael, John A. Gray, and Nicolas Egli (1991), *Forest Pricing and Concession Policies: Managing the High Forests of West and Central Africa. Africa Technical Department Series*. World Bank Technical Paper Number 143. Washington, D.C: World Bank.

Gunder Frank, Andre (1966), "The Development of Underdevelopment," *Monthly Review* (September), 17–31.

Guntur, Md Taufan B. (1990), *The Harris Mahatir Gang*. Hong Kong: Rafflesia Enterprises, Pte., Ltd.

Hadi, Yusuf (1985), "Future Log Production from the Forests of Sabah, Malaysia," Occasional Paper No. 1, Faculty of Forestry, Universiti Pertanian Malaysia, Serdang, Selangor, Malaysia, February 1985.

Hani Ahmad (1991), "'Cut and Run' Logging Fast Depleting Virgin Forest," *Sunday Mail (Sabah)* (7 July).

Hartwick, J. M. (1977), *American Economic Review* 67, 972–4.

Hassan, Kalimullah (1995), "Anwar Sought Cancellation of Dad's Timber Concession," *The Straits Times*, 10.

Haughton, Jonathan, Darius Teter, and Joseph Stern (1992), "Report on Forestry Taxation," Private Memorandum, September 8, 1992.

Hawes, Gary (1992), "Marcos, His Cronies, and the Philippines's Failure to Develop," in *Southeast Asian Capitalists*, ed. Ruth McVey. Ithaca, N.Y.: Cornell Southeast Asia Program, 145–60.

Hedlin Menzies and Associates Ltd. (1972), "Sabah Forest Development Study: Phase III – Economic Evaluation," Prepared for the Canadian International Development Agency, Vancouver.

Hicks, George L. and Geoffrey McNicoll (1971), *Trade and Growth in the Philippines: An Open Dual Economy*. Ithaca, N.Y.: Cornell University Press.

Hill, Catherine (1991), "Managing Commodity Booms in Botswana," *World Development* 19, 1185–96.

Hillman, Arye L. and Dov Samet (1987), "Dissipation of Contestable Rents by Small Numbers of Contenders," *Public Choice* 54, 63–82.

Hirschman, Albert O. (1958), *The Strategy of Economic Development*. New Haven: Yale University Press.

(1977), "A Generalized Linkage Approach to Development, with Special Reference to Staples," *Economic Development and Cultural Change* 22 (Suppl.), 67–98.

Hong, Evelyne (1987), *Natives of Sarawak: Survival in Borneo's Vanishing Forests*. Penang, Malaysia: Institut Masyarakat.

Hotelling, Harold (1931), "The Economics of Exhaustible Resources," *Journal of Political Economy* 39 (2 April), 137–75.

Hunt, Shane J. (1985), "Growth and Guano in Nineteenth-Century Peru," in *The Latin American Economies*, eds. Roberto Cortes Conde and Shane J. Hunt. New York: Holmes and Meier, 255–318.

Hunter, Ed (1976), *Misdeeds of Tun Mustapha*. Hong Kong: Ed Hunter Enterprises.

Hurst, Philip (1990), *Rainforest Politics: Ecological Destruction in Southeast Asia*. London: Zed Books.

Innis, Harold A. (1956), *Essays in Canadian Economic History*. Toronto: University of Toronto Press.

Institute of Social Analysis (INSAN), ed. (1989), *Logging Against the Natives of Sarawak*. Petaling Jaya, Malaysia: Institute of Social Analysis.

Jackson, Karl D. (1978), "Bureaucratic Polity: A Theoretical Framework for the Analysis of Power and Communications in Indonesia," in *Political Power and Communications in Indonesia*, eds. Karl D. Jackson and Lucian W. Pye. Berkeley: University of California Press, 3–22.

Jakarta Post (1994), "IPTN gets interest-free loan from forestry funds," *Jakarta Post* (5 July), 1.

Japan Tropical Forest Action Network (1992), "Japan's Role in the Commercial Exploitation of Indonesian Forests for Timber," Presented at the Eighth International NGO Conference on Indonesia, Yokohama and Odawara, Japan, March 20–2, 1992.

Jenkins, David (1980), "The Military's Secret Cache," *Far Eastern Economic Review* (8 February), 70–2.

John, David W. (1974), "The Timber Industry and Forest Administration in Sabah Under Chartered Company Rule," *Journal of Southeast Asian Studies* 5, 55–81.

Johnson, Nels and Bruce Cabarle (1993), *Surviving the Cut: Natural Forest Management in the Humid Tropics*. Washington, D.C.: World Resources Institute.

Jomo Kwame Sundaram (1989), "The Pillage of Sarawak's Forests," in *Logging Against the Natives of Sarawak*, ed. Institute of Social Analysis. Petaling Jaya, Malaysia: INSAN, 1–30.

Jowett, B. (1892), *The Dialogues of Plato*. New York: Oxford University Press.

Kahin, Audrey R. (1992), "Crisis on the Periphery: The Rift Between Kuala Lumpur and Sabah," *Pacific Affairs* 65 (1, Spring), 30–49.

Karl, Terry Lynn (1997), *The Paradox of Plenty: Oil Booms and Petro-States*. Berkeley: University of California Press.

Kavanagh, Mikaail, Abdullah Abdul Rahim, and Christopher J. Hails (1989), "Rainforest Conservation in Sarawak: An International Policy for WWF," WWF Malaysia, November 1989.

King, Dwight Y. (1982), *Interest Groups and Political Linkage in Indonesia 1800–1965. Center for Southeast Asian Studies*, Special Report. No. 20. DeKalb: Northern Illinois University.

Klitgaard, Robert (1988), *Controlling Corruption*. Berkeley: University of California Press.

Knight, Jack (1992), *Institutions and Social Conflict*. New York: Cambridge University Press.

Knudsen, Odin and Andrew Parnes (1975), *Trade Instability and Economic Development*. Lexington, Mass.: Lexington Books.

References

Koehler, K. G. (1972), "Wood Processing in East Kalimantan: A Case Study of Industrialization and Foreign Investment in Indonesia," *Bulletin of Indonesian Economic Studies* VIII, 93–129.

Krause, Lawrence B. (1995), "Social Capability and Long-Term Economic Growth," in *Social Capability and Long-Term Economic Growth*, eds. Bon Ho Koo and Dwight H. Perkins. New York: St. Martin's Press, 310–27.

Krueger, Anne O. (1974), "The Political Economy of the Rent-Seeking Society," *American Economic Review* 64, 291–303.

Krugman, Paul (1987), "The Narrow Moving Band, the Dutch Disease, and the Competitive Consequences of Mrs. Thatcher: Notes on Trade in the Presence of Dynamic Scale Economies," *Journal of Development Economics* 27, 41–55.

Kummer, David M. (1992), *Deforestation in the Postwar Philippines*. Chicago: University of Chicago Press.

(1995), "The Political Use of Philippine Forestry Statistics in the Postwar Period," *Crime, Law, and Social Change* 22, 163–80.

Kurer, Oskar (1993), "Clientelism, Corruption, and the Allocation of Resources," *Public Choice* 77, 259–73.

Kuswata, Kartawinata (1980), "East Kalimantan: A Comment," *Bulletin of Indonesian Economic Studies* 16, 120–1.

Laitin, David D., James A. Caporaso, David Collier, Ronald Rogowski, Sidney Tarrow, Gary King, Robert O. Keohane, and Sidney Verba (1995), "Review Symposium: The Qualitative-Quantitative Disputation," *American Political Science Review* 89 (2), 454–81.

Lal, Deepak and Hla Myint (1996), *The Political Economy of Poverty, Equity, and Growth: A Comparative Study*. New York: Oxford University Press.

Landé, Carl (1965), *Leaders, Factions, and Parties: The Structure of Philippine Politics*. New Haven, Conn.: Southeast Asia Studies, Monograph Series No. 6, Yale University.

Landgrebe, J. G. (1966), "The Philippine Textile and Timber Trades," *The Philippine Economic Journal* 1, 146–61.

Lauriat, George and Guy Sacerdoti (1977), "Processing Drive Lags," *Far Eastern Economic Review* (2 December), 64–6.

Laver, Michael and Kenneth Shepsle, eds. (1994), *Cabinet Ministers and Parliamentary Government*. New York: Cambridge University Press.

Lee, D. (1985), "Marginal Lobbying Cost and the Optimal Amount of Rent-Seeking," *Public Choice* 45, 206–13.

Lee, Edwin (1976), *The Towkays of Sabah: Chinese Leadership and Indigenous Challenge in the Last Phase of British Rule*. Singapore: Singapore University Press.

Lee, H. S. (1982), "The Development of Silvicultural Systems in the Hill Forests of Malaysia," *Malaysian Forester* 45 (1), 1–9.

Leigh, Michael (1974), *The Rising Moon: Political Change in Sarawak*. Sydney: Sydney University Press.

(1988), "The Spread of Foochow Commercial Power Before the New Economic Policy," in *Development in Sarawak: Historical and Contemporary Perspectives*, eds. R. A. Cramb and R. H. W. Reece, *Monash Paper on*

Southeast Asia, No. 17. Melbourne: Centre of Southeast Asian Studies, Monash University, 179–90.

———(1991), "Money Politics and Dayak Nationalism: The 1987 Sarawak State Election," in *Images of Malaysia*, eds. Muhammad Ikmal Said and Johan Saravanamuttu. Kuala Lumpur: Persatuan Sains Sosial Malaysia. 180–202.

Lele, Uma and Robert E. Christiansen (1989), "Markets, Marketing Boards, and Cooperatives in Africa: Issues in Adjustment Policy," MADIA Discussion Paper 11, The World Bank, Washington, D.C.

Levi, Margaret (1988), *Of Rule and Revenue*. Berkeley: University of California Press.

Levin, Jonathan V. (1960), *The Export Economies: Their Pattern of Development in Historical Perspective*. Cambridge, Mass.: Harvard University Press.

Lewis, Jr., Stephen R. (1984), "Development Problems of the Mineral-Rich Countries," in *Economic Structure and Performance*, eds. Moshe Syrquin, Lance Taylor, and Larry E. Westphal. New York: Academic Press, 157–77.

———(1989), "Primary Exporting Countries," in *Handbook of Development Economics*, eds. Hollis Chenery and T. N. Srinivasan. New York: Elsevier Science Publishers, 1541–99.

Lian, Francis Jana (1989), "The Timber Industry and Economic Development in Sarawak: Some Contemporary Trends and Proposals for 1990 and Beyond," in *Socio-Economic Development in Sarawak: Policies and Strategies for the 1990s*, eds. Abdul Majid Mat Salleh, Hatta Solhee, and Mohd Yusof Kasim. Kuching, Sarawak: Angkatan Zaman Mansang (AZAM), 118–37.

Libecap, Gary D. (1989), *Contracting for Property Rights*. New York: Cambridge University Press.

Liddle, R. William (1985), "Soeharto's Indonesia: Personal Rule and Political Institutions," *Pacific Affairs* 58 (1, Spring).

Lim, David (1988), "Export Instability and Economic Growth in Resource-Rich Countries," in *Economic Development Policies in Resource-Rich Countries*, eds. Miguel Urrutia and Setsuko Yukawa. Tokyo: United Nations University, 66–89.

Little, I. M. D., Richard N. Cooper, W. Max Corden, and Sarath Rajapatirana (1993), *Boom, Crisis, and Adjustment: The Macroeconomic Experience of Developing Countries*. New York: Oxford University Press.

Liwag, Juan R. (1963), "The Constitutional Prohibition to Own Forest Concession," *The Philippine Lumberman* (December–January), 46–7.

London Environmental Economics Centre (1993), "The Economic Linkages Between the International Trade in Tropical Timber and the Sustainable Management of Tropical Forests," Main Report to the International Tropical Timber Organization; ITTO Activity PCM (XI)/4.

MacBean, Alasdair I. (1966), *Export Instability and Economic Development*. London: George Allen and Unwin Ltd.

Machiavelli, Niccolo (1979 [1531]), "Discourses on the First Ten Books of Titus Livius," in *The Portable Machiavelli*, eds. Peter Bondanella and Mark Musa. New York: Penguin, 167–418.

MacIntyre, Andrew (1990), *Business and Politics in Indonesia*. North Sydney, Australia: Allen and Unwin.

References

Mackie, J. A. C. (1970), "The Report of the Commission of Four on Corruption," *Bulletin of Indonesian Economic Studies* VI, 87–101.

——— (1990), "Property and Power in Indonesia," in *The Politics of Middle Class Indonesia*, eds. Richard Tanter and Kenneth Young, Monash Paper on Southeast Asia, No. 19. Clayton, Australia: Centre of Southeast Asian Studies, 71–121.

Magenda, Burhan (1991), *East Kalimantan: The Decline of a Commercial Aristocracy. Monograph Series Publication*, No. 70. Ithaca, N.Y.: Cornell Modern Indonesian Project.

Mahdavy, Hussein (1970), "The Patterns and Problems of Economic Development in Rentier States: The Case of Iran," in *Studies in Economic History of the Middle East*, ed. M. A. Cook. London: Oxford University Press, 428–67.

Malaya (1986), "MNR Runs After Seven Logging Firms," *Malaya* (5 March), 2.

Malley, M. (1990), "Soedjono Hoemardani: A Political Biography," unpublished M.A. Thesis, Cornell University.

Manapat, Ricardo (1991), *Some Are Smarter Than Others: The History of Marcos' Crony Capitalism*. New York: Aletheia Publications.

Manila Times (1961), "Log Producers Form Group," *Manila Times* (21 May).

——— (1962), "Forestry campaign stressed," *Manila Times* (16 January).

——— (1965), "Illegal Logging Drive Pressed; Politicians Blamed for Violations," *Manila Times* (14 February).

——— (1971), "Woodmen Concerned over CC Proposals," *Manila Times* (2 May).

Mañalac, Gaudencio S. (1956), "The State of the Philippine Lumber Industry," *The Philippine Lumberman* (June–July), 6–27.

Manning, Chris (1971), "The Timber Boom, With Special Reference to East Kalimantan," *Bulletin of Indonesian Economic Studies* VIII, 30–60.

March, James G. and Johan P. Olsen (1984), "The New Institutionalism: Organizational Factors in Political Life," *American Political Science Review* 78, 734–49.

Marcos, Ferdinand E. (1968), "Extemporaneous Remarks Before Regional Directors and District Foresters, Malacañang Heroes Hall, May 24, 1968," *The Philippine Lumberman* (June), 16–24.

McChesney, Fred (1987), "Rent Extraction and Rent Creation in the Economic Theory of Regulation," *Journal of Legal Studies* XVI (January), 101–18.

McCoy, Alfred, ed. (1993), *An Anarchy of Families: State and Family in the Philippines*. Madison, Wisc.: Center for Southeast Asian Studies, University of Wisconsin.

Means, Gordon P. (1976), *Malaysian Politics*, 2nd ed. London: Hodder and Stoughton.

Means, Gordon (1991), *Malaysian Politics: The Second Generation*. Singapore: Oxford University Press.

Mercado, Juan L. (1971), "UN Report Cites RP Forest Grim Future," *Manila Times* (10 September).

Michaels, Robert (1988), "The Design of Rent-seeking Competitions," *Public Choice* 56, 17–29.

Mill, John Stuart (1987 [1848]), *Principles of Political Economy*. Fairfield, N.J.: Augustus M. Kelley Publishers.

Milne, R. S. (1973), "Patrons, Clients, and Ethnicity: The Case of Sarawak and Sabah in Malaysia," *Asian Survey* 13 (10, October), 891–907.

Milne, R. S. and K. J. Ratnam (1974), *Malaysia – New States in a New Nation: Political Development of Sarawak and Sabah in Malaysia*. London: Frank Cass.

Ministry of Primary Industries (Malaysia) (1993), "Statistics on Commodities," Kuala Lumpur.

Mission Established Pursuant to Resolution I (IV) (1990), "The Promotion of Sustainable Forest Management: A Case Study in Sarawak, Malaysia," Report Submitted to the International Tropical Timber Council, ITTC(VIII)/7, 7 May 1990.

Mitra, Pradeep K. (1994), *Adjustment in Oil-Importing Developing Countries*. New York: Cambridge University Press.

Mittermeier, R. A. and T. B. Werner (1990), "Wealth of Plants and Animals Unites 'Megadiversity' Countries," *Tropicus* 4 (1), 1, 4–5.

Mohr, Lawrence B. (1996), *The Causes of Human Behavior: Implications for Theory and Method in the Social Sciences*. Ann Arbor: University of Michigan Press.

Morduch, Jonathan (1995), "Income Smoothing and Consumption Insurance," *Journal of Economic Perspectives* 9 (3, Summer), 103–14.

Mosley, Paul, Jane Harrigan, and John Toye (1991), *Aid and Power: The World Bank and Policy-Based Lending*, Vol. 1. London: Routledge.

Moss, Alan (1972), "Sabah Economic Studies, Phase III: Report of the Forest Policy/Administration Consultant," Prepared for the Canadian International Development Agency.

Munang, Miller (1979), "Forest Resource Base, Policy and Legislation of Sabah," *Malaysian Forester* 42 (4), 286–310.

   (1987), "Deforestation and Logging," in *Environmental Conservation in Sabah: Issues and Strategies*, ed. Sham Sani, Kota Kinabalu (Malaysia): Institute for Development Studies, 31–9.

   (1988), "Forest Conservation in Sabah: Why, How, and for Whom?" Speech at a conference on "The Political Economy of Natural Resources," sponsored by the Institute for Development Studies, Kota Kinabalu, March 12, 1988.

Murphy, K., A. Shleifer, and R. W. Vishny (1989), "Industrialization and the Big Push," *Journal of Political Economy* 97 (5), 1003–26.

Murtedza Mohamed and Ti Teow Chuan (1993), "Managing ASEAN's Forests: Deforestation in Sabah," in *Environmental Management in ASEAN: Perspectives on Critical Regional Issues*, ed. Maria Seda. Singapore: Institute of Southeast Asian Studies, 109–40.

Myers, Norman (1988), "Threatened Biotas: 'Hotspots' in Tropical Forests," *Environmentalist* 8 (3), 1–20.

Nankani, Gobind T. (1980), "Development Problems of Nonfuel Mineral Exporting Countries," *Finance and Development* 17 (January), 6–10.

References

Nantha, Francis C. (1995), "Analysts Hail Foundation's RM350m Timber Deal," *New Straits Times* (17 April), 17.

Neary, J. Peter and Sweder van Wijnbergen, eds. (1986), *Natural Resources and the Macroeconomy*. Cambridge, Mass.: MIT Press.

Nectoux, Francois and Yoichi Kuroda (1990), *Timber from the South Seas: An Analysis of Japan's Tropical Timber Trade and its Environmental Impact*. Gland, Switzerland: WWF International.

Newbery, David M. G. and Joseph E. Stiglitz (1981), *The Theory of Commodity Price Stabilization: A Study in the Economics of Risk*. Oxford: Clarendon Press.

North, Douglass C. (1990), *Institutions, Institutional Change and Economic Performance*. Cambridge: Cambridge University Press.

North, Douglass C. and Robert Paul Thomas (1973), *The Rise of the Western World: A New Economic History*. New York: Cambridge University Press.

Nowak, Thomas C. (1977), "The Philippines before Martial Law: A Study in Politics and Administration," *American Political Science Review* 71, 522–39.

Nowak, Thomas C. and Kay A. Snyder (1974), "Clientelist Politics in the Philippines: Integration or Instability," *American Political Science Review* 68, 1147–70.

Nurske, Ragnar (1958), "Trade Fluctuations and Buffer Policies of Low-Income Countries," *Kyklos* XI, 141–54.

Office of Statistical Coordination and Standards (1968), *Statistical Reporter*. Manila: National Economic Council.

Palmer, Ingrid (1978), *The Indonesian Economy Since 1965: A Case Study of Political Economy*. London: Frank Cass.

Pardo, Richard (1987), "Forestry for Sustainable Development: A Review of Forest Policy in Sabah, Malaysia," Development of Forest Sector Planning, FO: DP/MAL/85/004, Working Paper 2, U.N. Food and Agriculture Organization, Rome.

Parker, Glenn R. (1996), *Congress and the Rent-Seeking Society*. Ann Arbor: University of Michigan Press.

Paul, Chris and Al Wilhite (1994), "Illegal Markets and the Social Costs of Rent-Seeking," *Public Choice* 79, 105–15.

Pearce, Fred (1994), "Are Sarawak's Forests Sustainable?" *New Scientist* 144 (26 November), 28–32.

Peluso, Nancy Lee (1983), "Markets and Merchants: The Forest Products Trade of East Kalimantan in Historical Perspective," unpublished M.S. Thesis, Cornell University, Ithaca, New York.

(1992a), "The Political Ecology of Extraction and Extractive Reserves in East Kalimantan, Indonesia," *Development and Change* 23 (4), 49–74.

(1992b), *Rich Forests, Poor People: Resource Control and Resistance in Java*. Berkeley: University of California Press.

(1993), *The Impact of Social and Environmental Change on Forest Management: A Case Study from West Kalimantan, Indonesia*. Community Forestry Case Study Series. No. 8. Rome: U.N. Food and Agriculture Organization.

222

Persson, Torsten, Gerard Roland, and Guido Tabellini (1997), "Separation of Powers and Political Accountability," *The Quarterly Journal of Economics* (November), 1163–202.

Philippine Lumberman (1956), "Eleven Forest Applications Approved By Ferrer Committee," *The Philippine Lumberman* (February–March), 9.

(1957), "Rampant Violations of Forestry Laws and Malversation of Fees Disclosed by Lumbermen," *The Philippine Lumberman* (December–January), 5.

(1959), "Senator Pelaez Calls For Congressional Action To Stop Forest Destruction," *The Philippine Lumberman* (February–March), 9–12.

(1963), "Lumber-Log Industry Singled Out Among Incorrect Taxpayers," *The Philippine Lumberman* (April–May), 33.

(1968a), "Indonesia Invites Friendly Countries To Develop Forest Resources," *The Philippine Lumberman* (January), 90–1.

(1968b), "Teofilo Santos is New Forestry Director," *The Philippine Lumberman* (February), 4–8.

(1968c), "Congress is After Director Santos; Issues PWR in Bicol National Park," *The Philippine Lumberman* (April), 6–10A.

(1968d), "Where Do RP Firms Abroad Draw Funds?" *The Philippine Lumberman* (September), 45.

(1968e), "RP Wood Industry Fears Japan-Indon Competition," *The Philippine Lumberman* (December), 10.

(1969), "FM Bares Plan to Down Grade Logging As Major Export Industry; Mining Given Added Incentives," *The Philippine Lumberman* (November), 6.

(1971), "B.F. Senior Foresters Protest Appointment of Cortes as Division Chief," *The Philippine Lumberman* (July), 4.

Poore, D., P. Burgess, J. Palmer, S. Rietbergen, and T. Synnott (1989), *No Timber Without Trees: Sustainability in the Tropical Forest*. London: Earthscan Publications.

Porritt, Vernon L. (1997), *British Colonial Rule in Sarawak, 1946–1963*. Kuala Lumpur: Oxford University Press.

Porter, Gareth and Delphin J. Ganapin (1988), *Resources, Population, and the Philippines' Future: A Case Study*. Washington, D.C.: World Resources Institute.

Potter, Lesley (1988), "Indigenes and Colonisers: Dutch Forest Policy in South and East Borneo (Kalimantan), 1900 to 1950," in *Changing Tropical Forests: Historical Perspectives on Today's Challenges in Asia, Australasia, and Oceania*, eds. John Dargavel, Kay Dixon, and Noel Semple. Canberra, Australia: Centre for Resource and Environmental Studies, Australia National University, 127–53.

(1991), "Environmental and Social Aspects of Timber Exploitation in Kalimantan, 1967–1989," in *Indonesia: Resources, Ecology, and Environment*, ed. Joan Hardjono, Singapore: Oxford University Press, 177–211.

(1993), "The Onslaught on the Forests in South-East Asia," in *South-East Asia's Environmental Future: The Search for Sustainability*, eds. Harold Brookfield and Yvonne Byron. Kuala Lumpur: Oxford University Press, 103–28.

References

PT Data Consult Inc. (1993), "Forestry and Wood-Based Industries in Indonesia: Current State and Prospects," Jakarta: PT Data Consult, Inc.

Pura, Raphael (1990), "In Sarawak, a Clash Over Land and Power," *Asian Wall Street Journal* (7 February).

—— (1994), "Once Disdained by Overseas Brethren, Fuzhous Earn Respect for Work Ethic," *Asian Wall Street Journal* (13 June).

Pura, Raphael and Stephen Duthie (1994), "UMNO-Linked Group Hopes to Log Gains in North Borneo Move," *Asian Wall Street Journal* (23 August), 1.

Pura, Raphael, Stephen Duthie, and Richard Borsuk (1994), "Plywood Tycoon May Purchase Malaysian Firm," *Asian Wall Street Journal* (3 February), 1.

Pusat Data Business Indonesia (1988), *Forestry Indonesia: A Profile of Indonesian Forestry Business*. Jakarta: Informasi.

Raffaele, Paul (1986), *Harris Salleh of Sabah*. Hong Kong: Condor Publishing Pty. Co.

Ranis, Gustav and Syed Akhtar Mahmood (1992), *The Political Economy of Development Policy Change*. Cambridge: Blackwell.

Reinhart, Carmen and Peter Wickham (1994), "Commodity Prices: Cyclical Weakness or Secular Decline?" *IMF Staff Papers* 41 (2, June), 175–213.

Repetto, Robert and Malcolm Gillis, eds. (1988), *Public Policies and the Misuse of Forest Resources*. Cambridge: Cambridge University Press.

Reyes, Luis J., Jr. (1955), "Are We Overcutting Our Forests?" *The Philippine Lumberman* (February–March), 5, 33.

Ridler, Neil B. (1988), "The Caisse de Stabilisation in the Coffee Sector of the Ivory Coast," *World Development* 16, 1521–6.

Riker, William H. and Itai Sened (1991), "A Political Theory of the Origin of Property Rights: Airport Slots," *American Journal of Political Science* 35, 951–69.

Robison, Richard (1977), "Capitalism and the Bureaucratic State in Indonesia: 1965–1975," unpublished Ph.D. Dissertation, University of Sydney.

—— (1978), "Towards a Class Analysis of the Indonesian Military Bureaucratic State," *Indonesia* (25, April).

—— (1986), *Indonesia: The Rise of Capital*. Sydney: Allen and Unwin.

—— (1993), "Indonesia: Tensions in State and Regime," in *Southeast Asia in the 1990s: Authoritarianism, Democracy, and Capitalism*, eds. Kevin Hewison, Richard Robison, and Gary Rodan. St. Leonards: Allen and Unwin, 41–74.

Roff, Margaret Clark (1974), *The Politics of Belonging: Political Change in Sabah and Sarawak*. Kuala Lumpur: Oxford University Press.

Rose-Ackerman, Susan (1978), *Corruption: A Study in Political Economy*. New York: Academic Press.

Rosenstein-Rodan, P. (1943), "Problems of Industrialization of Eastern and Southeastern Europe," *The Economic Journal* 53, 202–11.

Ross, Michael L. (1996), "Conditionality and Logging Reform in the Tropics," in *Institutions for Environmental Aid: Pitfalls and Promise*, eds. Robert O. Keohane and Marc Levy. Cambridge, Mass.: MIT Press, 167–97.

—— (1999), "The Political Economy of the Resource Curse," *World Politics* 51 (2, January), 297–322.

References

Ross-Larson, Bruce (1976), *The Politics of Federalism: Syed Kechik in East Malaysia*. Singapore: Bruce Ross-Larson.

Roth, Dennis M. (1983), "Philippine Forests and Forestry: 1565–1920," in *Global Deforestation and the Nineteenth-Century World Economy*, eds. Richard P. Tucker and J. F. Richards. Durham, N.C.: Duke University Press, 30–49.

Rowley, Anthony (1977), "Forests: Save or Squander?" *Far Eastern Economic Review* (2 December), 46–55.

(1990), "Logged Out," *Far Eastern Economic Review* (13 December), 72–4.

Rush, James (1991), *The Last Tree: Reclaiming the Environment in Tropical Asia*. New York: Asia Society, distributed by Westview Press.

Ruzicka, I. (1979), "Rent Appropriation in Indonesian Logging: East Kalimantan 1972/73–1976/77," *Bulletin of Indonesian Economic Studies* XV, 45–74.

Sacerdoti, Guy (1979), "A Shift to Local Leadership," *Far Eastern Economic Review* (7 December), 86.

Sachs, Jeffrey D. and Andrew M. Warner (1995), "Natural Resource Abundance and Economic Growth," *Development Discussion Paper No. 517a*. Cambridge, Mass.: Harvard Institute for International Development.

(1999), "The Big Push, Natural Resource Booms and Growth," *Journal of Development Economics* 59 (1), 43–76.

Salant, Stephen W. (1995), "The Economics of Natural Resource Extraction: A Primer for Development Economists," *The World Bank Research Observer* 10 (1 February), 93–111.

Sanib Said (1985), *Malay Politics in Sarawak, 1946–1966: The Search for Unity and Political Ascendancy*. Singapore: Oxford University Press.

Sarawak Tribune (1987), "Forest Bill Passed after 4-hour Marathon Debate," *Sarawak Tribune* (19 November).

Sartori, Giovanni (1970), "Concept Misformation in Comparative Politics," *American Political Science Review* 64 (4), 1033–53.

Schiff, Maurice and Alberto Valdes (1992), *The Plundering of Agriculture in Developing Countries*. Washington, D.C.: The World Bank.

Schmidt, R. C. (1990), "Tropical Rain Forest Management: A Status Report," in *Rain Forest Regeneration and Management*, eds. A. Gomez-Pompa, T. C. Whitmore, and M. Hadley, *Man and the Biosphere*, ed. J. N. R. Jeffers, Volume 6. Paris: UNESCO and The Parthenon Publishing Group, 181–207.

Schwarz, Adam (1994), *A Nation in Waiting: Indonesia in the 1990s*. Boulder, Col.: Westview Press.

Schwarz, Adam and Jonathan Friedland (1992), "Green Fingers: Indonesia's Prajogo Proves That Money Grows on Trees," *Far Eastern Economic Review* (12 March), 42–6.

Scott, James C. (1972), "Patron-Client Politics and Political Change in Southeast Asia," *American Political Science Review* 66 (1), 91–113.

Searle, Peter (1983), *Politics in Sarawak 1970–1976: The Iban Perspective*. Singapore: Oxford University Press.

Segal, Jeffrey (1983), "A Fragile Philosophy," *Far Eastern Economic Review* (14 April), 54–6.

References

Shafer, D. Michael (1983), "Capturing the Mineral Multinationals: Advantage or Disadvantage?" *International Organization* 37 (1, Winter), 93–119.

——— (1994), *Winners and Losers: How Sectors Shape the Developmental Prospects of States*. Ithaca, N.Y.: Cornell University Press.

Shambayati, Hootan (1994), "The Rentier State, Interest Groups, and the Paradox of Autonomy: State and Business in Turkey and Iran," *Comparative Politics* 26 (3 April), 307–31.

Shin, Yoon Hwan (1989), "Demystifying the Capitalist State: Political Patronage, Bureaucratic Interests, and Capitalists-in-Formation in Soeharto's Indonesia," unpublished Ph.D. Dissertation, Yale University.

Shleifer, Andrei and Robert W. Vishny (1993), "Corruption," *The Quarterly Journal of Economics* (August), 599–617.

Singer, Hans W. (1950), "The Distribution of Gains Between Investing and Borrowing Countries," *American Economic Review* 40, 473–85.

Skocpol, Theda and Margaret Somers (1980), "The Uses of Comparative History in Macrosocial Inquiry," *Comparative Studies in Society and History* 22, 174–97.

Smythies, B. E. (1963), "History of Forestry in Sarawak," *Malayan Forester* 26, 232–53.

Snyder, Richard (1992), "Explaining Transitions from Neopatrimonial Dictatorships," *Comparative Politics* 24 (4 July), 379–400.

Sta. Maria, Bernard (1978), *Peter J. Mojuntin: The Golden Son of the Kadazan*. Malacca (Malaysia): Bernard Sta. Maria.

Stauffer, Robert B. (1975), *The Philippine Congress: Causes of Structural Change*. Sage Research Papers in the Social Sciences, Comparative Legislative Studies Series, Vol. 3. Beverly Hills, Calif.: Sage Publications.

Steinmo, Sven, Kathleen Thelen, and Frank Longstreth, eds. (1992), *Structuring Politics: Historical Institutionalism in Comparative Analysis*. New York: Cambridge University Press.

Strohmeyer, John (1993), *Extreme Conditions: Big Oil and the Transformation of Alaska*. New York: Simon and Schuster.

Sutter, Harald (1989), "Forest Resources and Land Use in Indonesia," Indonesian Ministry of Forestry and UN Food and Agriculture Organization, Field Document No. I-1, Jakarta, October 1989.

Sweatman, H. C. (1971), "Report to the Government of Indonesia on Forestry in Indonesia," Food and Agriculture Organization of the United Nations, Report No. TA 2984.

Tan, Esther (1994), "PM Orders Audit of Timber Concessions," *New Straits Times* (27 March).

Tan Chin Siang (1992), "Taib: Lim's Proposal Not for Sarawak," *New Straits Times* (14 April).

Tanco, Arturo R., Jr. (1972), "The Crisis of Our Vanishing Forests," Speech at the induction ceremonies of the DANR-RCA Press Corps, February 21, 1972.

Thomson, Mark R. (1995), *The Anti-Marcos Struggle: Personalistic Rule and Democratic Transition in the Philippines*. New Haven, Conn.: Yale University Press.

Tollison, Robert D. (1982), "Rent Seeking: A Survey," *Kyklos* 35, 575–602.

Tornell, Aaron and Philip R. Lane (1999), "The Voracity Effect," *American Economic Review* 89.

Townsend, Robert M. (1995), "Consumption Insurance: An Evaluation of Risk-Bearing Systems in Low-Income Countries," *Journal of Economic Perspectives* 9 (3): 83–102.

Tsebelis, George (1990), *Nested Games: Rational Choice in Comparative Politics*. Berkeley: University of California Press.

Tsing, Anna Lowenhaupt (1992), *In the Realm of the Diamond Queen: Marginality in an Out-of-the-Way Place*. Princeton, N.J.: Princeton University Press.

Tucker, Richard P. (2000), *Insatiable Appetite: The United States and the Environmental Degradation of the Tropical World*. Berkeley: University of California Press.

Tullock, Gordon (1967), "The Welfare Costs of Tariffs, Monopolies, and Regulation," *Western Economic Journal* 5 (June), 224–32.

    (1980), "Efficient Rent-Seeking," in *Toward a Theory of the Rent-seeking Society*, eds. James M. Buchanan, Robert D. Tollison, and Gordon Tullock. College Station: Texas A & M University Press.

    (1995), "Are Rents Fully Dissipated? Comment," *Public Choice* 82, 181–4.

Udarbe, Malu P. (1972), "The Implications of the Forest Resource Inventory on Forest Development in Sabah," *Malayan Forester* 35, 285–91.

UNCTAD (1995), *UNCTAD Commodity Yearbook*. Geneva: United Nations Conference on Trade and Development.

Urrutia, Miguel (1988), "The Politics of Economic Development Policies in Resource-Rich States," in *Economic Development Policies in Resource-Rich Countries*, eds. Miguel Urrutia and Setsuko Yukawa. Tokyo: United Nations University, 154–65.

U.S. Bureau of Foreign Commerce (1955), *Investment in the Philippines: Conditions and Outlook for United States Investors*. Washington, D.C.: U.S. Department of Commerce.

Utleg, Juan L. (1967), "A Rationale for Forest Development," *The Philippine Lumberman* (November), 8.

van Wijnbergen, Sweder (1984), "The 'Dutch Disease': A Disease After All?" *The Economic Journal* 94, 41–55.

Varangis, Panos, Takamasa Akiyama, and Donald Mitchell (1995), *Managing Commodity Booms – and Busts*. Washington, D.C.: World Bank.

Vatikiotis, Michael R. J. (1993), *Indonesian Politics Under Suharto: Order, Development, and Pressure for Change*. New York: Routledge.

Vincent, Jeffrey R. (1990), "Rent Capture and the Feasibility of Tropical Forest Management," *Land Economics* 66 (2 May), 212–23.

    (1992), "The Tropical Timber Trade and Sustainable Development," *Science* 256 (19 June), 1651–5.

Vincent, Jeffrey R. and Malcolm Gillis (1998), "Deforestation and Forest Land Use: A Comment," *The World Bank Research Observer* 13 (1 February), 133–40.

References

Vincent, Jeffrey R., Theodore Panayotou, and John M. Hartwick (1997), "Resource Depletion and Sustainability in Small Open Economies," *Journal of Environmental Economics and Management* 33, 274–86.

Vitug, Marites Dañguilan (1993), *Power from the Forest: The Politics of Logging*. Manila: Philippine Center for Investigative Journalism.

Wadsworth, Frank H. (1980), "Hill Forest Silviculture for Sarawak," FAO Draft, September 13, 1980.

WALHI Economic Team (1991), "Sustainability and Economic Rent in the Forestry Sector," unpublished report.

Wallerstein, Immanuel (1974), *The Modern World-System*. New York: Academic Press.

Wallich, H. C. (1960), *Monetary Problems of an Export Economy*. Cambridge, Mass.: Harvard University Press.

Watkins, Melville H. (1963), "A Staple Theory of Economic Growth," *The Canadian Journal of Economics and Political Science* 29 (2, May), 142–58.

Wenders, John T. (1987) "On Perfect Rent Dissipation," *American Economic Review* 77 (3, June), 456–9.

Wheeler, David (1984), "Sources of Stagnation in Sub-Saharan Africa," *World Development* 12, 1–23.

Williams, Michael (1990), "Forests," in *The Earth as Transformed by Human Action: Global and Regional Changes in the Biosphere over the Past 300 Years*, eds. B. L. Turner II, William C. Clark, Robert W. Kates, John F. Richards, Jessica T. Matthews, and William B. Meyer. New York: Cambridge University Press, 179–202.

Winters, Jeffrey A. (1995), *Power in Motion: Capital Mobility and the Indonesian State*. Ithaca, N.Y.: Cornell University Press.

World Bank (1962), "Economic Growth in the Philippines: A Preliminary Report Prepared by the Staff of the IBRD," Published as Appendix II to the State of the Union Message of President Diosdado Macapagal, January 4, 1962.

(1989), *Philippines: Environment and Natural Resource Management Study*. Washington, D.C.: World Bank.

(1991), "Malaysia: Forestry Subsector Study," Report No. 9775-MA; Draft.

World Rainforest Movement and Sahabat Alam Malaysia, eds. (1990), *The Battle For Sarawak's Forests*, second ed. Penang: World Rainforest Movement and Sahabat Alam Malaysia.

World Resources Institute (1994), *World Resources 1994–95*. New York: Oxford University Press.

(1998), *World Resources 1998–1999*. New York: Oxford University Press.

Zafra, Urbano A. (1955), *Philippine Economic Handbook*. Manila.

(1960), *Philippine Economic Handbook*. Manila.

Zerner, Charles (1992), "Indigenous Forest-Dwelling Communities in Indonesia's Outer Islands: Livelihood, Rights, and Environmental Management Institutions in the Era of Industrial Forest Exploitation," Unpublished draft manuscript, commissioned by the World Bank in preparation for the Forest Sector Review.

Index

Index

cognitive arguments
  versus societal arguments, 32
Collier, David, 2, 15, 17, 18, 24, 31,
  43
commodity booms. *See also* resource
  booms
  ill effects of, 3
  and international institutions, 13
  merits of, 2
  stabilization funds, 199
  and state institutions, 17, 36
  susceptibility of developing states
  to, 12
common pool problem. *See also*
  resource windfalls
  and allocation rights, 39
  avoiding, 39
commodity windfalls, 10, 36
Communal Forests, 146
comparative method, 43
corruption
  definition of, 35n
Cortes, Edmundo, 77
Côte D'Ivoire
  poor windfall management, 25
Crouch, Harold, 159, 163, 179
Cuddington, John, 18

Dandai, Sakaran, 119
Davis, Jeffrey, 25, 26
Deaton, Angus, 197
deforestation
  history of, 45n
Department of Agriculture and
  Natural Resources (DANR), 63
  used to influence the forestry
  bureau, 73
differential rents, 10
Disini, Herminio, 80
Djamaludin, Suryohadikusumo, 180,
  181
Dutch Disease, 16
  explanation of, 15

economic development theories, 2
Ecuador

Plan of Transformation and
  Development, 21
  policy failures in, 21
Enrile, Juan Ponce, 80
European Parliament
  ban on hardwood imports from
  Sarawak, 151

forest policies
  explanations of, 1
forestry institutions
  breakdown of, 1
  definition of, 52
  explanation of, 52
  in Indonesia, 165–6
  in the Philippines, 57
  in Sabah, 96–8
  in Sarawak, 133–5
forests
  protection of, 198–9
Fuzhou Chinese, 154n

Garcia, Carlos, 65, 73
Gelb, Alan, and Associates, 19
Geores, Martha, 2, 46
Gill report, 69
Gill, Tom, 69, 70
Gillis, Malcolm, 1, 46, 48, 105n,
  146n, 147, 167n, 169, 176,
  183
Golkar, 158, 162
Gunning, Jan Willem, 2, 15, 17, 18,
  24, 31

Habibie, Bacharuddin Jusuf, 187
Hak Pengusahaan Hutan, 168
Hamilton, Alexander, 40n
Hanurata, 185n
hard-rock minerals
  windfalls from, 22
Harris Salleh, 91, 93, 94, 110, 116,
  117, 118, 119, 120, 122
Hasan, Mohamed "Bob," *aka*
  The Kian Seng, 177n, 186n,
  187
Hawes, Gary, 80